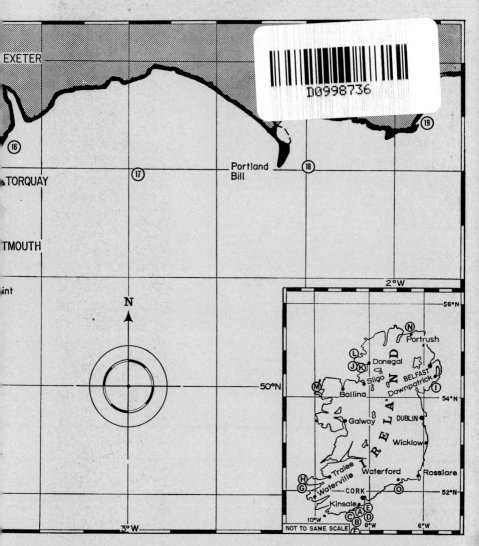

EXETER

⑯

▲TORQUAY   ⑰

TMOUTH

int

N

Portland
Bill

⑱

⑲

2°W

56°N

Ⓝ Portrush

Ⓛ
ⒿⓀ Donegal
     Sligo   BELFAST
Ⓜ   Downpatrick Ⓘ
     Ballina   54°N

     Galway   DUBLIN

I R E L A N D

              Wicklow

Ⓗ   Tralee   Waterford   Rosslare
Ⓖ Waterville
        CORK   52°N
     Kinsale Ⓞ
Ⓔ
10°W ⒸⒶ
NOT TO SAME SCALE ⒷⒹ 8°W   6°W
                Ⓕ

50°N

3°W

th ingot.   7 *James Eagan Layne.*   8 *Louis Shied.*   9 *San Pedro el Mayor.*
15 *Riversdale.*   16 *Gallicia.*   17 *Empress of India.*   18 *Earl of Abergavenny.*

' *Lusitania.*   G *Santa Maria de la Rosa.*   H *San Juan* (Horra).   I *L'Amitié.*
: *Maria Encoronada.*   N *Girona.*   O *Seahorse.*

[continued eastward on rear endpaper

D0998736

THE WRECK HUNTER

THE
WRECK
HUNTERS

by
Roger Jefferis
and
Kendall McDonald

South Brunswick

New York: A. S. Barnes and Co.

© *Roger Jefferis and Kendall McDonald* 1966
Copyright. All rights reserved

Library of Congress Catalogue Card Number: **67-13132**

A. S. Barnes and Co., Inc.
Cranbury, New Jersey

6634

Printed in the United States of America

Preface

IT would be nice to be able to say that the idea for this book came to me as I half stood, half floated on the wreck of the *Mohegan*, seventy feet down in the Cornish sea beneath the Manacle Rocks off the Lizard. I would like to say that, but it wouldn't be completely true. In the grey-white fog of that moment, with a guide-rail of the sunken ship sagging away into the limit of visibility on my right and the shot-rope jerking up towards the unseen surface within reach of my left hand, I felt only sadness tinged with fear.

The fear was the simple one of the unknown; the sadness that of knowing of the people who had died in this cold water when the ship beneath my feet had also died. Was the rail on my right the one the Captain of the *Mohegan* had held as his great ship plunged under the water? Now in her battered condition it was impossible to say, but on my way back to the surface I thought more of the ship and her passengers, until the sea above me grew whiter and whiter, and finally silver at the moment I broke through into the air near the bows of the diving-boat.

After that dive I wanted to know more and more about the *Mohegan*, her passengers on that last voyage, and the manner of her sinking.

I remembered the other wrecks I had dived on. Remembered, too, all the stories of wrecks and wreck diving I had heard whenever I met with other amateur divers. So inevitably I came into contact with Roger Jefferis, who is also a diver and one of the leading authorities on wrecks and wreck stories in this country. After that it became impossible not to write the book together.

We called on all our diving friends to help, wrote to divers whom we had heard of but not met. They all co-operated willingly, because they realized, as we hope our readers will too, that this book is the first of its kind. In any earlier time it would have been impossible to write, for until recent years the amateur diver did not exist. Only now that he does has the wreck hunter come into being too. Only now can the long-lost wrecks around the coasts of Britain be discovered.

Those wreck hunters who have helped us with this book are named with the shipwrecks which they have dived on and investigated. This permanent record of their work is our thanks to them all.

The photographs in this book have come from many sources too. Here are their credits and our thanks for permission to reproduce them:

The *Maine* salvage operation: Torbay Branch divers. Armada Medal: National Maritime Museum, Greenwich. Blasket Sound: G. R. Mundey. Loss of the *Association*; Sir Cloudisley Shovell; *Hindostan*; loss of the *Earl of Abergavenny*; the *Preussen*; the *Preussen* in full sail; the *Royal George*; divers down on the *Earl of Abergavenny*; the *Laurentic*; the *Lusitania*: National Maritime Museum, Greenwich. Divers on the *Gina-Anne*; cannon-ball underwater; the *Royal George* artifacts: Alexander McKee. The *Boscawen,* by Reynolds: National Maritime Museum, Greenwich Hospital Collection. Cannon recovery in Ireland: R. Trouton. The *Association* diving: Bob Rogers. Roland Morris diving: Roland Morris. The *Anson* cannon recovery and artifacts: R. Larn. The *Mohegan* on rocks and lifeboat: F. E. Gibson. The *Herzogin Cecilie*: I. Calkin. Ingot of tin: Royal Institution of Cornwall, Truro. Cannon-balls from Swanage: R. Campbell. Cannon from Thames: Port of London Authority. Brighton minion: *Blue Dolphin* Magazine. The Lamorna Cove guns, drawings by Anthony Bye. Pudding Pan map, by Edward Goldring. The *Anson* sketches, by R. Larn. Cannon in detail, by "Gus", of the *London Evening News*. Frontispiece, copyright 1963: Bob Kendall. *Maine* propeller: *Western Morning News. Anson* cannon: Admiralty. Mrs Trouton: *Northern Whig.*

KENDALL McDONALD

Contents

Illustrations

HALF-TONE PLATES

LINE DRAWINGS

The Big Lift

MORE ships have sunk around the coasts of Britain than around those of any other country in the world. Although this is hardly a record to be proud of, it is historical fact. So much so that it is almost impossible to stand on a stretch of our coastline and look out over the sea without viewing, unknowingly, the graveyard of at least a dozen ships. A map of school-atlas size, for example, when used to plot all the wrecks from Cornwall to the Thames Estuary, ends up with just a mass of shading along the coast—even when each wreck is marked with the tiniest cross.

Along other coasts, though the picture is often not so dark, it is difficult to find any area where a sinking has not taken place. Remember, too, that these are only the recorded wrecks. What casualties were suffered in the earliest days of our maritime history can be estimated only from fragments of the earliest writings. The more ancient less seaworthy vessels must have suffered even more.

The British Isles have been a centre for trade from earliest times. We have sent out ships and ships have come to us. Whether for trade, exploration, or war, ships have sailed to and from these islands for thousands of years. And during that time the weather and other natural hazards have taken a steady toll.

Many of these lost ships went down laden with exotic cargo—

with ivory, diamonds, gold, silver, pearls, silks, jade, and all manner of costly things. Just as many sank full of coal, vegetables, corn, iron ore, rubber, petrol, tallow, hides, and ammunition or less deadly general goods, from pianos to cement.

Once sunk their story might have ended, unless, of course, the professional divers with their leaden boots and globe helmets were called in for some prize of exceptional value. But even these tough, experienced men were used only if the exact location of the wreck were known or could be found with ease.

It took the invention of the Aqualung by Commandant Jacques-Yves Cousteau and Engineer Emile Gagnan in 1944 to make free-ranging over the seabed in search of wrecks a possibility. It took a long time, too, for the War to be over and for this diving equipment, with its cylinders of compressed air, to become available to the sporting amateur. It took even until now for it to be possible to write this book.

Now and only now have enough Aqualung divers been able to range over the seabed to make the location of lost ships more than just the occasional stroke of luck. Today the diver has his air supply on his back in cylinders. The air is supplied to him at the correct pressure for the surrounding depth, and through his mask he can see an ever-changing seabed flowing beneath him. As a direct result Britain's divers have been able to hunt out many lost ships. Not all of these searches have gone unrewarded. Not always has the treasure lost in these wrecks been in the most obvious place. . . .

She came zigzagging down the Channel on a drizzly, misty morning in March 1917. The s.s. *Maine,* a 3600-ton cargo-ship outward bound from London's East India Dock. Destination : Philadelphia; crew : 43; Master : Captain W. Johnston; cargo : 500 tons of chalk, 50 tons of cowhair, horsehair, goatskins, and fenugreek seeds.

The lookouts on the forecastle and poop didn't see it. Neither did the Master and First Officer on the bridge. At 8 A.M. on March 23rd, at 10 knots, 13 miles south of Berry Head, the *Maine* took a torpedo in the port side level with Number Two hold.

The U-boat Commander had timed his strike well. The torpedo blast blew off Number Two and Three hatches, smashed the port gig, and partially wrecked the bridge. Number Two hold started to fill immediately, and Captain Johnston, shaken but unhurt, could feel his ship settling by the head. His first order was to make sure that the presence of the submarine was reported. This was followed seconds later by a distress signal. The radio messages were reinforced by rocket signals.

Captain Johnston then set course for land, knowing from the lumpy feel of her and the crabbing pull on the steering that his ship was unlikely to get far. The engines thumped away the precious miles, but there was no great hope in the Captain's heart. Finally what he had feared most of all happened : sea-water reached the stokehold and the engines went silent.

Nobody aboard was certain that the U-boat had left her prey, and they could only hope either that she had lost the *Maine* in the poor visibility or that she had decided that the damaged ship was not worth another torpedo. Either way, the *Maine* swished to a standstill and hardly moved in the flat, calm sea. Captain Johnston ordered a lifeboat away, but scarcely had she hit the water when another ship was sighted—a rakish outline that worked wonders for the *Maine*'s morale. Closing rapidly was a naval torpedo-boat.

Lieutenant-Commander P. N. Taylor, D.S.C., R.N.R., commanding a flotilla of minesweepers from Torpedo Boat No. 99, sighted the *Maine* wallowing and at a standstill about five miles south-south-west of Start Point. He was returning to Devonport after clearing enemy mines from the approaches to Dartmouth, and in the calm sea had no difficulty in going alongside her.

The *Maine*'s crew quickly transferred to the naval ship, and those in the lifeboat were also soon aboard. While this was being done Commander Taylor and Captain Johnston held a brief shouted conference. Johnston reported that the whole of the midships section was now flooded and the engine-room out of action. Taylor immediately offered to try to tow the *Maine* and beach her near Hope Cove or Bigbury Bay.

By now only the Master, Chief Officer, First and Second Officers, Boatswain, and Cook were still aboard the *Maine,* and with this scratch crew the towing attempt started. Commander Taylor had meanwhile called Plymouth Command, asking for help from rescue tugs.

Towing-wires were passed to the silent ship, and the *Maine* got under way. But not for long. One after another the towing-wires parted under the strain not only of the *Maine* but also of the tons of water inside her. Progress was very slow.

About noon the first tug arrived on the scene, but shortly after the new tow was attempted the bulkheads of the *Maine* collapsed, and it was all over.

At exactly 12.45 P.M. she sank—upright and almost without a struggle. Bolt Head and Bolt Tail could clearly be seen as she sank. Indeed, they were only a mile away.

So quiet was her sinking that the Master and remaining crew almost floated off in the ship's dinghy, which had been lowered to deck level for just such an emergency. As they pulled clear one of the men in the small boat had time to lift the bridge telescope from the water. All were safely picked up by the torpedo-boat. The *Maine* was gone, but if there were any consolation for her Captain it was that there had been no loss of life in her dying. As the years went by she passed into the realm of lost ships. She was forgotten.

And so she would have remained except for a series of quite minor happenings. The first was that the amateur divers of South Devon banded together and formed a branch of the British Sub-Aqua Club in 1955. They called themselves the Torbay Branch, and were based on Torquay. The second happening was that in the spring of 1961 they decided to hold a branch committee meeting. And, thirdly, on the agenda for that meeting was the coming season's diving programme.

Until then the branch diving had followed a rather haphazard pattern. Most dives had no particular object, except to pick up crabs and lobsters, which abounded in the area.

The committee were not satisfied with this; hence the item on the agenda. They felt that the branch definitely needed some greater objective. So the meeting started, and soon the diving item was reached. One suggestion put forward was that there should be a branch marine biological study, but as there was no biologist on the strength this was discarded. The discussion went on and on, but finally it was decided that the branch should embark on a "systematic survey of all wrecks, both charted and uncharted, within the 20-fathom [120-feet] line along the South Devon coast".

Preparing to blast the propeller off the *Maine*. The *Princess* from Salcombe is moored over the wreck. Skipper Michael Dornom talks to Tony Hayward (with triple-cylinder Aqualung on ladder). Other divers are (*left to right*) Neil Howick, Terry Hall, and Derek Cockbill (on foredeck). (See p. 18.)

14

(*Below*) The *Maine* before her renaming in 1913. She was originally the *Sierra Blanca*. (See p. 17.)

The explosion has blown the marine growth off the propeller. This is what the Torbay divers read in the light of their torches 120 feet down. (See p. 19.)

15

(*Below*) Derek Cockbill examines the severed propeller-shaft. This photograph was taken twelve months after the explosion. Note the way the marine growth is returning. (See p. 26.)

Object of the survey was to explore, photograph, and record the history of each vessel, and to publish a complete report on these wrecks. Charts were bought, and the Hydrographic Department of the Admiralty was approached for help. And most helpful they were. All information on every charted wreck was readily given, and from local sources other sites were pinpointed. Now the diving could start.

Base of operations was Salcombe, that South Devon tourist and yachting centre renowned for its beauty. But it wasn't the beauty of the scene that attracted the Torbay divers. Salcombe Estuary is a safe harbour in an area which has taken a heavy toll of shipping over the years. Wrecks could be swiftly approached from here.

Also, in the event of continued bad weather the divers would still be able to dive, for the sheltered waters of the Estuary were always available, and a certain amount of salvage money could possibly be earned there from the recovery of anchors or mooring-chains.

The base for the keen Torbay Branch divers was now established. The next requirement was a boat suitable for diving from under most conditions. Such was the 30-foot fishing-boat *Princess,* owned by Skipper Michael Dornom. His trawling and local experience was to prove invaluable. Now the diving did start.

But, as one of the Torbay divers was soon to remark, there seemed to be more enthusiasm for the inshore wreck sites, where lobster and crab might be found (old habits apparently die hard), than for the deeper sites, such as the locally named "railway-line wreck". At this stage the Torbay divers had no way of knowing that they were being hopelessly misled by so-called local knowledge. How the *Maine,* in view of her cargo, ever became known as the "railway-line wreck" is a mystery that no-one has been able to solve.

The Sunday morning in July that was to change drastically the habits of the Torbay divers dawned fine and already warm. By mid-morning the sun shone, the sea sparkled, and anything less like an English Sunday in summer would be hard to imagine! Off to one of the inshore diving sites went the *Princess* with a cargo of enthusiastic divers. Spot chosen was where the 90-gun man-of-war H.M.S. *Ramillies* had been driven ashore in 1760 (see Chapter Four), but the divers had little luck even in their search for crustaceans, for the site had become the haunt of a colony of seals.

Probably as a result of this the suggestion of a dive on the "railway-line wreck" seemed this time to meet with general approval. According to the chart, the wreck lay about a mile away.

From his trawling experience Skipper Mike Dornom knew its rough location. Approaching the area, the divers could see a patch of disturbed water on an otherwise mirror-like surface : a large obstruction under water was breaking up the smooth flow of the tidal stream, which was then in full ebb. Steaming against the tide and moving ahead of the disturbed patch, Mike Dornom judged himself to be over the wreck. The anchor was let go. In a moment the warp stiffened and the divers knew that they were hooked on to something.

Interest on the diving-boat was now fully aroused, and the divers waited impatiently for the tide-flow to slacken and allow safe diving.

First into the water were Derek Cockbill, Tony Hayward, Roy Howkins, and Terry Downes. Derek Cockbill describes what they saw like this :

"We went down the anchor-rope and, approaching the 70-foot mark, a dim shape unfolded before our eyes—a complete wreck, except for the superstructure, lying upright on an even keel—a fabulous sight. We had hooked into the guard-rail on the forecastle, and after checking to see that the anchor-rope was not chafing we began our exploration. Going forward, we found the spare anchor in place on the forecastle and, descending over the bow, her port and starboard anchors still in the hawse-pipes. On the bottom we found various parts of the superstructure (presumably the result of wreck clearance after the War), but apart from this the wreck was found to be virtually intact."

Back on board after the dive, they all compared what they had seen. One reported a gun on the poop. Another a spare propeller on the upper deck. All agreed it was their finest wreck dive to date. Their enthusiasm for the *Maine* grew and grew.

When weather permitted during the rest of the summer most of the branch dives were on the *Maine*. Portholes were brought to the surface. Odd little things came up too. A fork bearing the Steamship Company's stamp. On one dive a doorlock; the following week the key to fit it ! But none of the divers thought of treasure. Or if they did they reserved it for private dreams of opening the ship's safe. They had examined the spare propeller to see if it was of any value, and found that it was iron and certainly not worth the expense of raising.

During the run out to the ship, again on a Sunday later in the year, Skipper Dornom casually remarked how valuable the single main screw under the counter stern of the ship would be if only it were made of bronze. A thing like that—four-bladed and about seventeen feet in diameter—would be worth a mint, he said.

Though Dornom's words were said casually, one diver, "Mac" Johns, evidently listened carefully to what was said. When he surfaced from his dive he said he thought that the marine growth on the propeller was not as thick as anywhere else. He'd tried scraping the screw, and was convinced that it was not iron. Two divers immediately went down with a hacksaw to get a sample. In the gloom under the stern the first bite of the saw into the metal gleamed dull gold in the light of an underwater torch. It was bronze!

The reaction on board the diving-boat as soon as the divers surfaced was immediate. Salvage! They were rich! Little things like the fact that the propeller was 17 feet in diameter, that it was firmly attached to its 19-inch-diameter shaft, that the water was 120 feet deep, that it was a mile from shore, that all the divers possessed in the way of tools was one hacksaw, were blithely ignored by all concerned.

They little knew the difficulties ahead—if they had done so the project would have been dropped immediately. But the winter was coming on, and there was plenty to do without actually diving. Firstly, the owners of the ship had to be found. Secondly, the weight and value of the propeller had to be nailed down. Thirdly, they had to find out all they could about the ship to help with salvage operations.

Letters travelled back and forth, and finally the Liverpool underwriters who held the subrogation rights for the vessel were tracked down. More letters passed, and then the salvage rights were offered for a "nominal figure" of £100.

More information came in, and it was found that the *Maine* had been built originally for the Sierra Shipping Company of Liverpool in 1905, and had been named *Sierra Blanca*. In 1913 she had been bought for £38,500 by the Atlantic Transport Company and named *Maine*.

Time was passing, and in the spring of 1962 the branch committee were approached. Though it was agreed to "have a go", the cost was way outside the total of any branch funds. A "Salvage Syndicate" was formed, and shares were sold at £5 each. No member could have more than two, but even so £200 was quickly raised.

Organization was forthcoming too. Tony Hayward, the Torbay Branch Diving Officer, was appointed Salvage Officer, Derek Cockbill was Secretary, and Pauline Gardner controlled finance. Only the more experienced club divers from the branch were to be called upon for their diving services. And off went the cheque for £100. The *Maine* was theirs!

Next problem was to get the propeller off the shaft. They decided to blast it off—but no-one had ever tackled a job of this complexity. Submarine blasting gelatine is the only suitable explosive at that depth, and a 25-lb. necklace charge made up from 4-ounce "pills" was threaded on to a length of Cordtex instantaneous fuse.

On June 15th 1962 four divers—Tony Hayward, Derek Cockbill, Neil Howick, and Terry Hall—left Salcombe to carry out the operation. Says Cockbill: "The wreck had been permanently buoyed by us now, the wire being attached to the barrel of the gun on the stern. We moored and waited for slack water.

"As soon as the tide eased, Tony Hayward and Neil Howick dived with the main charge, which was placed around the shaft in the aperture between the inside facing of the propeller-boss and the stuffing-box. Terry Hall and I arrived down under the stern with a length of Cordtex fed from the boat. We threaded this into the main charge to act as its detonator. We then all finned our way gently up to the boat, rather conscious of the explosive set-up behind us.

"Once in the boat, a detonator with a length of slow-burning fuse supported by a cork float was attached to the Cordtex. The fuse was lit, and we backed off. Then we waited. It seemed ages, but it could only have been moments before there was a thump from the depths and a momentary flattening of a patch of water over the wreck. The charge had gone off—at least we were sure of that.

"We decided to wait for the visibility to clear—the explosion was bound to have stirred up the bottom and the silt on the wreck. But suddenly all thoughts of the propeller were lost. Stunned fish by the dozen were breaking the surface. Throwing off our diving gear, we jumped into the water, and in fifteen minutes had collected three potato baskets full of fish. It was an unexpected dividend, but one that we should have known would occur, having read many tales of wartime Army fishing with hand-grenades!

"Our anxiety about the job soon returned, and climbing back into the boat and slipping on our Aqualungs, we descended once again to the wreck. Dropping cautiously over the stern, we peered into the gloom. Nothing seemed to have happened. Getting closer, we realized that the propeller now had a slightly drunken look. It was resting half-way along its taper, the securing-nut was missing, and there was a one-inch-wide crack in the rudder-post. The force of the explosion had sheared the propeller-shaft like a knife on the outer face of the propeller-boss, blowing the propeller and severed nut rearwards together. They had been checked by the rudder-post, which had fractured under the impact. The nut, with the threaded end of the shaft still in place, had dropped to the seabed. The result could not have been better."

The Torbay divers were jubilant. The explosion had also cleaned every vestige of marine growth off the propeller. Now a closer examination of the boss revealed the manufacturer's markings cast into the metal. Through their face-masks and in the light of their torches they could now read :

STONE'S BRONZE

LONDON 1904

440

A check on directories soon produced a J. Stone and Co. (Propellers), Limited, listed under "Propeller Manufacturers", and the branch wrote immediately to see if any record existed of the *Maine*'s propeller, which, of course, was now very much "our propeller" to the divers.

They did not have to wait long for a reply. The propeller had been traced in the records of the firm, who confirmed its finished weight to be about six and a quarter tons. The letter went further : it said, if they were interested in disposing of same the firm would appreciate the opportunity of making an offer. There was more delight when the next letter arrived. Stone's offer was £137 per ton on their lorry at site. The offer was accepted, for not only was this an increase over other tentative offers, but it would also cut out an obviously heavy transport bill.

For a group of men who had never attempted any sizeable underwater salvage the Torbay Branch felt that they were doing rather well. But more hard work lay ahead. Stone's wrote that they would prefer to have the propeller all in one piece, and the divers decided to try to oblige.

But raising something weighing over six tons from a depth of 120 feet is easier said than done. First of all, regardless of how the lift was made, there was a danger of the propeller fouling on the rudder-post, rudder, and steering gear. Once again the divers turned to explosives. Four dives, using smaller charges, were made before the work was completed.

Then there was the problem of the actual raising. Three methods were considered. The first was by use of buoyancy bags or drums filled with compressed air, until enough lift was available to float the attached propeller to the surface. This would be a long and costly operation, as it would mean a great deal of gear and the need to get the propeller into a position where a crane could lift it from the water to the truck. The same costs would apply to the second consideration—the tidal method. This would mean lashing the propeller to a ship at low tide, and then as the tide rose moving it stage by stage to harbour. More and more stages would be necessary as the water shallowed in to the shore. And, of course, in neither of these operations could the weather be relied upon to remain calm for the whole period required.

There was only one method left—the hire of a vessel big enough and strong enough to winch up the propeller and bring it to port.

Plymouth and Devonport—fourteen miles from the scene of operations—seemed the most likely places to search out such a vessel. Here the first major setback was encountered. No-one wanted to know. A request for permission to hire an Admiralty mooring-vessel was refused. But the divers did not give up. Perhaps the request for a naval ship, capable of lifting eighty tons on its 'horns', had been turned down because of inadequate information. A visit to the Mooring Officer met with a sympathetic hearing and a suggestion that they reapply, giving more details and asking for a quotation for the job, both as a special operation and as an 'on passage' job—*i.e.*, when the ship was returning to port from some other mission.

While waiting impatiently for a reply to the application the divers suddenly found that they were news! Stories appeared in papers all over the country. Three days later in the post came a photograph of the *Maine* and seventeen pencil sketches in a notebook giving full details of the ship from stem to stern. They were from a Captain H. J. Chubb, now retired, who had served his apprenticeship aboard her from 1909 to 1913. He had made the drawings from memory. This enabled Paul Truscott to make full-scale drawings of the ship which became vastly useful to the divers in further explorations.

Another surprise letter was airmailed from Florida, in the United States. It was from Captain P. N. Taylor, who had been in command of the minesweeping flotilla which found the *Maine* after her torpedoing and had taken off the crew. Captain Taylor passed on more details about the actual sinking of the ship.

Interesting and helpful though this was, the Torbay divers were still waiting to hear from the Admiralty, when they found out that another ship might help them.

The 85-foot MFV *Universal Dipper,* owned by Universal Divers, Limited, of Liverpool, was completing some work at Paignton, and was due soon to return to Liverpool. The owners were approached, and though the weight of the *Maine*'s propeller was near the capacity of the lifting-ship, they agreed to help if possible.

Though it was now December, the weather was still fine, and preparations for the big lift were made quickly. But the *Universal Dipper,* owing to delays on her main job, was three days behind schedule arriving off Salcombe. Now the weather forecasts were beginning to sound ominous, but a rendezvous was arranged on December 6th in an attempt to get the work done before the weather broke. Down went the divers, and they managed to fix a strop to the propeller-boss.

Underwater work is something that cannot be hurried, however, especially in 120 feet of water. The divers down around the propeller were working by torchlight long before the light had faded on the surface, and were unable to complete the underwater shackling in time. They planned to return and finish the job the next day, but even the most optimistic of them could see that the weather was turning.

The next morning it was clear that the wind was preparing for a gale, but even so they put to sea. On the site diving was impossible. The south-westerly wind was strengthening to Force Six, and the sea was rising rapidly. By the time they returned to the shelter of Salcombe a gale was blowing.

This was the start of the worst spell of weather experienced in Salcombe in living memory—even the local vessels were storm-bound for nearly three months. The *Maine* had hung on to her propeller—by just one day!

The time passed gloomily for the men itching to get out and bring home their 'treasure'. The only bright spot was a letter from the Admiralty agreeing this time to help. The price of such help was £56 'on passage' or £156 for a special operation.

So matters stood until March 1963, when it was time to take the Admiralty up on their offer. They knew that the mooring-vessel was due in the river Dart in early May to lay racing-marks for the Naval College, and hoped to use the ship on the return journey to Devonport.

A new Mooring Officer, Lieutenant-Commander Donald Watts, had been appointed since their last contact with the authorities, and the divers were grateful for the enthusiasm with which the project was received. Other people had been telling them that they would never succeed.

Now operations began to speed up. The divers collected a four-inch lifting-wire and strop, which they had hired from the Naval Dockyard. The idea was to shackle these to the propeller and lay them on the seabed. This lifting-gear would be buoyed so that when the mooring-vessel arrived all she would have to do would be to lift the wire and winch it in. A provisional date was set. It was to be May 2nd.

The deadline approached, but foul weather prevented diving. The week before the set date there was a slight improvement, and the Torbay divers decided that if it were humanly possible they would go down to the *Maine* once more.

On Thursday, April 25th, the *Princess* once again set out from Salcombe and headed for the diving site. With the lifting-wire were four divers—Roy Howkins, Terry Downes, Geoff Sanders, and Derek Cockbill.

Derek Cockbill tells what happened then: "With the highest spring tide of the year to contend with, we knew that slack water would be virtually non-existent and the combination of spring tides and rough seas would have reduced visibility drastically. Even on the surface it looked bad.

"As our buoy had been swept away by the winter gales, our first objective was to re-buoy the wreck on the stern. Mike Dornom, with his usual dexterity, quickly located her, and the anchor was soon hooked in. As soon as the tide slackened the first two divers, Roy Howkins and I, descended the anchor-rope into bitter cold and utter blackness. In spite of our powerful lanterns, visibility was a matter of inches.

"Gradually working downwards to 80 feet, we found the anchor, which mercifully had hooked into a guard-rail. By groping along the ship's side we eventually reached the stern. Once there, we tied a rope quickly to a bollard, and then surfaced through the murk.

"But we had to go down again. This time we carried the end of a thin wire. Once back on the stern, we dropped over the edge into even deeper darkness. Working mostly by feel, we shackled the wire through the boss. There was now a wire direct from the *Princess* to the propeller-boss, and, using this as a guide-line, the strop, shackle, and lifting-wire were lowered in turn to be connected. Of course, we didn't do all this in one go. The conditions were the most appalling imaginable, and we had to limit diving to half an hour, taking advantage of what slackening of the tide there was. It took four days. The tangles and snags were finally sorted out, and we were ready for the lift."

On the following Wednesday evening—the mooring-vessel *Barbastel* had completed her tasks in the Dart—final details were discussed with Lieutenant-Commander Watts and the Master of the lifting-ship. A rendevous was arranged for 11.30 A.M. the next morning over the *Maine*.

For once the weather played the game, and the early-morning forecast was of a north-westerly off-shore wind. Now the divers had high hopes as they steamed down Salcombe Estuary in the *Princess*. Even the sun shone.

The *Barbastel* was already at the rendezvous when the *Princess* arrived. Floating near by was the orange buoy marking the stern of the wreck and the conical black buoy connected to the lifting-wire.

"It had been decided," says Derek Cockbill, "that the mooring-vessel would drop her stern anchor some distance astern of the *Maine* and steam forward to pick up the buoy-wire connected to the lifting-wire, which would then be taken aboard and winched up. The plan was put into operation and was running smoothly when the weather had another go at us. Suddenly the wind freshened and the *Barbastel* began swinging to starboard. The stern anchor, which should have held her, suddenly dragged in soft shingle, and the vessel's full weight was thrown on the thin buoy-wire. It stiffened like a bowstring and parted at a splice. The heavy lifting-wire—then only inches from the winch—dropped back into the water. The *Barbastel,* with nothing to hold her, swung even further, and swept the stern buoy from the wreck. We stood by, helpless and stunned, as this sudden twist of fate brought the blackest moment in the whole of the operation."

Upset though they were, the divers felt that they must make some attempt, however desperate, to retrieve the situation. Roy Howkins and Derek Cockbill kitted up quickly, while Mike Dornom re-located the wreck and anchored.

As quickly as possible they went down the anchor-rope, and were relieved to find that the visibility had improved since their last dive, and that the anchor was fouled close to the lifting-wire, which was now coiled in great loops around the upper deck near the stern. The first job was to replace the stern marker-rope and to let the *Princess* pick up the mooring once again.

Then they dived again—this time with a thin line connected to the end of the heavy lifting-wire. The thin line was then passed aboard the *Princess,* and, using his small winch, Mike Dornom began lifting. He took as much strain on the line as he dared, and then down went the divers again. Now they carried the end of a heavy rope, which was passed through the eye of the heavy lifting-cable. A signal to *Barbastel* for a heaving-line, and this was hauled aboard the *Princess* and connected to the main wire. The *Barbastel* was now connected to the lifting-wire, and as she began heaving in, the securing-rope to the *Princess* was cut, and she drifted clear.

Tension on board the *Princess* mounted as all, including the dripping divers, watched the steady progress of the lifting-wire over the *Barbastel's* bow. Suddenly it stopped, and a diving check to make sure the wire was clear of the wreck was requested. Roy Howkins went down to the stern. To his amazement the propeller and the wire were gone!

A trail of drifting silt, sand, and scour-marks on the seabed disappeared into the limit of visibility. The propeller had obviously gone that way. Roy Howkins set off after it. The trail led across sixty feet of seabed before he sighted its end. And there was the propeller gently bumping on the bottom in a clear patch of sand. The *Barbastel* had drifted slowly westward and was taking the propeller with her.

On Howkins' signal winching was resumed once again. Moments later first one blade and then the whole propeller broke surface. The Torbay divers gazed in triumph at the result of two years of negotiation, frustration, and hard labour. There hung their propeller—a sight none of them will ever forget. A group of amateur divers, who had started out with nothing but a hacksaw, had completed a major salvage operation.

The propeller was secured to one of the 'horns' of the *Barbastel,* and, waiting only to transfer some of the divers from the *Princess,* the *Barbastel,* with the propeller, set course for Devonport. There was quite a celebration that night for all concerned!

On June 6th Stone's loaded the screw on to their lorry for its final journey to London.

Its weight was 6 tons 2 cwt. 3 qrs., and the Torbay divers received a cheque for £840 16s. 9d. After repayment of all loans the balance was used on equipment to further an ambitious programme on wreck location and exploration. But the *Maine* is not forgotten. The Torbay Branch of the British Sub-Aqua Club are her owners, and they still have 3600 tons of salvage in her, including a great quantity of valuable non-ferrous metals.

Torbay Branch, naturally enough, regard the wreck as one of the finest in the South-west. From a diver's point of view this may well be so. There are few wrecks that are as intact as this one.

She is 360 feet long and has a beam of 46 feet, and only her superstructure has been damaged and partially swept away. She lies on a shingle bed on an even keel at 120 feet. She stands 50 feet proud of the seabed.

Her exact position is 50° 12′ 45″ N.; 3° 50′ 53″ W. The Torbay divers tell us that they do not mind anyone diving on her, but do strongly object to anyone taking souvenirs or anything from the wreck.

Anyone who tries this would, however, be very foolish. Most of the local fishermen are well aware of the *Maine*'s story and of all the effort put in by the local divers. They would also object strongly to any looting. Otherwise the diving on the site should be ideal, provided that it is done by experienced divers. There are strong tidal streams, but the visibility is usually good. Marine growth on the ship is not excessive, but already the bare parts (where the explosives used to take off the propeller stripped them clear) have been covered again to some inches in depth.

Despite the loss of her propeller the *Maine* when you first see her looks for all the world as though she were still sailing on—120 feet under the surface. She will stay like that for many years to come. Already to the Torbay divers she has been as rich as any treasure galleon of Armada days. Which brings us to the next chapter.

Armada Wreck

ASK any Briton what happened in the battles with the Spanish Armada, and they will undoubtedly tell you, "We won." Details of battles are forgotten, names misused, but the fact that "We won" is never forgotten. But how was it that we did in fact defeat the Armada?

There are two main reasons. One was that our ships were smaller, faster, harder-hitting vessels, and their waspish attacks constantly harassed the more cumbersome Spanish ships. The second reason is vastly important. It is simply that the weather was on our side. Tempestuous winds blew almost throughout the campaign, and, as an Armada medallion records, "God breathed and they were scattered."

The reason for the sending of the Armada was simple. Philip was King in Spain and Elizabeth Queen in England. Philip wanted to take and rule England himself, but to do so he had to defeat the English in battle—a decisive battle. He had, in fact, to cross the water by ship and attack London by sailing up the Thames. To assist him Alexander Farnese, the Duke of Parma, was to assemble a vast army in France and, at the right moment, cross the Channel in invasion barges. The Armada's job was to protect the soldiers during the ferrying, and to provide heavy artillery, stores, munitions, and other supplies.

The plan, of course, went wrong. The Armada was scattered, and the surviving ships staggered back to Spain, the war over, the war lost.

But throughout the long and uneasy voyage of the Armada—over three months in many cases—the soldiers and sailors had to live and die on board ship. From the start of the voyage, which circumnavigated England and Ireland, right to the end in Spain, everything that was needed had to be on board. There was no chance of a quick trip ashore to pick up supplies to replace those used or forgotten. So every vessel was loaded with articles of every description—from cannons and cash to water and wine.

This created new problems, for, although the galleons themselves were big enough, certain *urcas,* or hulks, were employed as extra store-ships. They were cargo-carrying vessels of all kinds which had now been pressed into service to transport the extra gear needed for a campaign of this sort.

One of the ships in this squadron of hulks was a hospital ship, the *San Pedro el Mayor.* Of medium size, she was about 550 tons burden, and had left Spain with 30 sailors and 100 soldiers—50 men-at-arms to fight on land or on board ship—and some 50 others who were to tend the sick and organize the hospital. It is with this ship that our interest lies.

The squadron of hulks, according to an inventory made in Lisbon on May 20th 1588, had fourteen ships in it. All were large and cumbersome, awkward in the water and could make only slow speed compared with the galleons. These great ships and fast galleys made up the rest of the Armada squadrons. The hulks were a hindrance to the progress of the great fleet up the Channel, but they were needed for the supplies they carried, and at first the Duke of Medina Sidonia made a good job of keeping his ships together.

The *San Pedro* was off Plymouth on July 21st 1588, with the rest of the Armada, when the first skirmish took place with the English. She was to appear again three months later at practically the same spot, but in very different circumstances.

Her voyage around the British Isles became a painful mockery of what the crew had expected. As the battles progressed, so the numbers of wounded and sick mounted. Many soldiers and sailors with shattered limbs were put into the hospital, and nine days later, when the fleet should have been well on its way into the mouth of the Thames, and the hospital ship ready to put her patients ashore, the actual voyage of the Armada was only just beginning.

On July 30th 1588 the fleet was about twenty miles west of Flushing and the entrance to the river Sheldt, heading north-north-east towards Norway. English cannon-shot had started the work, and now the wind blew the fleet in disarray towards the north. Spaniards from the heat of Lisbon were to travel some 1500 miles to the north of that city, and for men raised in the sun latitude 60 was very cold indeed.

Still the *San Pedro* lurched on. Her crew, sick of the sea and in daily fear of their lives from disease and hunger, wondered if their journey would ever end. Soon the wounded on board began to die, and the movement of the cumbersome ship made sick-berth attendance more and more difficult.

Now the fleet steered westward between the Orkneys and the Shetlands, and out into the North Atlantic to begin the last, long leg home. The Duke of Medina Sidonia, on board the flagship, *San Martin de Portugal,* took his ships way out towards Rockall before finally heading south. His reason for this was simple. He had been told that no quarter would be given to any ships luckless enough to be forced into the shores of Ireland.

On board the *San Pedro el Mayor,* however, conditions were now so appalling that the risk of venturing into Irish waters was far outweighed by the chance of some fresh water and a little shelter from the foul weather. So she, together with the *San Juan de Portugal* and two other ships, put into the little port of Vicey, an anchorage by the Great Blasket Island, off County Kerry. The *San Juan,* commanded by Juan Martinez de Recalde, one of Spain's most famous seaman, was with the *San Pedro* when they put out to sea again. In fact, the *San Juan* limped painfully home all the way to Corunna, but the *San Pedro* was a far different ship from the great galleon. She and her crew could not face the probability of another month at sea. Even so, Ireland was far astern before she turned east—this time in search of any port, French or English, where she might find help for her wounded and dying.

That decision—to head for a probably hostile port—tells more about the condition of the *San Pedro* at that time than anything else. With the south-westerly gales still blowing fitfully behind her, she was taken back into the Channel. Now the numbers of those on board who could do any useful work were growing fewer. Fever and death were their companions, and about the 48th parallel there were no longer enough sailors on their feet to control the ship. The wind blew her where it would.

Back she went, Ushant to the starboard, the Scillies to port, heading helplessly towards Plymouth and final disaster. Back into Bigbury Bay and—to the amazement of all the local inhabitants who saw her coming—straight into Hope Cove. On to the Shippen Rock she dashed herself. Soon she was broken into pieces and sank with her dead and dying in the cold sea at last.

Some three hundred and seventy years later, in the reign of the second Elizabeth, the year 1960 brought a figure to the scene of the wreck as strange to the human eye as a Spaniard would have been had he appeared on the beach in full Court dress from the reign of Philip of Spain. He was a free diver, dressed from top to toe in foam Neoprene, with a mask on his face, fins on his feet, and a cylinder of compressed air on his back. Around his waist were lead weights, and strapped to his right calf was a diver's heavy knife. Behind him came his companion, a slighter, younger figure, who carried a spear-gun but no breathing apparatus.

The pair waded into the sea from Outer Hope beach until they were waist-deep, then together they swam slowly out to sea. After a short while only one head could be seen on the surface, then that too disappeared.

Such an occurrence in the reign of the first Elizabeth would have caused panic and talk of witchcraft, while the spot would have been well skirted on a dark night; but today we know that the disappearance and reappearance of strangely clad figures at sea and close inshore indicate that divers are at work.

The two figures were man and boy—George Tessyman,[1] diving instructor, and his young pupil, who had become interested in fishing with a spear.

At Hope, that day in 1960, the boy had been talking about catching fish, and George, dressed for a dive, had led him out to a spot some 200 yards from the beach and about 75 yards from the

[1] George Tessyman runs a fishing and diving business at Dartmouth, and his boat, *Tudor II*, is usually to be seen tied up alongside the Embankment near the Lower Ferry at Dartmouth.

Shippen Rock to look below the surface for mullet, which browse among the green weed growing there on the rocks.

George swam slowly down to the bottom in some thirty feet of water. His eyes behind his mask looked right and left, searching the weed-covered rocks for signs of fish. Looking up, he could see the spreadeagled figure of his pupil, lying in wait on the surface, poised for the signal to duck-dive to a place where there were fish. A signal passed between them, and the boy, bent at the waist, flung his heels out of the water and slid steeply down towards him. George pointed a gloved hand, and the boy pressed the trigger to send a spear lancing towards an inedible wrasse that had appeared from among some kelp. The spear missed by more than a foot, and hit a rock with a dull sound. Recovering his spear by pulling in on the attached line, the boy glanced upward at the mirrored surface, and with slow fin strokes rose to the air. A strong exhalation to clear his breathing-tube, two deep breaths to ease his lungs, and he was watching again while he reloaded the gun, setting the butt in the pit of his stomach and pulling the spear into the barrel against its spring until it clicked home at the trigger.

So the sport went on—George on the bottom, instructing, signalling, and watching, the boy diving again and again, firing, reloading, and firing again. For all George's patience, and for all the boy's attempts, not one fish was hit that afternoon. As the air began to be exhausted from the cylinder at his back George found that his buoyancy, which had been perfect when he entered the water, was becoming affected by the lightening air-cylinder, and he started to rise from the bottom. The used air, gaily bubbling from the exhaust-valve behind his neck, had, in compression, provided some three pounds of weight. Now, with the air all but finished, he had to find a means of remaining on the sea-floor without finning about, as any unnecessary movement frightened away the fish. There was no suitable small rock to hold, but near by a billet of wood protruded from the sand, so George withdrew his knife from its sheath and struck it well home into the pulpy wood to provide a handhold. The fishing continued, but all too soon his air was exhausted, so he retrieved his knife and slowly rose towards the surface, lingering a little and breathing gently, and thinking to himself how peaceful the underwater scene was all about him. Even the violence of the fish hunt had seemed more gentle than it would have been from land or from a boat. It was the silence, he decided, that made diving so worth while—that personal sort of silence where you could hear yourself breathing and the squeaky noise the suit made, but nothing at all from the outside world. Very pleasant, he thought, and cool, not at all like the noisy beach with sun-provoked people eager for loud enjoyment. As he mused he looked down to the sea-bottom to see if anything had been left behind, and as he did so his eyes passed over the helpful piece of wood rising from the seabed.

From his higher position he could now see that there were several pieces of wood in a slightly curved line, and the word 'breakwater' flashed through his mind, but he thought the idea foolish, as no-one in his right senses would erect a breakwater alongside a reef of rocks in some thirty feet of water. He arrived at the surface and made the necessary signal to his companion, then together they began the swim back to the beach. They gained the shore some ten minutes later, and walked up to the remainder of the diving party, who were eating a meal in the shade. As he changed and examined his equipment he listened to the discussion that was being carried on between the divers, a discussion centred around an ancient ship, a ship called the *St Peter*.

Up until then he had not heard the tale of the *St Peter*, or *San Pedro*, but now, between sandwiches, it was unfolded to him. The boys had been for a walk up the slope from the beach, past the Hope and Anchor Inn, and along to a cottage, where they had met a man who had a tobacco-tin full of coins. All the coins were very old, some copper, some silver, and, according to what they had been told, they had all been collected at various times from local beaches. Some of the silver coins had a cross on them, and the man had said they were Portuguese, and had come from the Armada ship that had been lost on the Shippen.

The tale was slowly pieced together, until realization of what he had seen on the seabed flowed over George like a gentle breeze. He sat quietly eating, and nodding his head, and saying nothing.

On the journey home he ran over the facts in his mind. An Armada ship had struck the Shippen Rock and had sunk. Coins had been found on near-by beaches. He had seen what were undoubtedly ribs or frames of an ancient wooden vessel buried in the sand. He came to the obvious conclusion that by sheer chance and a happy coincidence of information he had stumbled on the resting-place of a Spanish wreck.

Moment of triumph!
The *Maine*'s propeller
is secured to the horns
of the *Barbastel*. After
two years' work the
Torbay divers saw the
propeller out of the
water for the first
time. (See p. 25.)

32

George Tessyman searching underwater. He may have found the last resting-place of a Spanish Armada wreck—but the sand took it back again. (See p. 30.)

(*Below*) Medal struck at the time to commemorate the defeat of the Spanish Armada—"God breathed and they were scattered." (See p. 27.)

Two weeks later he returned to Hope beach to search again. The sea, however, was not going to let go of a secret that had been kept for so long. That weekend, and for two more after it, the waves were high, and a steady wind made diving impossible. It was nearly a month before he was able to enter the water over the site again, and, search as he would, nowhere could he find any trace of wooden ribs showing above the sand.

At about this time, in London, the authors of this book were searching records in various places for Armada details with a view to compiling a list of known wrecks. Our searches eventually led us to the old lifeboat house at Inner Hope beach. We talked with the fishermen there about the *St Peter*. The story to them was a romantic tale of long ago. They knew all the details, and one fisherman opened his leather purse to reveal a silver coin, nearly the size of a half-crown, that bore on one side a Maltese cross.

"Where did you find it?"

"Only a few yards from where you are standing," he replied, "down on the beach, right close inshore by the end of the boat-slip."

We walked outside in the rain and gazed over the wall at the end of the slip. The tide was high and the beach covered, but there was the place only a few yards from us. Another fisherman, suddenly enthusiastic, walked out with his shoulders covered by a sack.

"That was not the only coin found," he said. "There have been several others."

We walked back into the boathouse out of the rain. Inside the atmosphere had changed. They were talking now and arguing among themselves, not just for their own amusement and to please strangers from London, but seriously about the wreck.

"Don't believe a word of it," said one. "There was no such ship; it's all talk." And he left, cap pulled down against the rain.

"He thinks you are too interested," said another. "What you should do is see Mrs — over at Salcombe, or old man — up the way a little—they both have coins."

We took note of the names he had given, and with many thanks and waved good-byes, made our way back to the car-park. It was still raining, but we stood a few moments gazing at the Shippen rocks and thinking of the wreck. She's there, we thought, she's there right now, old and twisted and broken, but there still, and coins too, a few only maybe, but at least a memento to remember her by. And as for the Shippen Rock—why not 'ship in' or 'ship on'?

The next day we went to Salcombe and found the lady with the coins. She had two coins similar to the one we had already seen. They were in a little box, wrapped in cotton-wool, like birds' eggs, and with them a letter from a museum saying they were genuine coins and without doubt from the period of the Spanish Armada. We looked at them for a long time, wondering whose hand had held them and what they had bought so many years ago.

Later that year we returned to Hope beach with George Tessyman and some other divers and searched the area both morning and afternoon. It was a day of bright sun shining right down to the seabed, and fish gliding in and out of the weed-covered rocks. We searched and searched and found nothing—nothing, that is, except a copper heel-plate that was picked up, and is now nailed up over the bar in the Start Bay Inn at Torcross.

We have discussed the disappearing wreck many times since. Divers tend to talk of their exploits, and since talk seems to travel faster if there is money involved, there have been other attempts to search the area for the remains. No diver, to our knowledge, has yet been lucky enough to find anything—all except Alexander McKee, that is, and the coin he found on the bottom, although Elizabethan, was Elizabeth II and practically mint. It must have been lost from a boat.

Stories about sunken pirate gold, and booty, and specie, and treasure, are all very well, but there is only a rare chance of finding lost wealth on the seabed. It has been wisely said that if all the money that has been spent on treasure hunts could be collected together in one place, then it would represent the greatest hoard ever known. Nevertheless, it is always interesting to know the full details of a wreck, and also to know that there is a good chance of finding a small memento at the site of the sinking.

The following information may well be of use to the wreck hunter. The *Calendar of State Papers* (*Domestic*) for 1588 contains all manner of information in letter and report form concerning the Armada campaign. Two of these letters are worthy of note.

George Cary at Cockington, near Torquay, wrote the first letter to the Council, dating it November 5th 1588. His second paragraph states:

> And during my abode there, having understanding that one of the Spanish fleet was cast on shore (at a place called Hope near Salcombe) and the great pilfering and spoils that the country people made, I rode thither and took order for the restoring and rehaving again of all such things as either by search or inquiry I could find out, and have put the same in inventory. And took order, for the orderly saving of the rest, as weather would give leave, to have the same on land, appointing two head constables to attend that service, and they and others to keep several inventories.
>
> The ship is a hulk, and called *St Peter the Great,* one of those two ships which were appointed for the hospital of the whole Navy. She is in burden, as they say, 550 tons, but I think not so much.

According to the Archives Nationales, Paris K.1592 (Dossier B.81), one of the shipwrecked crew was Gonzalo Gonzalez. He was interrogated during his imprisonment at Kingsbridge. In his statement ("The Relation of Gonzalo Gonzalez, a prisoner in England"), dated November 7th 1588, he said that "The hulk *San Pedro el Mayor* of the squadron of Juan Gomez de Medina was cast ashore in England, on the land of Sir William Courtenay,[1] where she was pillaged and her people imprisoned."

Cary's letter continues:

> The ship is not to be recovered; she lieth on a rock, and full of water to her upper decks. They confess that there were put into her, at her coming out of Spain, thirty mariners, one hundered soldiers, fifty appertaining to the hospital. There are now remaining about forty, or thereabouts.

This is rather a staggering statement, as it clearly indicates how badly the Spaniards had fared. Seven-ninths of her complement had died, apart from the sick and wounded taken aboard as hospital cases during the voyage. When it is remembered that this was

---

[1] Sir William Courtenay was the third Earl of Devon and High Sheriff of Devonshire, who, incidentally, when marrying for the second time, married Sir George Sydenham's daughter Elizabeth, Sir Francis Drake's widow.

a hospital ship well stocked with medical necessaries the mind boggles at what must have been endured by other survivors who actually completed the voyage home to Spain.

> There was put into her as much drugs and pothecary stuff as came to 6,000 ducats, of which I think there will come little good of the same, the weather such as none could get aboard. There hath been some plate and certain ducats rifled and spoiled at their first landing, both from their persons and out of their chests. The ship, I think, will prove of no great value; the ordnance is all iron, and no brass; their ground tackle all spent, save only one new cable. There are no men of account in the ship—soldiers and such as have risen by service, and bestowed all their wealth in this action.

Cary completed his letter with references to the prisoners and their welfare, and also gave details of the little gunpowder available on the wreck.

The gunpowder was more important than the prisoners, as so much had been used by the English ships in the fighting that stocks had to be built up from any available source. The prisoners were a liability, and were packed off to jail to wait and pray that a beneficial government in Spain would arrange for their release. "No men of account" in Cary's letter indicated that no ransom money would be forthcoming from the prisoners themselves.

The second letter to the Council was written by Anthony Ashley from Ilton, Sir William Courtenay's house, on November 12th. "May it please your Lordships," it begins, and continues that he has made an inventory of the goods from the vessel.

> The ship being run upon rocks by the Spaniards, is now through the tempestuous weather broken in pieces and scattered on the seashore, and order is taken for the saving of such things as are anything worth.

From the two letters—written within a week of each other—it can be seen that the ship was not in any state to be saved, and now consisted of wreckage on the beaches. The two main beaches at Hope—Inner Hope and Outer Hope—are completely separated by the Shippen rocks. Outer Hope beach is known as Mouthwell; Inner Hope beach as Hope Cove. This is important when we start to consider the finding of the coins.

The prevailing winds over the British Isles are south-west, and as a result the beaches at Hope are usually in a condition which provides plenty of scope for the young sandcastle-builder. However, when the wind moves round to the north-east and blows hard for a few tides the action of the sea changes, and the beach surface is removed with a scouring action. Great quantities of sand and small stones are temporarily removed out to sea, and are not replaced until the wind changes. When this removal takes place the under surface of the beach is exposed. Below the sand and shingle is a stiff clay base. It is in this clay that coins have been discovered. The lady from Salcombe with two coins was walking with a companion on the beach at Inner Hope when one of them noticed something sticking up out of the ground.

It was the edge of a coin that had caught her eye—probably because the sun glinted on it for a moment. When the two women realized what they had found they naturally began to search all round the spot to see if other coins were scattered near by. To their delight a second coin was found within a few feet of the first, also embedded in the clay. The second coin was slightly smaller, but bore the same marking as the first. Though they searched around for more, they did not find any.

Remembering how the fisherman had found his coin by the slip really close inshore, one would imagine that the ship had struck on the Inner Hope side of the Shippen Rock, so that his coin and the coins found in the clay would naturally arrive on the beach by tidal action.

However, this argument stands up only if you assume that the coins were held loose on board ship. Any seaman or gentleman on board the *St Peter* would keep a tight hold on his cash, either in his pocket or else locked in his baggage, so it would seem that the coins came on shore by some other means.

Let us assume for the time being that when the vessel struck those on board were desperate only to save their lives and, as a second consideration, their baggage. This seems to be a fair assumption, as there is only one thought in mind when a ship is breaking up around you—how to get off safely.

When the actual striking took place the beaches and vantage-points would be manned by local inhabitants. Those on shore would be rather cautious at first, and only after bodies and survivors had been washed ashore would their courage be enough for them to venture out in boats and climb over rocks to see what pickings could be had.

Cary's letter states quite clearly: "There hath been some plate and certain ducats rifled and spoiled at their first landing, both from their persons and out of their chests." This implies that those who were able to reach shore had some baggage with them, and therefore some boat or raft must have put off from the wreck.

Cary also says: "the weather such as none could get aboard." This further implies that, though desperate men could leave the ship, no-one from the shore was prepared to risk getting aboard and searching for booty. Cary's use of the word 'spoiled' simply means looting. How then did the coins get on the beach?

Anyone putting off from the wreck would first get away from the sinking ship as fast as possible to avoid the breakers and undertow raging around the actual wreck spot. If she struck on the northern side of the Shippen, or possibly on the unnamed rock to the north of this point, the first movement away from the ship would be westerly and out to sea. From a boat in this position it is only four hundred yards to the beach at Inner Hope—a point to which the boats would naturally head.

Having made the shore safely, the survivors would have been taken prisoner and searched. Their boxes and chests would have been broken open and the contents shared out.

At such a time coins could easily slip on to the beach and be stamped on and lost. Weight is also added to this argument by the fact that over the greater period of years comparatively few coins have been discovered. If a money-chest on the ship had broken open as the vessel disintegrated, then it would be more likely that coins would have been discovered in greater quantity over a longer period of time.

Apart from the clue of the coins, there have been several theories about the actual wreck spot. One of these indicates Yeovil Rock as the most likely place. There is certainly a true account of another shipwreck that happened there many years ago, and survivors from that wreck were marooned overnight on top of the Rock. It may be that this tale has become mixed with the Armada story.

A walk along the cliff-top from Hope, past Pilchard Cove, to Yeovil Rock will give you the lie of the land—and sea. The path climbs up from Hope and follows the cliff-edge until it becomes possible to climb down on to the rock itself. Having searched all round the rock, we have come to the conclusion that this site is improbable, as the water surrounding the rock deepens rapidly, and any ship striking it would wash off and sink quickly.

Another point against this site is that there are no reports of coins being found at Pilchard Cove, which is the nearest beach. And another clue in Cary's letter is that he states that the wreck occurred "at . . . Hope", not "near Hope" or "on the Bolt" (Bolt Tail).

The Basses Rock, just off Inner Hope beach, is another site that has been suggested, but this seems most unlikely.

What is left to be found? What could a diver expect to see on the seabed? To find this out we must study the actual contents of the *San Pedro*. A book by Daniel Archdeacon from an original in Lisbon, and printed in England on May 20th 1588, contains

a discourse upon the number of Galleons, Ships, Pinnaces, Zabres, Galeaces, Galleys, and other vessels which were assembled in the river of Lisbon, where of is Chiefe and Generall, the Duke of Medina Sidonia, together with the burthen of them, the men of warre, mariners, munitions, weapons, artillery powder and other furnitures for warre which they bring and for what time the said munitions shall serve as followeth.

Then follow the details of each squadron of vessels, but not full cargo inventories. For example, the flagship is listed as

The Galeon of St Martin. Capitaine Generall of the Armie, of 1000 tunnes, carrieth 177 mariners, 300 soldiers, chosen men, 50 pieces of cannon, bullets, powder, lead, corde and all that which is needfull.

Another account, of a similar date, lists the Armada as a total of 130 ships, 57,868 tons, 19,295 soldiers, 8450 seamen, 2088 slaves, and 2630 brass cannon. It also lists 7000 guns, 1000 muskets, 10,000 pikes, 1000 halberds, and 6000 half-pikes. From these figures, which, of course, must be treated with caution, certain equipment details emerge. For example, half the soldiers carried pikes; there was one gun for every three soldiers; every twentieth soldier had a musket, or, perhaps, more likely, for every 1000 soldiers there were 20 muskets provided, rather on the lines of one

Bren gun to each section in the Army during the last War. There were half-pikes for the rest.

The figures are not guaranteed to be accurate, but one thing is certain: the pikemen were the main attacking force for the land army. According to the facts that Cary was able to extract from survivors of the *San Pedro,* there were one hundred soldiers on board, of whom fifty were hospital staff. The fifty not with the hospital would have been armed for the field, so it should be fair to say that about fifty pikes, three muskets, and some twenty "guns" would have been on board at the time of the sinking. Besides these weapons, there would have been various arms belonging to the seamen and the ship's defence—in this case all iron cannon.

Then there were the contents of the hospital itself. Most of this will have disappeared long since, but you can never be sure about anything under the sea.

The wreck site would obviously be worth a diver's time, but the various legal aspects should be studied first (see Appendix One). It is also worth bearing in mind that the discovery of parts of an Armada ship would be of great value to historians. Local opinion of the wreck is mainly that its existence is not proven. Fishermen who have boats are not prepared to allow any chance visitor to hire one for the sake of a close look at the Shippen rocks. They are not prepared to risk their boats for a nominal fee.

On the credit side for the diver, however, is the fact that the underwater scenery is superb. On a bright day the water can be as clear as that of an aquarium, and the fish life is a joy to behold. And, despite local opinion, there is no doubt that an Armada ship did end up wrecked in the immediate neighbourhood. George Tessyman has seen the remains of an ancient ship. So go out one day some 200 yards from Outer Hope beach, and some 75 yards to the right of the Shippen as you face the open sea, and who knows—you may be the first to find the last resting-place of the *San Pedro el Mayor.*

CHAPTER
Three

Spanish Gold

IF the chance of a diver finding a fortune in the wreckage of the *San Pedro el Mayor* in South Devon is rather remote—she was almost certainly the only Spanish Armada vessel to strike the coast of England while under command of Spanish personnel— then we must turn to Ireland for the best chances of finding Spanish gold.

That divers can, on rare occasions, find fortunes is no longer open to doubt; recent diving discoveries of masses of coins from Spanish treasure-ships wrecked in the Bahamas have proved that centuries underwater do not always mean that all treasure is lost.

There are two examples of rich wrecks from the Armada lost in Irish waters—the *Santa Maria de la Rosa* and the *Girona*. This is what happened.

The Armada was standing out towards Rockall before finally heading south. As was said in the previous chapter, the Duke of Medina Sidonia on board the flagship *San Martin* warned the ships with him against attempting a landing on the Irish coast— "for fear of the harm that may come to you there". He was right. Thousands of Spaniards were to die on Irish soil—drowned, hunted down, killed by soldiers if they reached the beaches alive, executed formally, or, more rarely, killed by the Irish for the coins in their pockets.

But even so, as the Armada fleet edged southward, still remarkably complete, the less stout ships began to drop off. Those that had taken the brunt of the fighting wallowed lower and lower in the sea. Those whose crews were feeling the pinch of hunger and the greater pain of thirst began to lose station and edge towards land. The Duke himself suffered as much as the rest. He was no sailor, and continued sea-sickness, together with the fact that he would not allow himself better food than that taken by his men, made him a very sick man indeed.

The water shortage naturally got worse each day, and there was none to spare for the horses and mules on board. To save water the animals were forced overboard, and a fearful trail of swimming jetsam, left behind to drown, marked the wake of the ships.

One of the ships now turning in towards land for shelter was the huge carrack *La Rata Santa Maria Encoronada,* commanded by Don Alonso de Leyva, Captain-General of the Milan Cavalry. He was greatly respected in Spain, and many high-born Spaniards had competed to serve under him during the Armada campaign. Indeed, his ship had fired the first shots against the English off the Lizard many weeks before.

His once proud ship was now a very different sight. Several encounters had left their mark. She was wallowing, shot-battered, and her sails were in tatters. De Leyva needed fresh water, and he needed shelter and time for repairs. So he headed for the northwest of Ireland. The weather was still stormy, and high waves and tempestuous winds hammered the *Rata* towards the coast of Ireland. Soon she entered Blacksod Bay, in County Mayo, but there was little her crew could do to prevent her landward drift, and she stranded off Ballycroy.

De Leyva was not beaten yet. He landed his men and all their possessions, and then fired the hulk of his ship. There would be no escape by sea, and so he prepared for a land battle. His first move was to take over the castle at Ballycroy, but after a short while, apparently thinking it a better defensive spot, he moved with his company on to the Mullet Peninsula. There he was joined by another ship's company that had come ashore at Inver, in Broadhaven.

Soon De Leyva found that two other ships were anchored in Blacksod Bay—the *Nuestra Senora de Begona* and the *Duquesa Santa Ana*. De Leyva promptly embarked himself and his men into the *Santa Ana*. His plan was to sail north to the islands of Scotland, where he would be able to find friends.

Once there, he would reorganize his troops and refit the ship for the final journey back to Spain. By now his presence in Ireland was known, and a letter from the Lord Deputy to the Privy Council tells how a search for him was started. But before the search got very far De Leyva was off. The *Santa Ana,* however, had been hastily repaired from parts of other wrecks, and was really in no condition to sail again so soon. At first she met the storm winds bravely, but before she had sailed some seventy miles De Leyva found himself being forced ashore again. This time the *Santa Ana* was completely wrecked in Loughros Bay, in County Donegal.

James Machary, a Spanish sailor, who had been pressed into service in Lisbon, was captured later in the campaign and examined before Lord Deputy Fitzwilliam in Tipperary. He had been a sailor on board the *Duquesa Santa Ana,* and he told how De Leyva had saved everything from the *Rata*—"all the goods they had in the ship of any value as plate, apparel, money, jewels, weapons and armour"—and had taken these into the *Duquesa Santa Ana.*

At Loughros Bay De Leyva once again organized the salving of everything possible, but he was injured in doing so.

Machary said of this: "There fell a great storm which broke in sunder all their cables, and struck them upon the ground", and De Leyva "was hurt in the leg by the capestele of the ship in such sort as he was able neither to go nor ride". The "capestele" was the capstan. Although he had once again saved his men and their belongings, De Leyva was now badly hurt. So badly hurt that a litter had to be made for him. Four men carried him nineteen miles across country to Killybegs, south of Loughros Bay, where they were told some more Spanish ships had run ashore.

If it seems unbelievable that so many ships could be ashore all at the same time, a letter written to the Privy Council concerning the Spanish landings and wreckings on the western coast of Ireland confirms it. Part of the letter reads:

As I passed from Sligo, having then gone 120 miles, I held on towards Bundrowes (in the county of Leitrim) and so to Bally-shannon the uttermost part of Connaught that way, as some say, but denied so to be by O'Donnell and his followers, and riding still along the sea coast, I went to see the bay where some of those ships wrecked, and where, as I heard, lay not long before 1200 or 1300 of the dead bodies.

I rode along upon that strand near two miles, (but left behind me a long mile and more), and then turned off from that shore leaving before me a mile and better's riding, in both which places they said that have seen it, there lay as great store of the timber of wrecked ships as was in that place which myself had viewed, being in mine opinion (having small skill or judgement therein) more than would have built five of the greatest ships that I ever saw, besides mighty great boats, cables and other cordage answerable thereunto, and some such masts for bigness and length, as in mine own judgement I never saw any two could make the like.

From this account we realize that De Leyva had some idea of the number of Spanish ships that were crashing into the area, and knew that his litter journey was not likely to be in vain. Nor, indeed, was it. The ships were there.

Three Spanish ships had headed for the harbour of Killybegs. One of them did not quite make it and was wrecked outside the harbour. The second had apparently got in, but was smashed to pieces on the shore. The third, a galley called the *Girona,* though badly damaged, came safely to anchor.

When De Leyva arrived the galley was repaired, using planks from the second ship which had tried to reach the Killybegs harbour and which had been wrecked.

For the last time De Leyva loaded all the plate, money, jewels, and weapons into yet another ship. He was carried aboard, and the *Girona* sailed again on October 16th 1588. De Leyva was sticking to his original plan, and once more was heading for the isles of Scotland. But he was not to get clear of Ireland.

A letter from Mr Henry Dulse dated October 26th 1588 tells of the news he received from a man he had sent to spy on the Spaniards:

The 16th of this instant October the said gally departed from the said harbour with as many Spaniards as she could carry, and sailing along the coast towards the Out Isles of Scotland, wither they were then bound, struck against the rock of Bunboyes, (near Dunluce), where both ship and men perished, save only five who hardly got to shore; three of which five men came the next day, being the 17th, in company with Sorley

Boy M'Donnell unto O'Neill's house at Strabane, where they certified of their late shipwreck. Sorley Boy's coming to Strabane at this time was to get O'Neill's daughter to wife. This rock of Bunboyes is hard by Sorley Boy's house (of Dunluce).

One of the five survivors from the wreck of the *Girona* was James Machary, who told of De Leyva's treasure. De Leyva and all the other men on board had gone down with the ship, and so had all the plate and money that De Leyva had struggled so hard to save. What he had also lost on the ship caused some worry to the English authorities. The brass cannon on board the *Girona* were complete working weapons. These and the bullion were a tempting thought for the local insurgents. The Irish needed cash and cannons to resist the English, and suddenly both these welcome commodities were delivered to their doorstep—under some thirty feet of water.

To stop the local Irish from obtaining these weapons, instructions were sent to Sir George Carew, Master of the Ordnance, to make haste to Northern Ireland to retrieve all he could from the sea.

It would seem it took nearly a year for this haste to be acted upon. H.M.S. *Popingay* was dispatched then to pick up the Dunluce cannon after having done some other jobs.

In 1906 the *Geographical Journal*[1] published a very complete account of the Irish Armada wrecks by William Spotswood Green.

Green's works are often quoted with reference to these wrecks, and he is an extremely reliable source. Concerning the wreck of the *Girona*, he says:

> She was driven at midnight on to the Rock of Bunbois near the Giants Causeway. . . . Tradition connects the wreck of the *Girona* with the little bay called Port Na Spagna to the eastward of the Giants Causeway, but those who reported from personal knowledge said she was wrecked on the Rock of Bunbois, that is, in English, the Rock of Bushfoot, which is a little to the westward of the Causeway, and the Lord Deputy reported on December 31st "That three fair pieces of brass lie among the rock of Bunboyes where Don Alonso was drowned, and can be recovered". . . . Taking all things into account, I incline to the conclusion that the remains of the *Girona* lie off Bush River near Port Ballintrae.

[1] May 1906.

H.M.S. *Popingay* did not get the guns, for when she arrived to raise them it was found that the MacDonnels, helped by two Spaniards, had already raised the guns, and also helped themselves to two chests of treasure. The guns were later used to defend Dunluce Castle against the English, and one of the chests is still in Glenarm Castle.

So it would appear that at least some of the guns and bullion has been raised already. But the quality of the divers and equipment available at the time was not very high. Sir George Carew had worked on a similar wreck in Southern Ireland, and he noted —though his diver was working in only thirty feet of water—"our diver was nearly drowned, but Irish aqua vitae [whiskey] hath such virtue as I hope of his recovery".

Local legends and stories have, of course, grown with the years, but oddly enough there is no further record of any diving being done, until the modern wreck hunter arrived on the scene in 1963. Wreck hunter this time was Sidney Wignall, the underwater survey and salvage expert of Old Colwyn, Denbighshire, who has done a great deal of underwater work on the Irish Armada wrecks.

His report on the 1963 search reads as follows:

"Our only hope was to find some of the heavy pieces with which the *Girona* (as one of the most heavily armed of the Armada vessels) was fitted.

"In the coastal areas the local people have some legends as follows:

"(1) The *Girona* sailed parallel with the coast eastward until she struck the great reefs just offshore Portrush (the Skerry Islets).

"This theory does not hold water. It is very doubtful that the MacDonnels had the means of salving heavy brass guns from the reefs.

"(2) The *Girona*, when sailing past the Giant's Causeway, came close inshore and fired her guns at the Chimney Rocks, mistaking them for the tall chimneys of Dunluce Castle. At this point the rudder broke away and the *Girona* was driven ashore.

"This one is easily exploded. When De Leyva first landed in Ireland in the *Rata* he was requested by the Irish to help them fight the English. He replied, 'The instructions from my King do not include making war in Ireland.' At any rate, a worn and damaged ship manned by a sick and starving crew does not look for trouble on a last-chance gamble of reaching home. Apart from this, the Irish of Killybegs would have warned De Leyva where he could and could not land, and they would surely have informed him that the MacDonnels of Dunluce were against Elizabeth. Why then should he fire on England's enemies?

"(3) That the wreck of the *Girona* is connected with the little bay of Port (or Point) na-Spagna. This was worth investigating.

"We were surprised to find a steep-sided cove with cliffs about 300 feet high, vertical and in places overhanging. The only foot access is via a frighteningly narrow sheep track. No place to carry up cannon by hand.

"One important factor, however, was that the little cove, although almost inaccessible, was covered with a multitude of flotsam and jetsam, everything from spars, buoys, cans, rope, deadwood, all piled up on the shingle. No other beach within an area of miles had such a collection. As we looked we could even see new debris being carried inshore by the current.

"Is the origin of the name Point-na-Spagna that the *Girona* sank elsewhere, but most of the bodies were carried in here by the freak currents? It looked to me as though anything floating in the sea in the Bushmills area might end up in Point-na-Spagna.

"This left the contemporary statement that the *Girona* hit the reefs of Bushfoot. Local people who have studied the subject agree with Green's theory that what is now Bushmills was then Bushfoot, or as some have it Bun-bois.

"We searched under Dunluce Castle to eliminate the area, and found, as we expected, nothing. Visibility was good. We then searched the east side of Bushmills Bay up to a point to eastward where it would have been impossible for the MacDonnels to have rescued cannon due to the high and overhanging cliffs. No results. The west side was searched in a similar fashion until bad weather put an end to diving. This left a small area uncovered which would be worth investigation."

Sidney Wignall has, however, an interesting theory of his own. "Perhaps," he says, "there are no remains awaiting discovery. Perhaps the MacDonnels took away everything salvageable. My reason for saying that? The galleas was not a ship built for northern waters. She had little freeboard with oars intended to supplement sail as and when required. On the return home she had a complement of 1200. She was overloaded. She lacked food and water due to this overloading. Would De Leyva risk the safety of his ship and lives of 1200 men just to take 50 or so guns back to Spain? My theory is that De Leyva took with him only light pieces, perhaps only robinets. This would explain how the guns on the reef could have been picked up by the MacDonnels.

"Where then are the guns of the *Girona*? Go back to De Leyva's negotiations with the Irish. He refused to help them attack the English. He refused to supply them with cannon. If the *Girona* was overloaded, then the safety of the vessel demanded that the ship be lightened. De Leyva would not leave several hundred Spaniards behind. My theory is that he jettisoned all the heavy pieces at the point from which the *Girona* finally sailed. At Killybegs. If I'm right, then the big guns of the *Girona* lie just offshore at Killybegs."

In the same year—1963—Sidney Wignall was to take part in another expedition to find a Spanish treasure-ship. But first the story of the ship herself.

Running parallel in time with the loss of the *Girona* is the loss of the *Santa Maria de la Rosa*. She too was in convoy with the Duke of Medina Sidonia and she too decided to make for land to get away from the battering waves. The wind was blowing hard to the land—so strongly, in fact, that little could be done to prevent the *Santa Maria* from moving eastward towards the cliffs of County Kerry.

On board disease and privation had brought her complement of soldiers and sailors down to half.

Those that remained—and their health was none too good— were mostly the gentry and richer men who had been able to provide themselves in advance of the campaign with extra food and other luxuries.

The *Santa Maria* had been hard pressed since leaving Spain. Not once had they been able to take on fresh water, and what remained was now green with scum and stank. Many on board could not touch what food there was, as the great thirst had swollen their throats and prevented the swallowing of anything dry. Meat had begun to putrefy, so that this stench mingled with the scent of death that hung around the ship. Ship was the wrong word. She was a floating charnel-house.

On board orders were croaked out to those still able to walk on the rolling decks—take in sail, make sail, steer the ship. But all

Somewhere beneath the sea in this photograph of Blasket Sound lie the remains of two Spanish Armada galleons—and one almost certainly contained a great quantity of treasure. (See p. 51.)

(*Right*) Sir Cloudisley Shovell as he appears in an oil painting by Dahl. He was murdered for his jewellery after surviving the wrecking of his ship. (See p. 62.)

(*Left*) Admiral of the Blue Edward Boscawen as painted by Reynolds. He commanded the flotilla from which H.M.S. *Ramillies* was lost between Hope Cove and Bolt Head, Devon. (See p. 67.)

failed. No matter what venture was tried, the ship, in the clutch of the westerly winds, ploughed on towards the beetling cliffs. Soldiers and sailors sat in scattered groups, not even trying to brace themselves against the lurch and pitch of the decks. Their heads rolled drunkenly on their breasts, and cordage, loose and broken by the gales, whipped unnoticed about them.

Nearly all the sails were in tatters, blowing from the yards like giant emblems of defeat. The ship had been shot through 'between the wind and the water' some four times, and the un-plugged holes let the sea in to wash from side to side below decks, shifting ballast and daily causing the ship to wallow lower in the water. The crew were shipwrecked men still on board their ship. Had they been cast loose in an open boat with few rations they could not have been worse off.

All about them the dark-grey seas hurried on; waves reared up astern and passed, giving the hull an uprushing push to the top of a wave-crest, where the spume and spray tore off and soaked them. Coats-of-mail and weapons changed colour as rust and rot set to work. And all the while the Irish coast loomed nearer.

It was about September 11th 1588 when the end came. The ship was close to the western tip of Kerry before those on board realized that they were too near to the land for safety. By the time they were abreast of Dunquin the land seemed to be closing in all around them. Ahead the land swelled out on the port side in Dun-more Head, and to starboard, to the west, the little island of Beginish seemed to form part of the Great Blasket Island. The bay in between boiled and frothed expectantly. Tired eyes peered over the bulwarks to see what fate there was in store for them, and then a shout from the forepeak pulled all eyes to the starboard bow, to gaze upon what was to them a complete miracle. Anchored between the Great Blasket and Beginish were three Spanish vessels—two great galleons and a smaller ship. Martin de Villafranca, Captain of the *Santa Maria,* ordered a gun fired to signal their entrance to the anchored ships, and then another gun as they moved towards the anchorage, as he could not detect any movement to their assistance. An anchor had been prepared some days before-hand, and was catted from the bow in readiness for sudden need. Two sailors, one with an axe, staggering and crouching as the vessel lurched through the waves, made their way to the bow to release the anchor. One cut and then another with the axe severed the supporting cordage, and the anchor dropped to the bottom, taking the sodden cable behind it with a rush and a shower of water from the hawse-hole. Within a few minutes the forward movement of the ship ceased, and she swung at anchor, pitching and tossing like a toy on a disturbed lake. Hopes were exchanged between the men of the *Santa Maria* that the weather might improve, and then they could expect aid from the other galleons. Some hoped that boats would put off at once with water and medical supplies, and others fondly imagined that all was safe and that they would be well cared for within a few hours. But it was all to no avail. They were never to know that the anchored ships were in little better condition than their own, and that they had only one good boat with which to visit them. From their anchored position those on board the *Santa Maria* could now make out that the water to their front was not a bay, but stretched away between the headlands of the mainland and the island in a fearsome channel through which the water was rushing and heaving like a live thing. Their single anchor-rope stretched towards the channel as the tide held them steady with the wind blowing hard on their stern. They were very much 'between the wind and the water' at that moment, the wind pushing them on, the tide holding them back. It was midday; the tide changed at two. They were anchored in a most dangerous position, but there was nothing they could do to better it in any way.

With the wind blowing from anywhere between west and north, no feat of seamanship could bring them across to where the other ships lay at anchor between the Great Blasket and Beginish. If they had been better prepared on entering the anchorage and had had a fit crew and a full complement of sails they might well have been able to come up to the anchored galleons, but now, as they lay to their single anchor, nothing short of a miracle could save them should this one cable part. Preparations were made to receive the imagined aid from the anchored ships; a little food was issued and a very little water. Midday passed, and the tide changed to slack and then to ebb.

Beneath the surface the solitary anchor moved as the ship swung to take the strain in a new direction, and as it moved so it loosened, or broke from the seabed, and the ship began to drift towards the mainland. With the tide and wind behind her the drifting increased, and the loosened anchor began to bounce over the bottom, unable to take a hold. Villafranca screamed at the men in the waist of the ship to hoist the good foresail, but as they clambered to obey him the ship struck on a submerged rock and immediately filled and sank like a stone. As she disappeared from view, hull and masts, pieces of the ship bobbed away in the tide. A few heads showed and then sank, the exhausted bodies beneath them unable to bear up against the freezing cold of the water and the spume that filled their mouths at every gasping breath. One head, however, did not sink. Only one sailor, "naked upon a board", came ashore alive. He was the pilot's son—Antonio de Monana, a Genoese who had been taken into service with his father at Lisbon. Now, a prisoner in a strange land, he was taken to Dingle to be examined in front of James Trant, the local agent of Sir Edward Denny. Trant had already examined a boatload of men that had come into his clutches from the galleon *San Juan,* which was one of the ships anchored in the Sound when the *Santa Maria* made her entrance. He had some information of what was happening out there near the Great Blasket, or "The Ferriters Great Island", as the Blasket was then called. He asked many questions and poor Antonio, "Marryner", tried as best he could to give the right answers, but as he spoke Italian and some Spanish and his answers were written in English by an Irish clerk, some of the recorded examination can be regarded as suspect. In his various statements he is quoted as saying that the Prince of Ascoli, base son of the King of Spain, had been among those lost. He even described his appearance and the sort and colour of his clothes. However, it is a fact that the Prince had been put ashore in France and was unable to rejoin the ship when it sailed. This mis-statement is possibly an error of record, as the recorder could have imagined the details about the Prince to refer to a member of the lost ship, instead of realizing that the description and account referred to a happening that took place some time previous to the loss. Whatever the cause, the local Irish believed the tale, and the place at Dunquin where several bodies from the wreck were buried is known to this day as the Grave of the Son of the King of Spain.

What was of greater interest to the examiners was the fact that a quantity of cannon and gold and silver coin had also been lost in the wreck. It is unfair to assume that a pilot's son would be able to give an exact inventory of ordnance or the contents of several locked and guarded chests, but it is as unfair to assume that he completely fabricated his report that she carried "50 great pieces, all cannons of the field; 25 pieces of brass and cast-iron belonging to the ship; there were also in her 50 tuns of sack". He also estimated that the cash on board amounted to some 50,000 golden ducats and 50,000 silver ducats, and besides this there was the plate of gold and silver owned by the rich persons who were on board at the time of the loss. All in all she was a rich wreck. The *Santa Maria* was a merchant-ship of some 950 tons and had started the campaign with 300-odd men.

On board the anchored galleons were Juan Martinez de Recalde, Admiral of the Armada, and Marcos de Aramburu, Paymaster to the Castille squadron. They each commanded a galleon called *San Juan,* Recalde's being the *San Juan* of the Portugese squadron, Aramburu's the *San Juan* of the Castille squadron, and although both saw the entrance and wreck of the *Santa Maria,* only Aramburu's account remains for examination. Possibly because he was a Paymaster, and thereby an exacting person, his account deals carefully with the complete happening, even to a record of the state of the tide and the accompanying weather. It was no doubt compiled with the aid of the ship's log. The whole account of what happened to the *San Juan* of Castille while she voyaged along the Irish coast would occupy too many pages, but the parts relative to the loss of the vessel, in which the interest of this chapter lies, are certainly worth repeating. We take up Aramburu's tale just previous to the wreck of the *Santa Maria.*

The 18th, 19th and 20th [of September 1588] we remained in the same port without being able to get out. Juan Martinez went on taking in water; and I, having no long-boat or other boat, could do nothing; and he but little, and that with much labour. On the morning of the 21st the wind began to blow from the west with terrible violence. Clear, with but little rain. The ship of Juan Martinez drifted down on ours.

It can be seen here that the careful Aramburu did not confuse his account with references to the *San Juan,* but referred to the ship by its commander's name.

He dropped anchor with another cable, and, having smashed our lantern and the tackle on our mizzen-mast, brought the ship to. At midday the ship *Santa Maria de la Rosa,* of Martin de Villa Franca, came in by another entrance nearer the land, towards the north-west, and on coming in fired a gun, as if asking help, and another when further in.

Aramburu records the distress signal, but does not note that he was unable to assist in any way, so one must assume that the prior information that he had no boat with which to take water from the island was sufficient to say that he could not send aid across the stormy water to the *Santa Maria*.

She had all her sails torn to ribbons, except the foresail. She anchored with a single anchor, as she had no more. And as the tide, which was coming in from the south-east, beat against her, she held on till two o'clock, when it began to ebb, and at the turn she commenced drifting, about two splices of cable from us, and we with her; and in an instant we saw she was going to the bottom while trying to hoist the foresail, and immediately she went down with the whole crew, not a soul escaping —a most extraordinary and terrible occurrence.

The account gives details about anchors and replacements of broken parts, and then continues:

The same evening at 4 o'clock the ship *San Juan* [the third of the same name in the Sound!], of Fernando Horra, came in with the mainmast gone, and on entering, the foresail was blown to threads; she let go anchor and brought to. Owing to the gale it was impossible to communicate with or help her. On the 22nd he lowered his long-boat and made known his distressed condition.

Horra's condition was distressed indeed, as his ship was leaking like a sieve and ready to go to the bottom at the next strong gale of wind. Because of this Recalde divided the crew among the other ships and attempted to save the guns from Horra's ship. Aramburu told him not to worry about the guns, and suggested he set fire to the ship and leave without delay. But Recalde was determined to do all he could to save the precious guns, and, imagining it would take a few days, he gave Aramburu permission to sail as soon as the weather allowed. Aramburu upped anchor next morning and left the anchorage. After a series of gales and terrible weather he eventually arrived in Spain. Recalde left soon after him, and also came home safely, but his attempt to save the guns from the *San*

Juan (Horra) failed, and they went to the bottom with the ship. It is sad to note that Recalde died soon after landing in Spain— another tragedy after the abortive attempt by Spain to land on English soil.

After the story the thoughts of what was left behind. At the bottom of the Blasket Sound lie the remains of two Spanish galleons, both with cannon, one certainly with a goodly store of golden treasure. Whatever was on board the *San Juan* of any value we must assume was saved by Recalde before the ship sank, and that only the guns were left when the ship went to the bottom.

In another account, by W. S. Green (*Proceedings of the Irish Academy* of February 1909, Volume XXVII, Section C, N. 12, and entitled "Armada Ships on the Kerry Coast"), some other points worth recording are raised.

Firstly, the compass. We all know that a magnetic compass points to that part of the globe that contains the magnetic substance that attracts the compass-needle. But this magnetic area is a moving one. The geographical north pole is fixed, for the sake of accuracy and convenience, but the magnetic north pole revolves around it, taking about 500 years to complete a revolution. That is why charts showing a compass rose have noted on them, usually across the rose, the annual increase or decrease of the magnetic variation. The point to note here is that all the references to compass bearings and wind direction given in the contemporary accounts were read from the compass on board at that time. Today's compass placed at the same spot would point in a different direction. According to Green, the variation in the latitude of the Great Blasket during 1588 was 10 degrees east. Assuming that the present variation is 10 degrees west, and approximately it is, then the difference in the compass bearings would be 20 degrees —nearly two points on the 32-point compass.

Secondly, Green makes a shrewd guess at the site of the wreck itself. The *Santa Maria* came into the anchorage "by another entrance nearer the land, towards the north-west, and on coming in", etc., according to Aramburu. Using this as a guide, she must have entered by the northern entrance, and, with the wind blowing from the west, she would have been well over towards the mainland when she dropped anchor. Aramburu and Recalde were between the Great Blasket and Beginish when the *Santa Maria* came in, but they too dragged their anchors when the storm hit, and must have been across nearly to where the *Santa Maria* made her first anchorage. While they dragged, so did the *Santa Maria*, and Green places the wrecking place as the Stromboli Rock, which is a submerged rock on the mainland side of the Sound, opposite to An Gob, the easterly headland of the Great Blasket. It is shown on Admiralty charts. There are two and a half fathoms (fifteen feet) over the rock at low water at the present time, but Green considers that this rock may well have been awash in 1588, and says that it seems to have been smashed when H.M.S. *Stromboli* ran into it "some fifty years ago". This would be 1850 or thereabouts.

Some twenty years before this a small brass cannon was fished up from the bottom of the Sound in a net by local fishermen. It was recorded as having a coat-of-arms emblazoned on it bearing the device of an uprooted tree. The report goes on to say that the cannon is preserved in Clonskeagh Castle, Dublin. It is regretable that the cannon does not exist today. We had the greatest hopes that it would still be there, and with it an account of how and where it was found. We were doomed to disappointment, however, for an inquiry to the castle brought the news that no trace of it remained. Apparently it had disappeared during the 'troubles', and the story was that it had been melted down into scrap by the Black and Tans, and the proceeds from the sale used to supplement the drinks ration. This story is unconfirmed. No matter what was done to it, it is not there now, and with its disappearance goes one of the main clues to the site of the wreck of the *Santa Maria*.

Concerning the *San Juan* (Horra) that also sank, Green places her site as more to the westward than the *Santa Maria*; here again we are inclined to agree, as this ties in well with the known facts.

All in all, the two wrecks occurred in an area that is not too large for a determined team of divers to search.

In July 1963 Sidney Wignall, together with Joe Casey and members of the St Helens Underwater Club, arrived in Ireland and prepared for their first dive in Blasket Sound. Wignall reports:

"When we had judged that we were heading, with the tide, straight downstream for Stromboli Rock, I dropped over the side, hanging tight on to a 150-foot line with an inflated plastic buoy on the end as a marker. I was to drift over the rock and look for remains of the *Santa Maria*. The boat's crew were to follow my float, and when I surfaced another diver was to go down for another run.

"I hit the bottom at 100 feet (by my depth-gauge) and decided to stop still for a moment to get my bearings. This was impossible; the current took hold and I was off in the direction of Stromboli Rock at a good two to two and a half knots. Horizontal visibility was about 25 feet. I tried to fight the current and slow down, but soon gave up the unequal struggle. After a few minutes coasting over a hard, sandy bottom with occasional large stones, I saw a grey shape ahead. It was the rock.

"I hauled up the line and ascended with one or two bumps against the vertical rock-face. The weed was remarkably sparse, probably due to the speed of the current.

"Every few feet I passed over a couple of large crayfish, waving their long feelers. The flat table-top of the rock came along at 70 feet, and, as I floated over it, I saw the odd large salmon holding the tide by finning slowly with its tail. They ignored me although only about three feet away. Eventually the bottom fell slowly away and I ran out my line to 120 feet. Then the bottom plunged down to over 150 feet. There was no sign of the *Santa Maria* or her guns.

"I was running out of line now, and there was nothing to be gained by staying down, so I surfaced. It was a different world. The calm of the seabed gave way to a swell heavier than when I submerged. About half a mile away I could see Dunmore Head on the mainland, and then I dipped down into a deep trough. On the crest again I could see Great Blasket Island receding behind me. Ahead here was only the swell of the Atlantic. I looked around for the boat. No sign. Could it have sunk? Impossible. Several minutes passed while I hung on to my plastic buoy. I was about to ditch my gear and inflate my lifejacket when I suddenly saw the boat—half a mile away and heading in the opposite direction! Shouting was useless, so I waved.

"Just at that moment one crew member turned round and saw me. Then the boat and I dipped into troughs, and I lost sight of them for a few minutes. . . . Ten minutes later I was in the boat— and very thankful for it. . . . We were all beginning to assume a very healthy respect for Blasket Sound.

"How had the boat lost sight of my buoy? It sounds impossible, but the crew told me that they lost it for an instant in a trough and never saw it again. What seemed to have happened was that neither the boat nor the buoy was on the crests at the same time on any one occasion.

"We managed one run towing a diver along the approximate line of the anchorage off shore from Great Blasket Island. This proved negative. A south-west wind made further diving impossible, but we believe that a continuous search of the off-shore anchorage would have shown positive results."

The next expedition arrived in April 1964. It was composed of Roger Jefferis, co-author of this book, John Halfhide, Gerald Mundey, and William Butland, all divers from the London Branch of the British Sub-Aqua Club.

This expedition had been designed to cover three points. Firstly, to prove that a good base camp could be established on the now uninhabited Great Blasket Island that would provide divers with food, shelter, and warmth. Secondly, to size up the area and find out diving conditions and hazards. Thirdly, to dive and explore the possible sites of the lost ships.

Objects one and two were achieved. The third is covered in the expedition's report:

"Diving was started on the day after arrival and setting up camp on the Island. Snorkel diving close inshore showed that visibility was good with the growth of kelp thick but not at full strength. Currents worried us before this preliminary exploration. It was felt that the tide washing between the islands would carry divers away and make diving difficult without ropes, but once in the water we found that though the currents were certainly there, they were not as bad as we had feared. Diving with Aqualungs then began. Once away from the rocks, the bottom proved to be sand and shingle with occasional clumps of weed covering protruding rocks. The wind then increased from the south-west, and diving had to be cut to the minimum.

"After three days of appalling weather, we were able to start diving again. We now buoyed a possible site for the wreck of the *San Juan*. On the bottom the sand and shingle move with the tide, but the visibility is excellent and with the high sun there is plenty of light at 40 feet. Bill Butland made a long search of the area, moving to and fro across the selected strip of seabed. No sign of any wreck. The tide made searching strenuous, and as the tide changed it was possible to use its force to plane over the bottom.

"Michael Brennan now joined the expedition, but even this extra pair of eyes could not find any trace of the two wrecks. Our searches revealed only sand and rock; even the 30-foot-long basking sharks which had joined us in the bay for a time had now deserted us. We felt at the end that any future expedition to succeed would need many more divers and much larger boats."

The report concludes with thanks to the Irish divers who helped in the planning of the expedition.

Two mentioned in particular are Desmond Branigan of Dublin and Desmond Lavelle of Valentia Island. Both are excellent divers and have themselves looked for the last resting-place of these two great ships.

So far they too have met with no success, but the search will certainly go on. The latest move being discussed is the use of a metal detector towed from a boat. Only when a positive reading is obtained on the instrument will divers be sent down. In dangerous waters and areas of poor visibility this would seem to be the ideal method of search.

Underwater searches for wrecks contain a number of hazards—as, indeed, does any diving. In June 1963 James Hewitt, on holiday from Newcastle-on-Tyne, failed to surface while diving in Blasket Sound, and was later found dead in ninety feet of water.

Down they go

S HE was a fine ship. He was a most successful Admiral. But he was no navigator. And that was to lose him first his ship, together with others in his fleet, and then his own life.

First, then, the ship. She was the *Association*, a 90-gun ship of the line, strong, seaworthy, and one of the Navy's best.

Now the man. He was Admiral Sir Cloudisley Shovell, who was so well thought of that his remains rest in an elaborate tomb in Westminster Abbey.

There was no doubt that the *Association* was a seaworthy ship. In November 1703 a fantastic storm struck the British Isles, and thousands of sailors died as ship after ship was driven aground or foundered in gigantic seas. Among those completely wrecked were the *Stirling Castle,* 70 guns; the *Mary,* 70 guns; the *Northumberland,* 70 guns, lost on the Goodwins; the *Vanguard,* 70 guns, sunk at Chatham; the *York,* 70 guns, lost near Harwich; the *Resolution,* 60 guns, lost on the coast of Sussex; the *Newcastle,* 60 guns, lost at Spithead, and the *Reserve,* 60 guns, sunk at Yarmouth. And these were only the larger vessels lost in this storm, which from contemporary accounts must have been riding on winds of hurricane strength.

The *Association,* however, rode out that storm. She was part of the fleet commanded by Sir Cloudisley Shovell, and was off

Harwich at the time the storm struck. She was blown from her anchorage, and the seas nearly had her. The gun ports on her upper
deck, many feet above the waterline, were burst in by the waves,
and only the efforts of her crew stopped her filling and sinking
there and then. The *Association* now ran with the wind and
sought shelter in Holland, but was blown away again north to
Scandinavia. It took her two months to get back to England
again!

It may have been his memory of the way the *Association* had
coped with the hurricane several years earlier that made Sir
Cloudisley choose her as his flagship when he was at Lisbon in
March 1707. In April he was off Toulon to make siege with the
Duke of Savoy. By the 10th of August the battle was over, the
French Mediterranean Fleet was destroyed, and Sir Cloudisley
was free to return home to England with honour and glory.

As an Admiral he was obviously a capable man, but as a navigator he was not. At the Battle of Vigo Bay, some years before, he
had been in charge of a captured galleon full of gold, but had run
her on a rock at the mouth of the bay and lost her.

Now with his fleet of fifteen ships of the line, five frigates, and a
yacht he had led the way from Toulon, out through the Pillars of
Hercules, up past Portugal and Spain, and out into the Atlantic
and the mouth of the English Channel. But he wasn't sure where he
was!

So on Wednesday, October 22nd, signal flags streamed in the
slight south-west wind, and from the ships of the fleet came small
boats all converging on the flagship, the *Association*. A meeting of
the fleet Sailing Masters was to be held to decide on their present
latitude. In all fairness to the Admiral, as he did not know his position, he did solicit the advice of all the capable navigators available
to him. As Admiral he was not really expected to keep a daily check
on the distances sailed, or the minute directions in which his ships
went, but one would have thought he would have had some idea of
where he was!

In his state room Sir Cloudisley listened, glass in hand, to the
comments and calculations of his Sailing Masters. His own comments were more or less confined to keeping the meeting in order.
He was a large man, fat and "lusty", a man who liked the good
things of life. He was going home to England at the height of his
success, and no doubt felt very important and powerful.

The discussion seemed almost to bore him. Was he looking ahead to his triumphant arrival in Falmouth? A pompous man, perhaps, but, having listened to the arguments of his Sailing Masters, he made no hard decision of his own, but merely took the majority decision as being the right one. The majority were of the opinion that the fleet was in the latitude of Ushant. Sir Cloudisley instructed one and all to carry on on that assumption.

Sir George Byng, Vice-Admiral of the Blue, from the *Royal Anne,* and Sir John Morris, Rear-Admiral of the Blue, from the *Torbay,* apparently agreed with this too. Certainly there was only one voice raised in protest—that of Sir William Tumper's Sailing Master of the *Lennox.* He insisted that they were much nearer to the Scilly Isles, and therefore much nearer England and farther north. No-one else agreed with him.

To underline the decision, and no doubt to impress upon this errant Sailing Master that he was right, Sir Cloudisley dispatched the *Lennox,* with another frigate, *La Valeur,* and the fireship *Phœnix,* ahead of the fleet to announce its imminent arrival in Falmouth. The course was read off to them, and sails were set at once.

The *Lennox* set off, steering on the directed north-easterly course. Within a very short time the Scillies loomed ahead, and the *Lennox* was nearly wrecked, but managed to anchor in time. *La Valeur* also came to anchor safely, but the *Phœnix* was damaged crossing a hidden reef, and had to be beached between Tresco and St Martin's.

After the first glow of self-congratulation had faded from the *Lennox*'s Sailing Master's mind he suddenly thought of the other ships sailing in his wake—sailing to certain destruction. But there was nothing he could do. The wind was now blowing stormily from the south-west, the sky was overcast, and he was at anchor in a position which would mean disaster for his own ship if he tried to move.

And so, that same evening at 6 P.M., Sir Cloudisley set out on a course that meant that the *Association* and the rest of the fleet would sail straight on to the rocks of the Scilly Isles. Two hours later, at almost exactly 8 P.M., the *Association* struck, and within moments was gone from sight, leaving only a few heads bobbing on the windswept sea. The *St George,* close by, struck on the same rocks, but managed to get off again.

The *Eagle*, 70 guns, went down like a stone with all hands. The *Romsey*, 50 guns, sank, and only one man escaped to shore. The frigate *Firebrand*, a fireship under the command of a Captain Percy, was wrecked also, but five of her crew came ashore clinging to some wreckage, and Captain Percy and seventeen more of his men got to shore in a boat.

In a matter of moments it was all over. Big, proud ships had disappeared from the face of the stormy sea. Sir George Byng, on board the *Royal Anne*, had a narrow escape, and but for the presence of mind of his officers and crew would have joined Sir Cloudisley in the water. Sir George's Sailing Master may have been a bit sketchy on his navigation, but his handling of the ship was superb. He had the ship about in an instant, and avoided the rocks when they were only a ship's length away.

Captain Loader, Sir Cloudisley's Flag Captain, Sir John Narborough, his brother James, and the son of Bishop Trelawney were cast up, drowned, on the beach at Porthellick, and were later buried in the old church there. Sir Cloudisley got ashore at the same place. He had suffered badly on the rocks and in the sea, but he was still alive.

With careful nursing he would most likely have lived on for several years (he was then fifty-seven) and enjoyed his return to England. It was not to be. As he lay exhausted and bleeding on the sand he was discovered by two women who had come down to the beach to see what pickings could be had from the wreckage. Whether they knocked him on the head at once, cut his throat, or waited for him to die of shock and exposure is not known, but kill him they did. When he was dead they stripped off what clothes remained, tore off the great emerald ring on his finger, and left his body on the beach.

A man called Harry Pennick, searching the cove later, found the naked corpse, and ordered it to be buried in the sand near the place where it had been washed ashore. This gave rise to a local legend about Sir Cloudisley which has been repeated many times as fact. The legend has it that Sir Cloudisley had had a sailor hanged from the yardarm not long before the wreck for daring to argue that the ships were near the Scillies and not where Sir Cloudisley believed them to be. Because of this, says the story, his temporary grave on the beach will never grow grass on it, and the grave of this evil man is a place to be avoided.

There is not the slightest shred of evidence to support the hanging tale, but it is true that the woman who kept Sir Cloudisley's ring had no benefit from it. Once the hue and cry for the murderers had died down and she felt able to go safely about her normal life, the ring itself became a millstone to her. It was worth untold riches in the way of food and warm clothing—all she needed and desired—but she could not try to sell it. Such a ring would have been recognized at once.

Thirty years passed, and only when she lay on her death-bed did the woman confess the crime to her clergyman and pass the ring on to him. He then gave it to one of Sir Cloudisley's old friends, the Earl of Berkeley, and the ring remains in the family still.

But back to the wrecks. The day after the tragedy several boats were in the area looking for and finding parts of the lost ships and gruesome reminders of the swiftness of the destruction. The Welsh fleet had seven men-of-war at anchor in the Scillies, and boats from these ships—the *Southampton, Arundel, Lizard, Salisbury, Antelope, Hampshire*, and *Charles*—began plying between ships and wreck site collecting all the flotsam that appeared on the sea. A great deal of wreckage was recovered in this way.

The sole survivor of the *Romsey* was her Quartermaster, George Lawrence, and even though he had been battered by the rocks in making his escape from the sea, he was still entered on the books of the *Salisbury* that same morning. The *Salisbury* was to figure again in the story of Sir Cloudisley, as this vessel was selected to transport his exhumed body from the Scillies to Plymouth. From Plymouth the body was carried to London for decent burial. To this day there is an elaborate memorial in Westminster Abbey marking his last resting-place.

The memorial is in the south aisle by the choir. It depicts Sir Cloudisley reclining scantily dressed as a Roman. The inscription reads:

Sir Cloudisley Shovell Kt. Rear Admirall of Great Britain and Admirall and Commander in Chief of the Fleet. The just rewards of his long and faithfull Service, he was deservedly beloved of his Country and esteem'd tho' dreaded by the enemy, who had often experienced his Conduct and Courage. Being ship wreckt on the Rocks of Scylly in his voyage from Thoul on 22nd of October 1707 at night in the 57th year of his age. His fate was lamented by all, but especially the Sea faring part of the Nation to whom he was a generous Patron and a worthy example.

His body was flung on the shoar and buried with others in the sands, but being soon after taken up was placed under this monument which his Royall Mistress has caus'd to be erected to commemorate his Steady Loyalty and Extraordinary Vertues.

The inscription makes no mention of the 2000 lives that were lost that night in the sea by the Scilly Isles. At the site of the wrecks more timbers and cordage came on shore. The Town Hall at Penzance has the sternboard of the Admiral's barge which was washed up at Porthellick, and in the church at St Mary's is a small lion which has apparently come from one of the ships.

Many other bits and pieces were recovered from time to time after storms, but nothing of any consequence is recorded, nor any serious attempt at salvage, until a report appeared in the *London Letter* of July 1710. The *London Letter*, a Scottish newspaper, stated:

> We hear from Scilly that the gentlemen concerned in the wreck where Sir Cloudesley Shovel was cast away, have taken several iron guns and seven brass guns with a cable, and have found the *Association* in four fathom at low water, the hull of the ship being whole, wherein there is a vast treasure—the Queen's Plate, several chests of money, besides ten chests of Sir Cloudesley's own, with great riches of the Grandees of Spain.
>
> The Divers go down in a copper engine, and continue two hours under water, 30 fathoms deep, where they have also met with the fireship, (cast away at the same time as the *Association,* I don't know her name). Had not the winds been westerly, which occasioned the seas to be very high and boisterous, all the Treasure before this, had been fished out.

The account stresses the treasure, but then goes on to say the wreck is in four fathoms of water, but the divers are working at thirty fathoms. Four fathoms is twenty-four feet, a depth which any reasonable swimmer used to diving below the surface could reach without too much effort; on the other hand, thirty fathoms, or 180 feet, is a depth at which modern divers take care. Using modern decompression tables, we find that two hours underwater with a maximum depth of 180 feet would mean that, to avoid a nasty attack of the bends, the diver would have about half an

The loss of the *Association*. A contemporary idea of how it actually happened. (See p. 61.)

(*Above*) The search for the *Impregnable*. Maurice Harknett (*left*) aboard his boat *Gina-Anne*. (See p. 85.)

(*Below*) Bob Rogers in the Scilly Isles when searching for the *Association*. Life-jacket is inflated. Single-hose demand valve from his air supply rests above the underwater camera-case. (See p. 65.)

(*Above*) Mrs Maureen Trouton when spearfishing before the discovery in Cannon's Hole. (See p. 94.)

hour on the bottom. As such tables were unknown in the times we are writing about, the whole report becomes suspect. It may be that the fact that no more is heard in the *London Letter* of his salvage work means that the divers died!

However, the report does make it clear that the site of the wrecks was known and that some sort of salvage attempts were being made.

We are now left with two mysteries. Firstly, why were the ships so far off course? Secondly, is there a fortune in treasure lying in the wreckage of the *Association*?

The answer to the first question is now fairly straightforward. Obviously the westerly winds had moved the fleet farther than the Sailing Masters had calculated, but a greater cause of the disaster was probably the action of a strong sea-current, now known as Rennell's current, after James Rennell, who first discovered it.

But is there any treasure? The answer would seem to be—probably. There is no record of any salvage of treasure from the wreck, and it would be an extremely difficult thing to keep quiet in a place like the Scillies.

One man who is sure that there is a fortune waiting for him on the bottom of the sea on the site of the *Association* is Bob Rogers. Already he has great cause for hope. He and his firm, Blue Sea Divers, believe that they found the *Association* during dives on their first exploratory expedition to the Islands.

The *Association* is reputed to have hit a rock called the Gilstone. It was at this point that Bob Rogers started his search.

"Time was the main trouble," said Bob Rogers; "winter was coming on before we really got to the Scillies. But we dived very methodically for a week. Each diver would cover a square as large as an acre. We found a sunken village—it appeared to have a finely constructed causeway. We found several flint arrowheads and shot some ciné film of it, but we thought if it had kept this long under the sea it could keep a little longer. At any rate it was the *Association* we were looking for—not sunken villages!

"Finally we tackled a new, deeper section—about 40-50 feet deep—and had to cut the size of the area as we were now working in pairs with Aqualungs. And then it happened.

"I was diving with Roscoe. We were swimming along, peering carefully into the weed below us. We spotted a piece of a brightly coloured plate about two and a half inches long on a sandy patch. I picked it up and kept the piece in my hand. Roscoe was swimming alongside me, and now he finned on past a thick bank of weed. I was just about to follow him when my eye caught a long black object just beneath. I reached out and caught his arm, shaking it in my excitement.

"I swam down to the object and stared at it close up. There, no mistake, there in the underwater twilight, was a naval cannon at least 6 feet long and badly corroded after 250 years on the seabed. A gun-layer's handle stretched from the top of the breech to the knob at the rear. I reached out and grabbed it—but to my dismay it broke off in my hand.

"We surfaced and called the rest of the diving team together to concentrate on the area around the gun. We decided to work deeper, following the line of the seabed. We got down to 60 feet that day, 70 feet the next, and 80 feet on the next.

"When I first saw the next thing we found I thought we had discovered the island's rubbish dump. There, at 80 feet, was an area about 600 feet across which looked exactly like a rubbish dump. The seabed, quite normal sand and weed patches elsewhere, was here littered with masses of fragments of plates, bottles, pots, flagons, and jars.

"We brought up a great number of things for closer inspection, and found that many of the cups and plates were made of pewter. The area was so big that we decided this was the time to use our battery-powered underwater scooter. Using this as our work-horse, we surveyed the area minutely, covering every square foot.

"On the bottom we started digging and uncovered nine more cannon similar to our first find. I'm sure it is the *Association*."

Meanwhile Bob Rogers and his Blue Sea Divers go on exploring the area. Recently he told us that he feels sure that he will need to use a compressed-air lift to clear away much of the debris and sand over the site, which he cautiously says is "about half a mile from the Gilstone". He would like to see a properly organized archaeological excavation done on the site of the *Association*. If this were done it would certainly be the first of its kind in British waters, though there is talk of such an excavation on the *Marye Rose* (see Chapter Eleven).

The loss of the *Association* was caused by poor navigation, but the loss of the next ship with which we deal, H.M.S. *Ramillies*, was more likely due to poor maintenance than poor seamanship.

The *Ramillies* was a 90-gun second-rate ship of the line, and the war with the French was the only reason that she was still at sea and not undergoing a major refit in a shipyard.

Admiral Lord Hawke had fought and won a great sea battle in Quiberon Bay in November 1759, and had defeated a French invasion threat. When the battle was over and victory decisive he was recalled to England. But though the French had been defeated, not all their ships had been sunk. A blockading force from England was needed to make sure that they did not challenge English seapower once again.

The blockading force was commanded by Admiral of the Blue Edward Boscawen. He was ordered to take a small flotilla and stand guard at Quiberon Bay. He set sail with his ships during January 1760, and at once encountered heavy weather—so heavy, in fact, that he was forced to shelter at Spithead. He waited there until February 6th, when he saw a break in the weather. Off he went again, and got as far as Plymouth before being forced to shelter once more.

His vessels were battered and tattered from the beating of sea and wind. Any normal voyage would have allowed time for refitting and at least a check on strained planks, but this was war, and the Admiral wanted to press on. But the weather forced him to wait. And as he waited he hoped, too, that the *Ramillies* would join him at Plymouth after losing the rest of the flotilla during the voyage from Spithead. But the hours passed and the *Ramillies* did not come.

Instead the Admiral heard to his dismay that the *Ramillies* had gone on shore near Salcombe, South Devon. And on the 17th of February 1760 he had to write this letter:

Royal William,
PLYMOUTH SOUND

SIR,

I have received their Lordships' order of the 6th instant relating to the number of ships, frigates and sloops which I am to keep under my command and shall take particular care to comply therewith.

Yesterday I sent Mr Hall, one of the Master Attendants here, to Salcomb in order to obtain what particulars he can of the *Ramillies,* and to secure what men are saved, so soon as he returns shall send his report to their Lordships.

I am,

Sir,

your most obedient,

Humble servant,

E. BOSCAWEN

Though Admiral Boscawen had sent his man to Salcombe, the main town for the area, the wreck was not there, but between Hope Cove and Bolt Head. Another two days elapsed before the Admiral was able to forward Hall's letter and an account from the Customs men at Hope to their Lordships in London. Hall's letter tells the dismal tale of the wreck, in which about 600 men died:

THURLESTONE,
Feb. 17-1760

HONOURABLE SIR,

At one this afternoon I gott to the place where the ship was lost which is a litel to the Eastward of the Bolt Head in the dismal spot that fate designed her—She is intireley under water and what comes from her no boat can ventur to save yet as the sea is very high but as the wind is at N.W. hope tomorrow at low water to take up all the Ironwork and gather things that comes on shore and give it to the care of the officers of the Customs I cant see aney part of her, mast sails or yards soe I think the sea has split and torn them to pieces without they lay in coves that I cant see without a boat—this evening I went to the village where some of the seamen was that was saved and told them the Admirals orders they that are able gave me there word of coming to Dartm. tomorrow and those that are lame ask me how there landlords is to be paid to that I can give no answer—Sir I hope what I shale doe tomorrow will meet with your aprobation to sound in her as the guns is faling in her hole and the Fishermen told me at low water its three fathom I shale take wot step I can to preserve all the stores I can and waite your Honble Command.

I am Sir your most obedient Humble servant to command

BENJ. HALL

Together with Hall's letter is a letter from the Customs men, Frank Shepherd and Thomas Barriball, who point out that they had been on watch at the cliff-top until the wreck occurred, and how they would organize a party of eighteen men to hoist what they could up the steep cliffs.

To round off the relevant correspondence, Admiral Boscawen forwarded a draft report to their Lordships in London on February 21st. This report, which describes the shipwreck very well, follows:

On Thursday 14th instant in the close of the evening the *Ramillies* being in company with the Admiral, observed the Admiral to lower his main topsail, but could not see whether it was taken in. However, Captain Taylor ordered his to be lowered and as soon as it was dark, furled it. The ship then making much water, having sprung a leak under the larboard entering-port, William Wise imagined a butt to have started near the place. As soon as the main topsail was handed, Capt. Taylor ordered guns to be unshotted and signal lights to be got ready for making the signal of Distress;—but on consultation, concluded it would be better to bear away without making the signal of distress as some other of the squadron might take it to be the Admiral. They were now employed at all the pumps and buckets and hawled the main sail up and bore away under a foresail.

About ten or eleven in the morning steering about E by N, some of the officers thought they saw the land, but the weather was so extream thick that few believed it to be the land. The master not convinced it was the land stood in to make it; got their larboard Fore-tack to the cat head and set the mainsail; about eleven they saw the land, and the master seeing Burrow Island which lays in Bigberry Bay took it for the Loo Island, and concluded they were to the westward of Plymouth. About this time the people on shore saw the ship, and as they say, she was rather to the northward of the Bolt, and were in hopes that she would have brought up in Bigberry Bay rather than attempt to weather the Bolt, as a very great swell set right on it; but to their surprize they saw her wear, and get their starboard tacks on board and set their topsails.

They now endeavoured to weather the Eastermost Point, taking it for the Ramhead; set the courses and close reef'd topsails: The Captain, as well as some other Officers, said they could not weather the land; the Master was persuaded they could, but soon saw his mistake, and endeavoured to stay the ship and get into Bigberry Bay; but the great swell, together with her having much water in her hold would not admit of it. At this time Wm. Wise and Robuck were standing by the Main sheet; they heard somebody say the mainmast is sprung; and presently they heard the Captain call, "Let go the Mainsheet". Which they did and ran directly upon deck, where they found the Main mast gone and presently the Mizon mast.—Wise then heard the Master call, "Let go the anchor and clew up forward," which was done; they then let go another anchor and cut away their foremast, which carried the Bowsprit with it; this was about two o'clock, and the ship about a quarter of a mile from the Bolt's Tail, but the weather was so thick that as yet they did not know the land. She rode till the dusk of the evening when she drove; they then let go the sheet anchor, but before they could give her cable to bring up, she struck with her starboard quarter, and her bow then drove to the westward and took the rocks.

William Wise who seems to be clear in his account, says that he was the last man that jumped on shore; he let loose the starboard stern ladder, and went down it, and threw himself on the rocks where the ship fell upon his right leg and bruised it to pieces, but that he got up in that condition and looked back, and could not see any more of the ship.—The stem is drove into a cave to the eastward, where she struck and most of the men lay in the surf of that cave; but the ship drove to such small pieces that it appears like piles of firewood.—One of her cables lays over a rock and seems to have hold of the bow of her, but it is impossible to be certain where her bottom lays untill fine weather admits of boats making a stricter survey.

E. Boscawen

Captain Wittewronge Taylor, the Captain on board the *Ramillies* at the time of her loss, had a reputation for being a hard man to please, and from all accounts was a person who insisted that regulations should be followed to the letter. It has been suggested that his ability as a commander of men was one of the factors in the great loss of life at the time of the *Ramillies* wreck. William Wise and twenty-five ratings were the only survivors recorded, and these saved their lives by jumping ashore at what proved to be the last possible moment. Wise was the last ashore from the stern of the vessel. Having had his leg smashed, he looked back with fear in his face—that the wrecked ship was going to fall upon him again as he dragged himself up the rock with a trailing, useless leg. But there was no ship there. She had gone down as soon as she struck.

For a vessel in normal seagoing condition this would be unusual. After all, the ships were made of wood; but, remembering the report that the ship had taken on a lot of water through the damaged larboard entering port, it can be supposed that she was already very low in the water when she eventually ran on the rocks. If this was the case, and it seems very likely, then all on board would have realized that their position was most dangerous. Only iron discipline and rigid attention to the control of his men could have prevented other attempts at self-preservation from among the crew. A fine example, it could be said, of Navy discipline, but a terrible loss of life nevertheless, as saved sailors could sail again, and well-trained crews are harder to come by than wooden battleships.

Another tale about Taylor is that a seaman on board the *Ramillies* at the time of her loss, a fisherman from Bigbury Bay pressed into service, recognized the Bolt when the Sailing Master and all the officers thought it to be the Rame Head at Plymouth. He reported his recognition to the Captain, but was put in irons for his implications that those in command did not know where they were. But this sort of tale—note its likeness to the *Association* legend—always follows a disaster, and can usually be put down to local gossip about one of their own kind who was maltreated by someone in command. It is always easy to make a scapegoat of someone who is dead, especially when that person has had the responsibility of command at the time of the disaster.

After the wreck a poem was composed called "Shipwreck", and this is said to be based on the *Ramillies* loss. The writer, William Falconer, is often imagined to be the surviving midshipman, but this is not so, unless it is a pen-name, as his name does not appear on the pay-books of the *Ramillies*.

After the mainmast had gone an anchor was put down, and then a second anchor to stay the ship. The mizzen went after the main, and the foremast was cut away, taking off the bowsprit in falling, so leaving the ship bare of all masts and yards and a mere hulk in the water. A ship without masts cannot manœuvre, and, to the horror of those on board, it was found that the second cable had passed over the first and the two were chafing tremendously at each lurch of the waterlogged hull. With all masts gone no chance of hoisting a scrap of sail remained, so there was no way in which the cables could be relaid. With cables stretched bar-tight from the bow and the ship heaving at them tremendously, it is little wonder that after a short while one parted. When this was gone and all the weight of a ship nearly full of water was acting on the remaining cable this parted also, and the ship backed towards the cliffs. The sheet anchor, virtually the last resort, went over, but before it could take effect she crashed stern first into the rocks. Stern first is not quite exact as the report details "with the starboard quarter"; this means that the right-hand side of the ship when facing the bow, and the back half of that side, hit first. If you imagine this page as the ship, with the bow at the top of the page, then the bottom right-hand corner hit the rocks first. After striking, the bow, or front end, was taken by the waves and thrown round and on to the cliffs with terrible effect. Wise, going down the ladder nearest to the cliffs, must just have had time to leap before the vessel hammered into the rock behind him. So near was his escape that his leg was caught by the ship and smashed. He probably jumped on the upswing of the wave, and when he had landed in the smothering foam and grabbed desperately at the weed- and barnacle-covered rocks the ship dropped back as the wave receded and smashed down on him. He was very lucky to have escaped with his life. In the calmest weather the great cliffs here are a frightening sight, and the rollers breaking against their foot far below bring home in no uncertain manner the power of the sea.

Chapter Two told of the lost galleon *San Pedro el Mayor*, the Spanish Armada hospital ship. She was lost only a short distance away from the *Ramillies* wreck, on the Shippen rocks. At the top, where the grass finishes and you can look over into the cleft in the Shippen, is a flat part and what was once a cleared space. Here lies a cannon; grass grows up about it, and not many people know that it is there. In fact, it is one of the cannon from the *Ramillies*. It was placed there many years ago, but the proposed site with a flagstaff never materialized, and the cannon rusts slowly away.

This cannon had been raised in a salvage and exploration attempt many years ago. The salvage attempt is mentioned in a local guidebook of the area, *Salcombe and Neighbourhood*, that is now out of print, and it records that some success was had by the adventurers below the surface as they found "a large brass wheel, a brass buckle, a round shot, and a gold coin". Since that time, and since the advent of self-contained underwater breathing apparatus, many visits have been made to the area by local enthusiasts. Quantities of chain-shot—that is, two cannon-balls joined by chain—have been seen on the bottom, and some have been raised. Cannon and occasional pieces of twisted and broken timber can still be found on the seabed. It was after publication of the account in the old guidebook that interest was aroused in the *Ramillies'* story, and to fulfil a desire to find out more about the ship a writer sent a letter to the Admiralty asking whether or not the Navy still owned the wreck. The reply suggested that the writer tender to the Admiralty to purchase the wreck on the bottom. It appeared that the writer was not the only person interested in the wreck at the time, as other similar requests had been received. In due course an offer was submitted as directed.

The thought that one might well become the owner of a ship of the line was most appealing. Imagination runs riot at times like this, and, of course, the letter-writer saw himself covered with glory as he raised a hitherto unknown cannon of rare design and beauty. The vessel herself would, no doubt, be in a much better state of preservation than others imagined, and in his enthusiasm he thought that he might even come across valuable coins and personal belongings of drowned sailors. Having submitted the tender, which was, in fact, not very large, but considered sufficient in view of prices that had been quoted for similar wrecks, he sat back and waited. After some time came a reply in an Admiralty envelope from Bath saying that another tender had been accepted. Thoughts of fame and proud ownership dissolved like spray in the wind. He was wreckless, and felt as if someone had stolen his birthright. However, after a couple of days he decided to write again to the Admiralty to find out who the new owner was. As will be imagined, their reply was noncommittal, and they regretted that no information as to the name or address of the new owner could be divulged. But eventually an envelope containing a letter to the new owner was forwarded, so that he would know the name and address only if the owner cared to write. Luckily he did, and at last permission was given to dive on the site, at the diver's own risk, but he was not to forget that anything he found, if retrieved, was to be handed over without delay. There were two people involved in the purchase of the *Ramillies*—Mike Borrow, agent for the purchase, and David Langfield, the new owner. Mike is well known in diving circles, being an expert in many underwater matters.

As stated previously, the wreck is not unknown locally, and various attempts have been made to search out parts of the lost ship. Some attempts have been complete failures, while others have met with some measure of success. The pieces of timber that have been found are all wormeaten and spongy, bearing little relationship to the once strong timbers of a fighting ship. There are plenty of cannons on the bottom, and plenty of cannon-balls, but everything is in sand and jammed among rocks that have weed growing over them, so at no time can the searcher be certain of success. However, cannon-balls have been raised from this site, and there is no doubt that there are many more to come.

Any reader who thinks that he, or she, will away to the site and raise cannon-balls or the like for their own use should not attempt such a venture without prior permission. Local fishermen, and there are plenty of them, know the site well enough to understand that pilfering is going on, and to get there for diving you must have a boat. You can be quite certain that any diving will be noted, and if it is, then information will find its way to the authorities, and you will find that a Customs man will appear as you land. Anything brought ashore will be impounded. It is just not worth it. Besides this you will create bad feeling towards divers, be they wreck hunters, spear fishermen, or merely others interested in an underwater swim in a pleasant part of England.

Incidentally, very close to Ramillies Cove are the boilers and plates of another wreck—the 4000-ton West African mailboat the *Djebba*. She ran aground on March 18th 1907 close to Bolt Tail.

Riddle of the Guns

CAPTAIN JONATHAN FAULKNOR, of His Majesty's Ship *Impregnable*, watched the twelve merchant-ships he had escorted from Lisbon lumber past. He would be glad to see the back of this convoy. As he made sure that all was well with his charges, he wondered how Captain Stopford in H.M.S. *Excellent* was making out.

It was October 1799, and England, together with Russia, Austria, Portugal, Naples, and Turkey, was at war with France. Despite this, the *Impregnable*'s 98 guns had been silent the whole voyage. No French vessels had swooped on the homeward-bound convoy, and the only excitement had been the sighting of an unidentified vessel. The *Excellent*, smaller—74 guns—and faster, had been the obvious choice to set off in pursuit. That left the *Impregnable* in sole charge of the convoy, but as they were now fast approaching the Isle of Wight, the risk of leaving the convoy to one ship had seemed very small. Even so Jonathan Faulknor would have liked to have taken the *Impregnable* into battle. She felt a good ship, and had had her battle christening some years before.

The *Impregnable* had been launched at Deptford in 1786, was of 1887 tons, and normally carried a crew of 750 men. She was 178 feet long, 49 feet in the beam, and drew about 25 feet. King

George III knew her personally, for he had been aboard her when she was flying the flag of Rear-Admiral Sir Richard Bickerton at Plymouth in 1789.

But it wasn't until May 5th 1794 that the *Impregnable*, commanded then by Captain George Blagden Westcott and carrying the flag of Rear-Admiral Benjamin Caldwell, linked with a fleet bent on battle. There, off Ushant, she joined the 25 ships, 7 frigates, sloops, hospital hulks, and fireships, all under the command of Admiral Earl Howe. At the end of the month, after sundry minor actions, the French fleet was partially engaged. In five hours of sporadic fighting one French ship was disabled, with hundreds of her crew killed and wounded. But even this was not outright success, for the French came back and towed their troubled ship away.

The next day the French took a worse beating, but the real battle was not joined until June 1st, when the British went completely over to the attack, smashing the French line and attacking from the leeward. The *Impregnable* was not heavily engaged, but even so lost 7 killed and 21 wounded, out of the British total of 290 killed and 858 wounded, including three Captains killed and three Admirals wounded.

The French suffered terribly. Seven thousand men were killed, wounded, or taken prisoner by the time the battle ended.

Other records show that the *Impregnable* was in action again on January 8th 1794 when helping the frigate *Hind* to escape from attack by five French frigates. But there was no record of the *Impregnable* being in action under the command of Captain Jonathan Faulknor, which is probably why he envied the Hon. Captain Stopford his slim chance of glory in pursuit of the unknown vessel.

Off St Catherine's Point on the morning of October 19th 1799 the convoy broke formation and started the run up to St Helen's Roads, ready to turn into Portsmouth. The wind was blowing strongly from the south, and Captain Faulknor handed over charge of his ship to the Master, Mr Michael Jenking, for the final leg of the voyage into Portsmouth Harbour. Soon the *Impregnable* was bucketing along at a good ten knots, in the slightly head-down attitude that all aboard had come to know so well that they hardly noticed it.

At 6 P.M. the cliffs of Dunnose were sighted about two miles off bearing north by east. But First Lieutenant John Mason had little time to look. His eyes were on the sails above his head. He noted the failing light, and waited for a command from the Master.

Third Lieutenant William Notter was on the main deck at the time, and heard the Captain hand over to the Master, but, finding there was little for him to do, spent most of his time on the quarterdeck. Lieutenant Notter thought to himself how plainly the land stood out at Dunnose, despite the fading light. Almost automatically he noted the rough bearing of the land—north and by east—and then went on keeping a watchful eye on the activity around him.

Shortly after six o'clock the *Impregnable*'s Chaplain, Mr William Hawtayne, decided it was time for a breath of air. He emerged on the quarterdeck just in time to hear the Captain hand over to the Master, and, seeing the concentration on both men's faces, decided that this was not the moment to raise one of the many problems that faced a Chaplain in charge of the souls of 700 seamen.

Seventh Lieutenant Joseph Blyth, on the lower deck, felt the ship kick to the growing wind, and cast around to make sure that everything was securely battened down. He felt rough weather coming on.

Below decks Mr John Brooks, the Ship's Carpenter, and his two mates, Stephen Clare and Thomas Bates, chatted idly. There did not seem to be much likelihood of a call on their services. The voyage was nearly over.

Richard Davey, the Coxswain, thought, "They'll be calling for leadsmen afore long, I'm sure. Well, it wasn't a bad voyage."

James Sawers, the Surgeon, who was tired of jokes about his name, started collecting his things together, and was thankful that his only jobs on this voyage had been very minor ones. Which was more than he could say for many another he'd been on.

Charles Hamilton, the Ship's Clerk, made one more entry in his ledgers and then gave up. The swing of the ship made writing a very chancy business.

John Hobbs, the Cook, was glad that the *Impregnable* was rushing on home. Personally, he thought he'd done rather well on this trip. No-one could blame him for handing men over to the Surgeon's clutches. Still, the fresh food taken on at Lisbon had lasted well. It was on the longer voyages that the Cook came in for real trouble.

On deck it was getting dark now, and Michael Jenking, the Master, started making his preparations for a steady run into St Helen's Roads. He knew that the Princessa Shoal lay ahead, and ordered to the wheel two helmsmen whom he knew to be first class, and a leadsman into each chain position. Half an hour later Culver Cliffs were sighted. The time was 6.30 P.M.

Jenking confidently ordered the jib hauled down and the main sail up, and set a new course to the east to avoid the Princessa.

John Mason, the First Lieutenant, had only a glimpse of Culver Cliff, less even than his sight of Dunnose, for trimming the sail was taking his full attention.

Lieutenant Notter was still not fully employed, and had time to overhear the Captain speaking to the Master. "We're going very fast," said Captain Faulknor. "Are you sure it's not too much speed?"

"We're going very well," said Jenking confidently in reply.

Notter heard no more, but he noted the wind freshening from the south and perhaps swinging a little to the eastward. He noted, too, that despite the wind the gathering darkness was bringing a haze with it, and soon Culver Cliffs disappeared from view.

The Ship's Chaplain, Mr Hawtayne, was still on deck. He was close to the Captain, and heard him ask the Master if he was sure the ship was in no danger as she was going very fast. He heard the Master's reply, "She's going very well", before moving over to look at the compass.

Captain Faulknor was obviously not happy about the *Impregnable*'s speed. He asked the Master again if he was quite confident in view of the ship's obvious speed. "I am satisfied," replied the Master. Captain Faulknor looked at him in silence, but his thoughts were fighting one another. On the one hand, he knew that while Jenking had been Master under his command he had been impressed with his abilities, and, indeed, he had brought the ship safely out through these same waters at the start of the voyage; yet, on the other hand, he felt that the ship was going too fast through tricky waters. Whatever his misgivings, he finally discarded them in favour of leaving the Master to do his job.

Jenking appeared to be the soul of confidence—even the Chaplain saw that—as he ordered the ship's course to be returned to north-east, having rounded the Princessa Shoal.

But Captain Faulknor had to sound still one more note of caution. "Do not you think," he asked Jenking, "that it would be better to stand out to sea for the night?" "No," replied Jenking, "I'm quite confident."

It was now 7 P.M., and it was obvious that they would not make Portsmouth that night in total darkness. They would have to anchor.

The darkness now surrounding the ship gave no comfort to Captain Faulknor, but Michael Jenking still gave no sign of being anything but happy with the ship's course. Indeed, almost on the hour of seven Jenking ordered the foresail to be hauled up, the topsail to be lowered down, reefed, and furled, and the ship's course to be altered to north-north-east. In the scurry of activity that followed the shouted commands Captain Faulknor said, "Shall we anchor here then?" If Jenking answered, then First Lieutenant Mason didn't hear his reply, though this was not unusual. Mason was far too busy making sure that all the crew concerned were busy with the sails. He felt the ship slow beneath him as the commands were carried out, and thought to himself that, despite the darkness, by his calculations they should be somewhere near St Helen's, about Bembridge Ledge.

Third Lieutenant William Notter heard the Captain ask Jenking if he would anchor where he was, but he too did not hear the reply. He gathered, from the way the ship ran on for at least fifteen minutes, that Jenking had replied in the negative. But he noted that some of the Captain's fears were now penetrating into Jenking's mind, for he started checking the compass very frequently, and he ordered leadsmen into the chains. The topsails were down now and reefed, and the first depths began to be called by the men in the chains. Jenking was now all attention, whether from fear that the ship had run too far too fast, or whether from a natural anxiety that the anchoring manœuvre should be neatly done, it is impossible to say. He was standing on one of the guns on the larboard side of the quarterdeck, listening intently to the shouted soundings.

"By the mark, seven!" shouted the larboard chains leadsman.

"Deep, twelve!" came the cry from the starboard.

For a moment Jenking thought he was mishearing the soundings. "That cannot be," he said. "Get another man into the starboard chains!" Lieutenant Notter moved forward. "Mr Notter," said Captain Faulknor, "put Davey, my Coxswain, on to it. He'll give true soundings." Notter hurried to do the Captain's bidding.

Richard Davey, the Captain's Coxswain, was inclined to grumble to himself at being given the leadsman's job, but consoled himself with Mr Notter's remark that at least he'd give 'em some true soundings. Ahead of him, in the chains, he could see a dark figure struggling to free the sounding-line, which had fouled on some projection.

"Here, give it me," said Davey, snatching the line from the man's hands. Even as he took it the line came free. But it wasn't until his third cast that he was able to get a proper reading.

"Deep twelve!" shouted Davey.

"By the mark, seven!" shouted the other leadsman.

"Deep twelve!" shouted Davey.

"Deep six!" came the cry from the other chains.

The minutes crept by, and still the leadsmen gave their greatly different calls.

"By God!" yelled Jenking, in a sudden fury. "Give me some true soundings!"

"By the mark, ten!" called Davey from the starboard side.

Through the darkness from the larboard chains came the thin impersonal cry: "By the mark, five!"

"It's impossible!" yelled Jenking into the darkness of the starboard chains. "You can't get that difference from each side!"

Davey protested that he couldn't hear the man in the other chains, but he stood by his soundings . . . sir.

The *Impregnable* was going slowly now—about four knots. Even so Jenking, disliking the odd readings of the leads, decided to anchor.

His decision was hastened by an apparent shoaling of the water on his port side. "Port your helm," said Jenking. Captain Faulknor repeated the command.

By now all the sails were in except the foretop mast staysail. As they prepared to anchor, the staysail was ordered down, and the ship swung around, her head now pointing to the south-east and almost into the wind.

But the deeper water that Jenking expected to find on his starboard side was apparently not there. As the ship swung Davey,

(*Top right*) Divers of
the Belfast Branch of
the British Sub-Aqua
Club bringing home a
cannon. Where is it?
See the diagram at
the foot of the page.
(See p. 95.)

(*Centre*) Robert
Sutton and his wife,
Maureen, look at the
result of their diving:
a demi-culverin dated
about 1798. (See p.
)

(*Left*) Oildrum-raft on
tow after rising tide
has lifted cannon.

The East Indiaman *Hindostan* sank in January 1803 off Westgate, Kent. (See p. 99.)

(*Below*) A drawing showing the loss of the *Earl of Abergavenny* on the Shambles in 1805. (See p. 102.)

still casting his leadline, shouted, "Deep nine!" This was enough for the Master. "Let go the anchor!" he commanded.

Some time before this Captain Faulknor had issued commands to his First Lieutenant to make sure that the cables were ranged and ready, anchors cleared, and that everything was prepared for this moment. Mason had not carried out the actions himself: he had passed the orders on to Mr Blyth, the Seventh Lieutenant of the ship. Blyth had done his job. At his station, on the lower deck, the work had been started nearly forty-five minutes before the moment of the command "Let go." Five fathom of cable was ranged ready, and on the command it raced out cleanly.

As the best bower anchor went plunging down, the men were still aloft on the foreyard furling the foresail. Fortunately they were all gripping hard owing to the strong wind, and no-one was careless of his holds.

Within two minutes of the anchor being let go—almost on the dot of 7.30 P.M., and with only a third of the anchor-cable out— the *Impregnable* struck.

It seemed to all the crew that at the moment she struck, the wind, though strong, had not been vicious, but now, cruelly, the gusts came, and there was little doubt that this was only the fore-taste of even stronger action to come. But the officers and crew had little time to stand and think. The *Impregnable*'s discipline had always been excellent; now it stood them in good stead.

Captain Faulknor's worst fears had been realized, but the Master was still in charge of the ship—and Master Jenking was still confident.

Mr Hawtayne, the Ship's Chaplain, heard him say, "I think we're on the Dean." At least, that's what it sounded like, but with the wind whipping the words away and the other shouts all around the Chaplain couldn't be sure.

But the Master's next sentence came in a lull, and the Chaplain heard it quite clearly. "We'll beat over it in a short time," said Jenking.

Even so Jenking decided not to leave it at that. Within moments the cable was being hauled in to pull the ship off the shoal. Third Lieutenant Notter was in charge of this operation, but to his horror the anchor-cable began to slide in easily with a minimum of effort. The anchor was dragging in the shallow water. Notter ordered the operation stopped, and reported back to the Captain and the Master.

By now the ship was thudding down on to the shoal, and breakers were forming all around. The *Impregnable* was broadside on in shallow water to a wind that was gusting to gale force.

An attempt was made to carry another anchor out in the ship's launch, but it was clear, as soon as the launch was hoisted out, that the small boat would never live in the wild, shallow sea around the ship. The attempt was abandoned.

The *Impregnable* was now in a desperate position. Fifteen minutes after the first strike the rudder could take no more of the battering on the bottom, and was beaten clean off.

John Brooks, the Ship's Carpenter, was ordered to inspect the damage and see if something could be rigged to take its place, but everyone knew that in the wild and stormy place they were now in there was no chance at all of doing so. Brooks reported back to the Captain. "Stand by with your mates," said the Captain. "I've no doubt we'll have need of your services soon." From the thudding beneath his feet Brooks understood what the Captain meant. The ship would have to lose her masts soon—and it would be better done deliberately than for them to break away below.

The anchor went on dragging, and the ship crunched on to the seabed with every large wave. After nearly two hours of this the order was given to cut the masts away. Brooks and his two mates, Stephen Clare and Thomas Bates, did their job well and swiftly. The severed masts fell safely clear of the ship, and immediately all on board could feel that the ship was eased of a great burden. Though she continued to strike, there was not the same weight about the blows on the keel.

At moments during that long night the anchor would find a grip, and the bows would jerk violently round into the wind, but within a few moments the giant anchor would be free again, acting only as a check on the ship's unhappy progress.

Distress signals were fired at regular intervals during the night, as they knew they must be close to Portsmouth Dockyard, but every man aboard was aware that it all depended on whether the *Impregnable* could last the night. No-one could reach them in the darkness and storm of that night.

Dawn came at last, and the Master and the Captain could scarcely believe what their charts and sights told them. They had, during the night, beaten a full mile and a half across Chichester Shoals, and were now near the entrance to Langstone Harbour. Jenking must have been way out in his estimated position even before the ship struck! He was miles to the east of where he thought he was! Whether the two men discussed this we do not know. Certainly both now knew that a court-martial must follow.

It had not been full daylight for long when the sloops *Fairy* and *Snake* from Portsmouth, followed by the *Carmilla* and *Regular,* were standing by. Various Dockyard craft followed them, and soon Mr James Parke, the Master Attendant at the Portsmouth Dockyard, was on board the *Impregnable* and preparing the salvage work.

He ran an experienced eye over the situation. The *Impregnable* was lying with her head to the north-north-east. Her masts were gone. She was still on the shoals, and her best bower anchor was laying on the starboard quarter of the ship with about a third or half a cable out.

Captain Faulknor was ready with the information almost before Parke asked for it. No, they had not started leaks so far—or nothing to speak of. No, apart from the removal of the masts, nothing had been done to lighten ship. "I feared she might have beaten farther on," said the Captain. Parke thought to himself that she could not have gone much farther, but saw the point of the Captain's remark. He thought, too, from what he could see, that once the ship had struck there was little else that could have been done.

This was Saturday morning. Parke started work immediately he had completed his survey of the position. Two of the ship's anchors were carried by other craft into firm holding positions. The cables were then fed back to the ship through the wardroom window. The slack was taken in and heaving started. The strain started the *Impregnable* taking in water, and hands were called to man the pumps. Parke decided that she was too heavy as she was, and sent to Portsmouth for slings to lift out the guns. By the time all the work had been done in readiness for removing the guns the day was over. Sunday morning was spent getting out the guns— almost all of them—together with shot and powder.

On the Sunday afternoon's tide they tried again, but the *Impregnable* would not move from the bed she had hammered for herself in the sand. The rest of the day was spent in removing provisions and anything else that would reduce the weight on board.

At 2 A.M. on Monday in came the tide, and the men strained at the capstans. Slowly, very slowly and reluctantly, the *Impregnable* raised herself out of the sand-bed and then crashed back even harder on some other projection. Brooks felt the blow and feared the worst. He was right. The water now started to beat anything the pumps could do. Shortly after 7 A.M.—no matter how hard the men worked at the pumps—the water was gaining four feet an hour. Soon there was eleven feet of water in the well, and just before 8 A.M. there was nearly sixteen feet.

"She's bilged," said Brooks shortly, when asked by one of his mates for the ship's chances. Even now the *Impregnable*'s discipline held firm.

Captain Faulknor sent a message to Admiral Milbank at Portsmouth requesting immediate assistance to save all on board, and made a signal at the same time to the ships about him. Launches and small boats answered the call at once. Between one and two in the afternoon the rescue was complete. Not one life was lost. The *Impregnable* was declared in a state of entire wreck.

Shipwrights from the dockyard arrived to strip off her upper planks and anything else that might be salvageable.

A court-martial was assembled on board H.M.S. *Gladiator* in Portsmouth Harbour on October 30th 1799: "To enquire with the cause and circumstances of the loss of His Majesty's Ship *Impregnable* and to try Captain Jonathan Faulknor, his Officers and Ship's Company for their conduct on that occasion. . . ."

It was an impressive and awe-inspiring scene. President of the court was Sir Richard Bickerton, Bart, Rear-Admiral of the Blue and Second Officer in Command of His Majesty's Ships and Vessels at Portsmouth and Spithead. Sitting on either side of him were twelve Captains: Robert McDonald, John Child Purvis, Francis Pickmore, Sir Harry Neale, Bart, John Elphinstone, Thomas Wolley, Thomas Wells, James Hind, Charles Bayles, John Whitby, Philip Charles Durham, and Robert Barton.

Nearly sixty Officers of the *Impregnable* attended. Faulknor questioned witnesses. Jenking told what happened. He did not deny that he was in charge at the time. The result was a foregone conclusion. The sentence was not.

The Admiral conferred with his Captains, and then the verdict was read to a hushed court. "There appears therein to have been negligence on the conduct of the said Master by his having been beyond the proper distance before he hauled in for St Helen's, and not having anchored the ship at the time there appeared to be a material difference in the Soundings of the Men at the Leads, but that no blame is imputable to the said Captain Jonathan Faulknor, his other Officers and Ship's Company for their conduct upon that occasion, but that the conduct of the Ship's Company after she ran on shore was highly praiseworthy—creditable to themselves and to the discipline of the ship in which they served. . . ."

Michael Jenking was sentenced to be dismissed from His Majesty's Service. Everyone else was acquitted. But that was not the last court case to be heard over the *Impregnable*'s bones.

At Portsmouth on November 2nd that year five people belonging to the Dockyard and a waterman were committed for trial at the next Assizes, "being detected in robbing the wreck of the *Impregnable*".

On November 6th the *Impregnable*—or what was left of her—was sold to a Portsmouth merchant, A. Lindenegren, Esq. And there until 1963 the *Impregnable*'s story rested. In 1799, in October, they had more to talk about in the matter of ships lost than the *Impregnable*. H.M.S. *Lutine* had gone down with £140,000 on board!

It was now the turn of the amateur Aqualung divers to write the last chapter in the story of the *Impregnable*.

Visibility in the area is usually very poor, and effluents released into the tidal streams there do not help. Sight distance underwater varies from six inches to a superb five feet.

Some of the most experienced underwater archaeologists in the area are Maurice Harknett and Alexander McKee, the author, whose discoveries at the Church Rocks in Hayling Bay have confirmed the belief of historians that it is the site of a priory church and village submerged in the fourteenth century, but at the same time have shaken some learned theories about changes in sea-levels.

These two men left Langstone Harbour one morning to continue the Church Rocks investigation. They had decided, however, to stop on the way to have a look at something Maurice Harknett had seen on a previous dive when in search of a fisherman's gear. Maurice thought he might have seen a cannon, but, on the other hand, he could not be sure that it was not a piece of old pipe.

Because of the fast and dangerous tides, they knew that they would have to make every second count. McKee had painted markings on his knife-blade so that he could take rapid measurements.

That evening, with his impressions of the dive still vivid, he wrote in his diving logbook:

"We anchored, transferred to dinghy, and dived from that. Morrie quickly found the 'cannon' and buoyed it, exclaiming at surface at the good visibility. It was maybe five feet, and dark and dingy, but good in comparison with what we have had before. I went down the buoy-line, and there she was—a big cannon and a dead ringer of the *Royal George* gun by the Garrison Church. Muzzle sticking up at 75 degrees, breech end buried in shingle. Muzzle flared. Not a piece of old pipe. Very sure about that. Hard to measure bore, because muzzle badly corroded inside (Morrie got his knife an inch deep into the corroded ironwork). But bore about 8 inches, or slightly less, and would guess a 32-pounder without much doubt. A ship of the line and the lower gun-deck to boot.

"While trying to take pix—and wishing I had flash—Morrie showed me another. This one had no growth on, and was lower down the slope. Then we started to see guns all over the place: cannon to right of us, cannon to left of us, cannon rearing above us, cannon looming below us. I lost count, but it was a real nest of some six or eight cannon all the same size. Some rearing, with buried breeches; others horizontal, but breeches still buried under the shingle.

"No resemblance to a ship. Just this vegetable garden of guns on a slope that goes down to 60 feet, as if a ship had struck broadside, rolled over, and guns on the high side had slid down to low side on top of the other battery. Shingle in their muzzles, no lobsters or congers! A decidedly eerie place and forbidding. We knew we had to streak in and streak out, and the minutes kept ticking away. Then we did pull out, and only just in time. A very hard row even with the dinghy, the tide pouring and waterfalling over the obstructions."

In the boat with them after the dive they had the fisherman's gear, found by Maurice Harknett far down the slope, a long way from where the man had lost it. It had all gone well and almost according to plan. But not quite. That night some scratches that Harknett had got from handling the old ironwork suddenly started swelling, and, in intense pain, he had to be taken to hospital for injections. Alexander McKee had worn gloves, suffered no scratches, and was not affected.

From historical records it would appear that the only three-decker in commission that had been wrecked near by was the *Impregnable*. Now they reviewed the evidence afresh.

Captain Faulknor's ship had piled up one and a half miles to seaward of where their cannon nest now lay. Such of the *Impregnable*'s guns and stores as could be got at had been taken out of the flooded hull and swung into dockyard lighters.

At once the significance of a diving find made just previously by another Southsea diver, John Eberhard, became clear. No great excitement had resulted at the time, because Eberhard's find was just a solitary cannon, puzzlingly entangled with a heavy-link chain, but with no sign of a wreck. Now in the context of the salvage of the *Impregnable*'s cannon and stores there seemed to the divers little doubt that the gun and chain represented a transhipment accident—a gun that got away.

The *Impregnable*'s hull had later, according to records, been blown up to release the remaining stores. In her position at that time the wreck, in one piece or many, would have started moving, urged on by the tremendous pouring tides at that place.

The two divers knew that this could have happened, because McKee had, earlier that year, solved a mystery that had been worrying local authorities. This was when the wreck of what appeared to be a large motor-boat had, in the course of forty-eight hours, travelled all round Hayling Bay.

The boat was reported awash or just submerged at many points during those hours. Police fears that there had been a fatal accident at sea were stilled, however, when Alex McKee saw the boat at low water opposite his house. A quick dive had established that the 'motor-boat' was in fact only an old houseboat, probably from Langstone Harbour.

Similarly, the *Impregnable*'s hull, perhaps in pieces, could have drifted almost anywhere. It was conceivable that the cannon represented her final resting-place. In favour of this a local boatman, Sid Thayers, recollected playing as a boy at that spot in the timbers of some large ship, which later disappeared.

To confuse matters, however, yet another Southsea diver, Pete Cope, reported finding the remnants of a large wooden hull lying at the other side of Langstone Channel below the Ferry Boat Inn, though local tradition associates this with the wreck of a convict ship which was once moored in the harbour. The convict ship had no guns, but was similar in size to the *Impregnable*.

From being 98 per cent sure that they had found the *Impregnable*'s guns, Harknett and McKee have become very wary, and will not now commit themselves definitely to the identity of their find.

They complain that there are "too many damn wrecks" in those waters ever to be sure, particularly in view of the strong tides. Both agree, however, that the cannon and chain found by Eberhard can only be from Captain Faulknor's great battleship. And near by a fisherman has told them is another unknown obstruction on the seabed.

What happened to Captain Faulknor, who had assumed command of the *Impregnable* on January 22nd 1799? Well, he officially relinquished command on October 21st of that year, and the *Impregnable* proved to be his last command. He never went to sea again, and consequently was on half-pay from October 30th 1799 until his death.

He was given the usual automatic promotions: Rear-Admiral of the Blue on April 23rd 1804, Rear-Admiral of the White on November 9th 1805, and Rear-Admiral of the Red on April 20th 1808. These promotions were made on a seniority basis, and vacancies occurred only through death.

Faulknor died at his house near Titchfield on January 7th 1809, aged fifty. He was still on half-pay when he died. As Rear-Admiral of the Red it amounted to £1 2s. 6d. per day.

The slang term for an unemployed Admiral like Faulknor was a "yellow" Admiral. It simply meant that he had never hoisted his Admiral's flag at sea.

Within a short while of the discovery of the *Impregnable* the Southsea divers began to locate lost ship after lost ship. You can read about their work on the *Royal George* in Chapter Eleven.

During their work in the Spithead area they became interested in the story of H.M.S. *Boyne*.

The *Boyne*, of 98 guns, was a three-decker commanded by the Hon. George Grey. On May 4th 1795 she was at anchor at Spithead, provisioned, and with enough ammunition for four months at sea. Not all of her 750-strong crew were on board, and it was a normal enough day at anchorage. Shortly before noon the Marines were exercising with muskets on the poop, firing and reloading by numbers. Somehow a spark from this musketry blew away, landed, still alight, in the Admiral's cabin, and set fire to some packages there. In five minutes the rigging was ablaze and the fire out of control.

News quickly spread through Portsmouth that a warship was on fire, and crowds poured down to the waterside to watch. So great was the excitement that it was found impossible to continue with a court-martial, and the sitting was suspended while most taking part joined the crowds watching the *Boyne* blaze.

Other ships in the anchorage moved quickly away from the blazing ship: they knew how much ammunition she had on board.

By 2 P.M. she was a complete mass of flames. Every now and then a gun would boom out from her as the flames set off the powder-charges in her loaded guns. The cables to her anchors burnt through, and she drifted with the tide towards the harbour. Finally, she ran aground opposite Southsea Castle. The crowds now watching numbered thousands, and had no idea of the danger they themselves were in.

The *Boyne*, like most warships of her time, had one main magazine, lined with felt and situated below the waterline. In addition to this she had small ready-use magazines, fore and aft.

At 5 P.M. the fire reached the aft magazine. The magazine may have been small, but the explosion was violent. Portsmouth shook, and a great cloud of smoke shaped like a palm-tree rose thousands of feet in the air. Out of the smoke came a hail of debris—burnt wood, cannon-balls, wreckage of all kinds. It fell into the sea and into the crowds of spectators. Yet strangely enough the only casualties on shore were among a flock of sheep grazing on the common.

Fourteen died on board—through not getting clear of the ship when she caught fire. Among them was the Captain's Clerk, seamen, four women, and three children.

The wreck of this great ship of about 1800 tons, nearly 180 feet long, obstructed the navigational channel for many years. Its general position is still marked by a wreck-buoy, even though she was blown up in September 1838 to reduce the danger to navigation.

But even this did not remove the wreck, and a modern angler's report that, though there is thirty feet of water under the wreck buoy and in the area generally, there is a great mound near by stirred the wreck hunters' curiosity. What would a great ship's remains in such conditions look like today?

In May 1965 Alexander McKee, Maurice Harknett, and Jim Dipnell, all divers, decided to find out.

As anchoring is prohibited in this area, the small diving-boat was kept moving to the safe side of the navigational channel, so that any ship which rammed the diving-boat would also have to ram the *Boyne* Buoy. The divers towed a small red buoy on the surface, and navigated carefully underwater by compass to keep out of the ship channel.

A zigzag search was carried out in thirty feet of water with three-foot visibility. The last six feet of the initial descent were the worst, with the seabed being quite unknown and the water getting blacker and blacker. Once the divers were on the bottom, the first western leg of the zigzag revealed no wreck and no shallowing of the water. The second eastern leg was over a bare, shingle-and-shell seabed from which a clump of weed suddenly loomed up. On investigation the 'weed' proved to be growth on a very heavy piece of iron, heavily concreted. It appeared to be hollow at one end, and may have been a cannon, but so deeply embedded and immovable was it, and so large and uneven were the concretions, that it was impossible to tell underwater. They continued easterly, with the seabed noticeably rising up in a mound. A clump of waving weed once again drew McKee's attention, and this time he was faced with a round iron object, again very heavily concreted. If it were a cannon-ball, as he suspected, then it was firmly fixed to something under the shingle and defied all efforts to move it.

By now it was clear to the divers that there was a great mound of shingle, some ten feet high, in this place. Odd pieces of ironwork stuck out. There was no sign of any wood, which would, of course, have been eaten away.

Says McKee: "There is little doubt that this mound conceals the remnants of the hull of the once great ship. Most of the interesting artifacts will be underneath. To get at them would require a suction-pump. To plot them will require more polished techniques than are at present available. But she might well be of interest to archaeologists when improved equipment and techniques are ready."

The divers left the shingle mound untouched, and passed on their report to the archaeologists of the Committee for Nautical Archaeology (see Appendix Three).

Cannon's Hole

ALL fishermen can tell you about wrecks. If they can't remember them in their own lifetime they will tell you stories handed down to them by their fathers or other fishermen. Such men are an important source of wreck information, but, as all stories grow in the telling, each story must be tested, if not in documents; then at least in actual diving.

So when Robert Trouton and Maureen McGladdery, two keen divers of Belfast Branch of the British Sub-Aqua Club, listened to an old fisherman telling them where to dive—"You can see the guns from the surface"—they didn't perhaps pay as much attention as they might have done.

The number of tales of Spanish galleons just asking for divers to take the treasure off them that they had heard in the past, and that had proved to be tall stories, had jaded them to such information. If this one was so well known and so accessible, why hadn't someone else investigated it already?

Robert Trouton was an architect and Maureen a specialist in teaching deaf children. They were not the sort of people to accept any story told to them. But the weather next day was superb. They wanted a dive anyway, so why not have a look at the old man's wreck?

The wreck site was some thirty miles south of Belfast, and as some friends had a near-by cottage, the trip would be a very pleasant way of spending the day. These friends knew more about the old man's wreck. Of course there was a wreck there!

The wreck was said to be that of a French ship called *Amité* or *L'Amitié,* and had taken place in the late spring of 1798. The ship was intended to aid an Irish rebellion in Londonderry. Ireland was certainly on the verge of open rebellion during this period, and it would have been, from the French point of view, an ideal moment to foster such feelings. Bonaparte, triumphant in many fields, might well have attacked England through Ireland, but, in fact, at the same time as the French boat was being wrecked near Belfast he sailed for Egypt, and Nelson sailed after him.

Some of the sailors from the Irish wreck, it is said, got ashore despite a blinding snowstorm, but the local people, thinking that they were ghosts, left them to die from exposure. The gully where the boat foundered is still known locally as Cannon's Hole.

Robert Trouton tells what happened to the divers next:

"Cannon's Hole is quite accessible from the shore, and the water is not deep. When we arrived the sea looked inviting. We dived, and quickly realized that it would be difficult to locate anything there, even something as big as a cannon. There were numerous clefts and crevices, all screened by rust-coloured laminaria, and the seabed was strewn with rounded boulders. Everything was covered with weed and plants.

"But suddenly there it was—a cannon! Excitedly, we scraped and examined it, and took a rough reading from the shore and of the depth. It was half embedded in gravel and too big for us to move, but it seemed to prove there was a wreck in the vicinity.

"Our air was running out, and regretfully we surfaced. We found we had drifted south of Cannon's Hole. I decided to take one last look and snorkelled down to 20 feet. What a sight met my eyes! There they were, cannons and yet more cannons, lying silent and grey, like large snails on a bare shelf. Maureen went down to count them. There were seven, plus the first one—eight. What a glorious day!"

The two of them went back the next week-end to take another look, chart positions, and plan a salvage operation.

They found that the guns were made of cast-iron and were in rather poor condition. All the markings had been smoothed away, and the trunnions were, in most cases, worn to points. The cannons each weighed about a ton. They were nine feet long, thirteen and a half inches in diameter at the breech, and six inches in diameter at the muzzle. The bore was nearly four inches in diameter.

Six of the cannons were held fast by gravel. The seventh lay across one of the others, and they decided to try to raise this one. The first attempt with ropes and pulley—with five people heaving—merely succeeded in moving the muzzle about a foot towards the surface. This method was obviously impossible.

It was then decided to float the cannon off on a rising tide, using a raft of oil-drums. Eight fifty-gallon drums were used for the raft, and operations began early one morning at low tide. Two divers tied ropes round the cannon and then to the raft. An hour later as the tide rose the cannon moved, but a rope slipped, and the divers had to wait for the next low.

As the tide went down, so did the divers, and this time there was no mistake. In the evening as the water rose, so did the cannon. Then the raft, with the cannon swinging twenty feet beneath it, was carefully towed to Ardglass, four miles away.

Says Trouton: "Local interest had been aroused, and one fishing-boat skipper had been persuaded by friends to attempt to land the cannon with a winch normally used for lifting nets. At noon the next day a boat arrived to tow raft and gun to a more convenient spot. Then for four hours people on the quay watched the attempt to raise our find. A winch rope broke as the cannon came out of the water. We raised it again, but it seemed impossible to get it over the combing of the boat.

"Finally they gave up. Seven divers working in three feet of murky water tied the gun to the raft once more, and David Rice, our patient boatman, towed our historical cargo to a quiet quay within the harbour and left it where it would be exposed at low tide.

"The next morning two still-weary divers untied the ropes for the last time, and we gazed in silence at the long, rusty object that had once been a sleek gun. Was it right to have moved it from where it had been violently deposited so many years before, and expose it to the cold light of the twentieth century?

"To the few of us who had followed up an improbable tale told on a wet Saturday night, it was. We had tackled something right outside our experience—and succeeded. Later we learnt that the cannon should more correctly be called a demi-culverin, and was one of the longest and most graceful guns in use at the time. It was long-shotted and long-range, a good weapon for a chase, firing fore and aft. It fired a 9-lb. iron shot, had a point-blank range of 400 feet, and a random range of 2500 feet."

The cannon now lies by Mr and Mrs Robert Trouton's front door at their Belfast home. He and Maureen McGladdery were married in the same year that they found it. The exact identity of the ship from which it came is still in doubt. There were many ships of the same name during the period in question, and during the war—as during any sea war—captured vessels were quickly renamed by either side. The Troutons are carrying out further research on "their ship" at the moment.

As we move forward in time we find that the casualty rate of ships continues to be high.

The year 1803 proved to be a stormy one at its beginning. Many sailing-ships were lost, some large, some small. Two of these wrecks are discussed below, and a third that was lost two years later, in 1805, is also described to excite the wreck hunter. They are, however, merely occasional examples of the great wealth of shipping that has gone to the bottom of the sea.

The vessel *Active* was a 350-ton West Indiaman from Greenock. She had been to the West Indies for trade, and had returned loaded with merchandise, including 300 hogsheads of sugar, and gold—£67,000 worth of gold. She was a frigate, a fine, strong vessel, and the pride of Captain Hornby, her commander. The *Active* arrived in Margate Roads during January 10th 1803, and came to anchor. Now that the long passage was behind them the crew were ready for Greenock and a rest from the sea, but first they anchored off Margate to prepare for the last part of the voyage.

With two anchors down, the ship swung in the tide during the afternoon, while a general clearing up took place. Sailors pottered about renewing cordage, washing decks, and generally smartening up the ship for the home run. As they crossed the deck many noticed the quickening movement beneath their feet, and, without thinking, they turned their eyes towards the direction from which the wind was beginning to blow with increasing force.

X marks the spot where H.M.S. *Anson* was wrecked on Loe Bar, near Porthleven, Cornwall. In the foreground is the memorial to over 100 of her crew who drowned in the wreck. (See p. 109.)

(*Left*) Mr Roland Morris, ex-Admiralty helmet diver, who bought the *Anson* wreck from the Admiralty. (See p. 112.)

The *Anson* gives up one of her secrets. Captain Beale, R.N., Commanding Officer of the R.N. Air Station at Culdrose, examines the half-ton brass pintle and rudder-plate recovered by the diving team (standing). (See p. 116.)

(*Below*) More artifacts from H.M.S. *Anson*. On the right two 32-pounder and one 22-pounder cannon-balls; the smaller items are grapeshot. In the foreground a wooden and spun yarn tampion removed from a 32-pounder cannon which was still loaded and dry! The spike appears to be a cross between a marlin-spike and sewing-needle. Large object on left believed to be a rigging plate, probably from the hull. (See p. 117.)

As the early evening turned to dusk the fresh wind increased in intensity, until a gale was blowing that had the *Active* bucking at her anchors and throwing up great spurts of spray from her bow. The crew hastened into heavy-weather clothing, and Captain Hornby ordered two sailors to watch the cables from the bow to see that any undue strain was reported to him. Movement on board had become dangerous, as the action of the ship made every step a gamble.

Huge waves, rushing at the bow, caused the ship to rear up like a spirited horse, and at each lunge the dripping cables tautened and pulled the ship's head down with a tremendous jerk. On the bottom the anchors bit more deeply into the sand and held the ship bow to weather. There was some two hundred feet of cable out on each anchor, and with each succeeding wave the shock transmitted to them was felt throughout the length of the ship.

Soon after six o'clock that evening first one and then the other cable parted near the anchors, and the *Active* moved over the bottom in towards Margate Pier. She had been anchored in some ten fathoms at the beginning, but now the bottom shelved to the five-fathom line, and within a few moments she had passed this depth and struck on the sand. The north-east and east winds were creating tremendous surf on Margate beach, and sending spray hissing over the rocks straight into the faces of those hardy locals who had come to the water's edge to watch the passage of the *Active* in from her anchorage. Those on shore could see that all was far from well on board, but the moon, which showed only through the ragged breaks in the clouds, gave very little light to illuminate the ship.

Great waves hammered on shore, and the sound of the wind, rising to gale force, was frightening. It was impossible to launch any boat from the shore, or, in fact, to make any rescue attempt at all, as no lifeline or lifeboat could possibly reach the *Active* in that weather.

On board, Captain Hornby knew that only a few minutes remained before his ship would be severely damaged by the waves. Already she was held fast on the bottom, and all about him the water was thick with sand. He watched as some of the crew made their way to the mainmast and congregated there, and then lashed themselves around the mast and gazed with terror-filled eyes at the immense waves that rushed past the ship to hurl themselves against the beach, only to curl over and destroy themselves, and then ebb back ready for the next onslaught. Looking at the back of each crest as it precipitated itself past him, he thought how well chosen was the name 'white horses', each wave like a line of charging stallions, their manes of spray flying over their arched necks, galloping line upon line to their end. With a convulsive movement the ship turned broadside to the waves and heeled over on to her beam ends.

No worse plight can be imagined for a ship. With her weather side continually hammered by the water and her lee scraping the sand on the bottom, the ship moved shoreward literally masts first. As she had fallen the mainmast snapped off short above the deck, and five sailors who had sought refuge in the main-top were carried to their deaths still lashed with their lifelines to the mast, trying desperately with numbed fingers to free the swollen rope from about their waists. Hornby clung to the weather shrouds grimly as the waves passed over the ship, facing the sea and bowing his body as each wave struck. He glimpsed other figures near him, ropes around their waists, being washed continuously by the water.

Two or three of the bodies did not move between waves, and he realized that they were already dead, drowned by the continuous onslaught of solid water and cold spray-filled air. He determined to stay alive, and kept his body moving and rested his arms and legs by turns between waves. His decision not to let himself be completely at the mercy of the waves and lash himself into one constricting place no doubt saved his life, his anxiety for his ship and the souls about him kept his mind from worrying about his own plight.

With the wind behind the tide, the *Active* moved in as far as the Nayland Rock and stuck there with fore- and mizzen-masts still standing. It was three o'clock in the morning. Hornby had been hanging on to life and hope for nine hours.

As the weather abated and the waves lessened in their intensity boats were put out from the shore to see what remained of the *Active*. The vessel was badly damaged, and the still-standing fore- and mizzen-masts had sagged and were badly cracked and strained. In the shrouds were nineteen persons, crew and passengers, lashed there to avoid being swept overboard; of these, nine had died during the night.

The local fishermen, lifeboatmen, and longshoremen did all they could for the survivors, and saved as much of the cargo as possible; the gold that came ashore, carefully guarded for fear of thieves, was soon boxed up and prepared for transport by land, although there appears to be no record of whether all the gold was saved.

While the removal of goods and crew was taking place from the *Active,* within five miles of her loss the vessel *Hindostan* had also been wrecked by the tempestuous weather. This other frigate was an East Indiaman, and was carrying a cargo of woollens, copper, lead, and a quantity of silver bullion, valued in all at some £100,000. The *Hindostan* sank on January 12th 1803 off Westgate, Kent, and during her loss suffered from what can only be described as internal piracy.

She had undergone the same brutal north-easterly battering that had caused the *Active* to leave her anchors behind on the seabed, and although she went to the bottom in very much the same manner, it would appear that the crew of an East India ship reacted differently from that of a West Indiaman. Whereas the *Active*'s crew were quite heroic in their efforts to preserve life, the men of the *Hindostan* preferred plunder to safety.

The *Hindostan* took the sandbank in the middle of a north-easterly blow that rammed the hull hard on to the sand and fixed her there. With the wind screaming through the rigging, great waves roared over the wreck, carrying buckets, loose gear, capstan-bars, and cordage over the side, while the sailors hung on to the shrouds and stanchions and rigged lifelines to prevent their following the flotsam. A hatch was breached by the heavy, pounding water, and in a short while there was so much water in the hold that the vessel began to work her way even farther into the sand. "All hands to the pumps" had been ordered as soon as water had started entering the ship, but, pump as they might, no effort could rid the ship of the amount of water that poured in through smashed hatches and ports; and as the ship sank deeper into the bank the pumps themselves became choked with sand brought in by the sea. Continual effort on pump-clearing and renewed pumping made no difference to the water-level in the hold.

After a short while, when the pumping had to stop, some members of the crew, realizing that although the ship was in some danger, the danger to themselves was not so acute, began to plunder parts of the ship and broke open the spirit store. Their fear abated, they avoided the Master, who was fully occupied with the safety of his ship and the terrible weather, and broke into his cabin to steal his plate and cutlery. Soon after the weather lessened and boats could make their way out to the wreck a number of the Captain's spoons were sold on shore, and later about £50 worth of plate was discovered "upon a suspicious person" who was apprehended. As the wind and waves lessened, so more hope was entertained for the saving of the greater part of the cargo, although the woollens in bales had suffered from the soaking they had received from the sea and were hardly worth recovering.

As soon as it was known that the ship had a valuable cargo of silver bullion on board the number of small craft about the hulk increased overnight. The East India Company had their representative on the spot within hours of the shipwreck being reported, and at the Company's request a pair of gun-brigs were ordered to the wreck to stand guard against plunderers.

The pilot vessel *Liberty* made several visits to the wreck, and her Master, Mr Thompson, reported how he had found the ship well aground on the Wedge Sand with only the foremast standing, the others having been broken off during the storm. He could not board the wreck at the first attempt, as the sea was still very high and great waves were washing over the hull, but he did get near enough to the starboard side to take a sounding, and found that there were some three and a half fathoms, with three and a quarter fathoms at the bow. He stood off a little and anchored in six fathoms, and then sent his boat to try to board the wreck, but once more they were prevented by the heavy seas.

After two or three days the wind, which had all the time been very strong and blowing up to gale force from the north-east, began to abate, and some serious attempts at salvage were begun. On board the wreck the salvors found that the ship was almost completely full of water, and below deck-level the ship was a tangle of loose gear that washed about with each wave, and made any visit below extremely hazardous. Bales of sodden woollens had jammed in hatchways, and great lengths of rigging from the fallen masts, together with broken yards and parts of the masts themselves, had formed a dangerous meshed trap over most of the ship that prevented safe entry within. As the days passed by, so the ship sank farther into the sand by the bow, and hopes for saving the bullion cargo fell with each passing tide.

Those parts of the general cargo, with the bales of woollens that had been recovered, were taken to Deal, but the silver chests that were stored deep in the hold defied recovery. Eventually the action of the sea that so far had hindered the recovery attempts began to assist. The ship herself had suffered a terrible battering for several days, and as a result most of the deck encumbrances had been carried away. The weight of the cannons on the gundeck, for this was a ship armed against privateers on the East India run, had proved too much with the damage inflicted by the sea, and the guns had fallen through the ship, taking parts of the decking with them. As the decks cleared, so the salvage parties were able to venture lower into the vessel and search for the chests of silver.

There were thirteen chests in all. The search-party found some of the chests some two weeks after the wreck occurred, brought them safely to shore and lodged them with Treasury officials in Margate. As work progressed from the initial discovery, more chests came to light, until by the 3rd of February ten of the thirteen chests had been recovered. The best of the weather passed, and the condition of the hulk worsened. The whole ship had been so battered by the sea that the deck-beams worked loose and began to fall into the hold, while the hull itself seemed ready to fall apart from lack of support. Each visit to the wreck became more and more dangerous. If it had not been for the lost silver any further attempts at salvage would have been given up some time before, but with the thought that perhaps all could be recovered no effort was spared. Daily the salvors attempted dangerous journeys into the smashed vessel.

Eventually the eleventh chest was located and raised with difficulty and brought to shore. This was to be the last recovery. The sea had done its work, and the ship began to break up into pieces, while baulks of timber, spars, and the odd sand-stained sodden mass of woollens moved away with the tide. All the deck-beams had gone, and what was left of the hold was choked with sand and general seabed debris. After waiting and watching the officials of the company decided to abandon hope of any further recovery, so they sent away the gun-brigs, which had stood guard all this time, and left the remains to the sea. The two chests full of silver that were never recovered remained on the sand somewhere among the broken bones of the ship. As the timbers washed away or lay broken in the sandbank the chests slipped deeper, and no doubt disappeared from view into the seabed. They are in all probability there to this day.

The time will come when the shifting sands, for they move as much as the sands of the great deserts on land, move sufficiently to reveal the silver-chests. It is the free diver who will best be able to find them once they are clear, but no serious search could be made for the chests now. Sand-thickened water prevents any widespread attempt. It will have to be good fortune that brings the silver to shore again.

The third Indiaman to make up the trio on the bottom was the East Indiaman *Earl of Abergavenny*. Like the previous vessels, she was a three-master, and a fine, strong ship well suited to her trade. In February 1805 she, with the *Wexford, Henry Adding-ton, Bombay Castle,* and *Royal George,* sailed for the East Indies in convoy with the armed frigate *Weymouth* as escort.

The *Earl of Abergavenny* left Portsmouth Harbour in company with the others of the flotilla, and made her way out round the Wight and down Channel. By the time they were in the longitude of St Albans Head they found the winds from the south and west had increased and the sea had become very high. The convoy had already been split up by the high seas, but now, as they neared Portland Bill, the *Wexford,* Commodore for the voyage, signalled that they should try to make the port if they had a pilot on board. The *Abergavenny* had no pilot, and waited as best she could until a pilot-boat came alongside and she was at last able to make sail for a safe anchorge.

Captain Wordsworth, on board the *Abergavenny,* felt much easier in his mind once the pilot had boarded and the ship was again moving to a definite place. He would have been less happy had he known that the pilot in whom he placed so much faith was a beginner to the coast, and was not so fully conversant with the dangerous tide-race as he made out. They sailed in towards Portland, but in a very short while entered the beginnings of the race and edged towards the group of rocks by the Bill of Portland known, and greatly respected by all sailors who have to pass them by, as the Shambles. And a shambles they are indeed, jagged and well spaced, some breaking the surface, others just under it at all stages of the tide.

The tide ebbed faster, the wind increased. The pilot had come aboard at about three o'clock in the afternoon, and Captain Wordsworth had hopes of being safe at anchor soon after sunset, which would have been at about five o'clock. But in the early dusk of evening the *Abergavenny* suddenly took a rock somewhere close under the bow and was caught on a pinnacle. The Captain had a hurried consultation with his officers and mates, and, after a short report from the Carpenter that the hole was not too bad, he decided to try to work the ship off the rock and complete the journey to the anchorage.

They tried every trick of seamanship to loose the ship, but all the while the ebbing tide was leaving less water under the hull. The *Abergavenny* settled on to more rocks and began to bump heavily. The strong winds that were blowing, and the increasing darkness, did little to assist the recovery of the ship from the rocks, and some hour and a half after the first stranding the ship was still firmly held. There were several passengers aboard for the passage to the Indies, and up to now they had been quite happy to watch the sailors about their tasks and to be reassured by the Captain that all was well, and that the ship would soon be free. They believed that they would be safe in port within a few hours.

But as the evening wore on into night several of the passengers approached Captain Wordsworth to inquire just how certain he was that the ship would be safe. His replies were still reassuring, but now they lacked some of the time-wasting politeness, and he seemed much more concerned for his ship than for the questions of the passengers.

For all his fortitude and bold face, he must have decided that he was in need of outside aid, as he ordered twenty guns fired to signal his plight to shore. They were some two miles from the nearest land, and with the gale increasing it is doubtful whether the guns were heard, but with luck the flashes might be seen, and it is fairly certain that the rest of the convoy would have known that the *Abergavenny* was still at sea. The pumps had been started at five, and had been kept at full pump continuously. By six the amount of water entering the ship from the first and subsequent leaks caused by the hammering on the rocks had steadily increased, until the pumps seemed to be making little headway against the inrush. A party of sailors were sent to the forehatch with buckets. A bucket-chain was formed to assist the pumps, but even with this the water gained steadily. Now the passengers began to feel the sense of hopelessness that had affected all on board.

More signals of distress followed, and two spinster ladies, the Misses Evans, approached the Captain and begged for a boat so that they might chance the hazardous journey to shore rather than stay a moment longer on the stricken ship. Captain Wordsworth used all his powers of persuasion, tact, and command to stop them, but nevertheless put a boat over the side with dispatches and important papers in it, embarked the Third Mate, the Purser, and six seamen, and told them to get ashore at all costs to summon assistance by any means available. The boat reached the shore, and the news was passed that there was a ship on the Shambles. By nine those on board could detect small vessels about their ship. One small boat approached the wreck and took off several of the passengers, the Misses Evans among them, and carried them safely to shore. The remainder of the small craft stood off and waited for those who had jumped into the sea to come to them, rather than venture too near the dangerous rocks. From the manner in which the boats moved about it seemed that several of them were more interested in the parts of the *Abergavenny* that were breaking loose than in the lives that could be saved, and on board the sailors had thoughts that they were never going to be rescued at all. Those with weaker wills left their duties and started looking about for something to bolster their courage, but Captain Wordsworth, knowing the ways of seamen, put an armed officer by the spirit-room to prevent any wholesale looting of drink.

On board it now became painfully obvious that the *Abergavenny* was a doomed ship, and sailors and passengers alike began to leave the ship by any means possible. The majority just jumped into the sea as near a boat as possible and hoped for the best. What Captain Wordsworth had been thinking about during the final moments of the ship's life cannot be imagined, but it would appear that the whole tragedy had been too much for him. He did little to arrange an organized lifeboat drill, nor was he able to let those who were left on board know just what sort of a chance the ship had of lasting the night. The Chief Mate reported to him that all that could humanly be done had been done to save the ship, but

Wordsworth only replied, "It cannot be helped—God's will be done."

Shortly after this the ship slipped from the rocks that had held her so long and began to sink. As she left the rocks and the water-filled hull began to move the whole vessel suddenly fell sideways, and those who were hanging tight to the shrouds were flung into the sea. As she sank farther she partly righted herself, and then sank on a fairly even keel in twelve fathoms of water. Captain Wordsworth went down with his ship.

The next day found a few hardy men out in small boats looking about for flotsam, but the cargo of costly porcelain and the gold bullion were solidly on the bottom, out of the reach of non-diving men.

Several attempts were made in the months that followed to retrieve the bullion-chests, and boats were often over the wreck fishing in the depths. It was not until May 1806, however, that a more organized and determined attempt was made at salvage by a Mr Braithwaite. Braithwaite, a diver with a diving-bell, working on a commission of 12½ per cent, set about locating the wreck on the bottom. His work from the bell proved most successful. He spent many hours on the bottom, roping the chests of bullion, and reported that apart from the strong effects of the tides he was experiencing no difficulty in working in that depth of water. He brought out twenty-seven chests of bullion before he finished, and accounted for nearly all the gold on board at the time of the ship-wreck. How much was left no-one can tell, but not all was brought to the surface and surrendered to the authorities.

Of these three wrecks it would not be sensible to try free diving on the first two—the *Active* and the *Hindostan*, the condition of the seabed being such that any attempt would almost certainly be doomed to failure by the all-covering sand. Although references are made to the positions of the ships by indicating that they were lost on such and such a sandbank, no faith can be put in the exist-ence of the banks today by the same name or any other. Tides move sand about continuously, and what is covered one day is un-covered the next. As far as the *Abergavenny* is concerned, there have been known attempts on the wreck, but it must be remem-bered that the Shambles of Portland Bill is a hazardous place to try diving unless the diver is very experienced. A boat is, of course, necessary should any attempt be considered, and, more important still, the boatman must be a man whose knowledge of the local tidal action is very good. He must also be willing to take his boat well in among the dangerous rocks. The *Abergavenny*, the hulk itself on the bottom, caused the beginning of a shoal that could have become a danger to shipping, so demolition men were sent out to see what could be done to reduce the danger. Charges were lowered alongside the hull and set off, and, having blown most of what remained of the ship to pieces, the rest was left to the mercy of the sea.

Just how much of the ship remains to this day is open to conjecture, as we have yet to find a diver who has visited the wreck in recent years. The site is certainly known, and it is possible for divers to go down and search the seabed for her remains, but the sea conditions there are very dangerous, and only the most experienced divers would consider such diving a possibility.

Secrets of the Shingle

THOUGH Nelson had been victorious at Trafalgar in 1805, it was still necessary two years later for English ships to patrol the Channel, to ensure that the shipping lanes— vital for communication and trade—were open and free from any interference.

So, regardless of weather conditions, the Channel patrols were kept up. During the winter of 1807 it could hardly be called exciting work, but fortunately the weather had kept quite mild until Christmas.

The crew of the frigate *Anson,* moored at Falmouth, had another reason for feeling well off. Most of them would be able to spend Christmas Day in port, though the stores being loaded showed that they would be at sea again soon. Rumours of the actual sailing date swept the ship just before Christmas, and the older hands fully expected to sail on Christmas Day, but it soon became clear that they would still be in Falmouth Harbour on the Great Day.

Other rumours that were passed from man to man were not so easily disposed of—that the *Anson* was to be pay ship for other vessels already at sea. But as the Captain was hardly likely to take the crew into his confidence, the stories of money aboard were not contradicted, and the amount involved grew with each passing hour and load of unidentified stores. On Christmas Eve the crew were told that they would sail on Boxing Day, and as far as was possible loading was finished and the ship prepared for sea on Christmas Eve.

Inside the shelter of Pendennis Point and St Anthony Head, the *Anson* scarcely bobbed at her moorings. She had been a 64-gun ship, but now she was cut down to 44. Her poop towered above the smaller fry clustered at anchor round her.

On Christmas morning Captain Lydiard of the *Anson* called for his boat and with his friend Commander Thomas Sulivan went ashore to dine at "Woodlands", the home of a Captain James. The two men spent the day ashore and returned on board late. Commander Sulivan had decided to come with the *Anson* for a cruise as a guest. On board, those of the crew who had not been able to go ashore were, like their luckier companions, sleeping heavily: extra food and drink had made its appearance to mark Christmas, and various home-made drinks had been highly successful.

But there was no long sleep for anyone. Early on Boxing Day morning the last voyage of the *Anson* began.

It was a dreary morning, dark and cheerless, and those of the crew with thick heads felt worse when the ship rounded the sheltering headland. Rain was in the air, and a freshening breeze from the south-west had a nip in it which caused a general buttoning of coats and an eye on the weather side for the icy drops of water that sprayed up and across the deck with each heave of the ship.

Falmouth was left behind, and the *Anson* was worked out into the Channel. The southerly tack to allow her to clear the Manacles took her out to sea, and she held this course long enough to enable her to clear the Lizard itself.

As the day wore on she weaved tack by tack past the Lizard Head and down Channel, but all the time the weather was getting worse. Squalls of wind with rain and patches of sleet reduced visibility to practically nil.

Suddenly, in the early evening of December 27th the Lizard was sighted again—this time about nine leagues off—bearing north-north-west by compass and the ship lying south-south-east.

The wind increased its force from the south-west, and the *Anson* was in trouble. Within a short while it was clear that she was caught in the lee of the Lizard Peninsula, and was being blown towards the jagged cliffs between Gunwalloe and Porth-leven.

Captain Lydiard called a meeting of his officers to discuss the situation, his friend Commander Sulivan among them. The ship was without doubt embayed, and nothing they could do, even with all their collective experience of the sea, would get them out again unless the wind slackened.

Two anchors were dropped, but the sea was so great that first one and then the other cable parted, and the drift towards the iron shore began again. The best bower with a fresh cable roused out from the cable-tier was put over to stay the ship, but such was the rate of drift that the entire cable was out in seconds and had to be made fast hurriedly to the anchor-bits so that a further length could be spliced on. Once released again, this cable passed out through the hawse-hole with a roar, and at such a rate that no-one could stop it. When its entire length was out and the ship brought to, head to wind, it extended like a steel rod, bar-tight, pointing at the heart of the gale.

A vessel moored in these conditions would need some form of protection for its cable against the chafing and continual moving across the lip of the hawse-hole, and Lieutenant Thomas Gill, watching the cable closely, knew this very well, but serving, or wrapping the cable with strips of canvas, would mean raising the rope from the hole to enable canvas to be passed beneath it and made a continuous parcel around it.

This was clearly impossible, as the strength of the wind and the sea never for a second allowed an inch of slack in the cable.

At Captain Lydiard's meeting with all the officers it had been finally decided that the only chance of survival was to run the ship to shore by Loe Pool, Porthleven, as soon as the cable parted. They had not long to wait. The cable snapped, and the *Anson* drove wildly towards the land; they strained their ears to catch the boom of the surf above the howling gale.

Soon after midnight on the 28th the *Anson* touched bottom, hesitated, and was thrown broadside on to the sands.

Her high poop, crowded with officers and men, gave a sinew-stretching lurch as the vessel struck, and many of those who had sought safety there were hurled into the raging sea. They stood no chance at all, everyone being choked to death in cold, sand-thickened salt water.

As the ship lay practically on her beam ends, with the short wind-driven waves bursting over her hull, Lieutenant Gill could see that the mainmast had broken off short and lay like a causeway between ship and shore. As each wave broke and then washed back, the truck of the mast disappeared and reappeared again through the froth. Sailors and some women, for there were wives on board, made dashes to shore along the mast, and were so successful that even a woman whose thigh had been broken was carried from ship to shore along the mast road to safety.

But Captain Lydiard remained to the last, lashed to the wheel stanchion alongside Commander Sulivan.

They looked about them to see that all who could leave had done so, and, unable to assist, saw a young midshipman, the son of the Surgeon, calling out to his father as he was lifted bodily by a huge sea and smashed down between two guns, where he was killed instantly. His father, distraught, left his own place of safety to help the boy, and as he did so another wave roared over the ship. The solid water spun him round and threw him against the lee side with such force that he never moved again.

Seeing now that there were only the two of them left, Lydiard urged Sulivan to take his chance along the mast. Together they dashed to its foot. Clinging to the stump, they discovered a boy rigid with fear and stunned by the brutal battering the sea had given him. As Sulivan started along the mast the Captain turned back to the boy and, regardless of the danger to himself, spent a few precious seconds coaxing him to make a dash for the beach. The next wave broke. It foamed around the mast-stump and carried Captain Lydiard and the boy over the side to their deaths.

Sulivan, seeing the wave begin, dropped across the mast and clung to the cordage on it so that the water passed over him. As it receded he was able to make good his escape to the shore.

Shortly afterwards the *Anson* began to break up. But about one hundred and forty sailors had reached safety and were gathered in groups on the shore above the wreck. Lieutenant Gill marshalled them together, and they moved overland in stages back to Falmouth, where they were stationed aboard the *Tromp*.

On that forlorn trip back to Falmouth Lieutenant Gill had plenty of time to think. And once the actual shock of the shipwreck had lessened he realized that he was the only surviving officer of the ship's company (Commander Sulivan was a guest).

So aboard the *Tromp* he sat down to write the dispatch to the Admiralty that he knew would mean his own court-martial, following the normal naval practice of court-martialling the senior survivor from any such disaster.

On the morning of Tuesday, January 5th 1808, the Captains who were to make up the court assembled on the flagship anchored in the Hamoaze.

The court-martial flag was hoisted and the convening gun fired. And Thomas Gill, Lieutenant on board the *Anson,* stepped forward to tell the court exactly what had happened on the occasion of the ship of His Majesty's Navy running on shore near Porthleven, just over two miles from Helston, Cornwall.

Gill told his story straightforwardly, and in the still of the big cabin being used as a courtroom the assembled Captains listened. But they didn't only listen. From time to time they shot questions at the young Lieutenant.

"Why were the guns not put overboard to lighten ship?"

Both the Lieutenant and the questioner knew the answer. An easy question to ask in the calm of an anchored ship in sheltered waters, but not one to be considered in the teeth of a gale and with a deck wet with sea that heaved and rolled incessantly. Without hesitation Gill answered: to cut a cannon loose in the confines of a gun-deck in such weather would be suicidal. Such a weight of wheeled metal would trundle from port to starboard and back again like a ponderous battering-ram until it finally smashed its way clear out through the side of the ship. This was to say nothing of the men who would be injured in trying such a manœuvre.

"Why were not the masts cut away to lessen the play of wind on the ship?"

Another easy question, and one to which Gill had a better answer than the other. No sailor likes to destroy his motive power and give himself no chance, and in this case, as the court would learn, without the mast very few would have survived at all.

Gill went straight on with his story, and once his statement was taken he was allowed to retire. Members of the crew followed. Finally the court had all the evidence before them. They considered it. And in his final words the President of the court summed it all up:

"The court is of the opinion that the cause of the loss of His Majesty's late ship *Anson* was in consequence of her endeavouring to make the land in a violent gale of wind and thick weather, and that the *Anson* was not prepared in a state of readiness to come to an anchor upon a lee shore in such tremendous weather as the ship had to encounter."

Gill was cleared, and the Admiralty files on H.M.S. *Anson* were closed.

But on the bottom of the sea the remains of the hull broke loose and drifted free. Bundles of cordage, planks of wood, the main-mast, and other bits and pieces of flotsam were collected by local men for use ashore, and the wreck of the *Anson* disappeared from view, but not from the gossip of the locality.

In the sand below the surface the guns, coins, and other objects were preserved, waiting the day when they would again see the light. Time passed, until a few years ago divers, searching the area, came across unusual shapes in the sand.

Mr Roland Morris, an ex-Admiralty helmet diver, and now proprietor of the "Admiral Benbow", a restaurant well known to holidaymakers in Penzance, bought the wreck of the *Anson* for a fee from the Admiralty in July 1961. This contract was to run for seven years, and part of the agreement was that he was to get a percentage of anything valuable recovered.

Roland Morris began operations by putting an advertisement in the local Press, saying that he planned to survey the wreck and would give a reward if anyone with local knowledge could say when the wreck might be exposed to divers.

To understand why this was necessary you must know a little more about Loe Bar. Had the *Anson* come in to the shore about eight hundred years earlier, there might well have been no wreck at all. For in the eleventh century Loe Bar did not exist, and ships could come straight from the open sea into Loe Pool and on up to the tin-mining town of Helston. The *Anson* struck exactly in the middle of Loe Bar—at the point where a deep-water channel used to lead into the sheltered inner waters. What caused the huge sand-and-shingle bar to be piled up as it is? No-one knows, but early evidence suggests that hundreds of tons of sand and shingle were thrown up in a very short space of time.

About 120 lives were lost when the *Anson* was wrecked, and to understand how this could happen so close to shore you have only to stand on Loe Bar in a winter's gale from the south-west. Giant

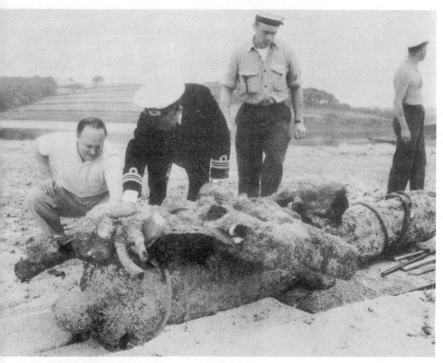

On the beach in front of the *Anson* wreck site a 32-pounder cannon has been dragged out of the sea. It weighs $3\frac{1}{2}$ tons and is 15 feet long. Cemented to the cannon as a result of its long immersion are three iron ballast 'pigs', four cannon-balls, a quantity of lead piping, and iron objects like bolts and rings. (See p. 114.)

(*Below*) Two cannon recovered from the *Anson*. The one on the right has undergone some preservation treatment. The other, not yet treated, shows the scour marks of the strong tides in the area.

Wreck hunters are not exclusively male! This woman diver found the wreck of the *City of Chicago*. Note the full-face mask and opening visor. (See p. 130.)

(*Below*) *The City of Chicago* broken in two after striking.

113

seas thunder in, the ground shakes beneath your feet, and a dull, booming roar fills the air. The seas crash down, grab and suck at the shingle, and tear out tons with each wave. And then the next giant flings it back. The formation of the bar itself has left a permanent shelf only about twenty-five feet off shore, so just below low-tide mark the beach drops instantaneously from a foot or two of water to almost twenty feet. It is a dangerous place for bathing or swimming even on the calmest day.

This is why it was necessary for Roland Morris to advertise for information. For the best part of the year the entire wreck site is completely covered by several feet of shingle. Then suddenly, normally with a large tide and preceding storm, it is uncovered. This may last for one day or perhaps a week, then it is gone again.

In August 1961 Roland Morris received a telephone-call to say that the wreck was exposed. "I began operations immediately," he says. "I was after a bronze cannon, and I was a bit disappointed because all I found then were five iron cannons."

But he also found within a few days 30-40 cannon-balls of various weights, wrought-iron fittings, and a collection of rigging-screws. Then the shingle moved over the wreck, and diving operations stopped.

In July 1964 H.M.S. *Seahawk* Sub-Aqua Club (formed from the Royal Naval personnel at the Royal Naval Air Station at Culdrose), who, together with local historian Mr F. Strike, had been planning an investigation of the *Anson* site, moved into action. Mr Strike had told them that the signs were that the shingle had gone from the wreck, and so, led by their Diving Officer, the men entered the water. They reported as follows:

"Using the two points of the cliffs at the entrance to Loe Pool as a marker, we took up a position a little to the west of the central point. We were prepared for the remarkable 'drop off' shelf and found it very close in shore. Swimming hard against the undertow, which clutches the diver and throws him against the shelf, then drags him out again, we swam down into slightly deeper water. The bottom changed from shingle to clean sand, absolutely barren with not a single trace of weed and only a few hermit crabs scuttling away from our path.

"Some twenty-five yards out we saw the first signs of wreckage, and decided we were fortunate on two scores. We had chosen a day when at least something was uncovered, and secondly we had found the actual site straight away. Then there quickly came into view four large heavily encrusted cannon. These lay in no particular pattern or order, and the first thing we noticed about them were the deep scours on their barrels. This later proved to be a feature of every cannon left, caused by the continuous movement of shingle over the metal.

"Having attached a line to the nearest cannon in order to have a marker for further dives, we swam further out and spread our search pattern. More cannon came into sight and a jumble of iron 'pigs' used as ballast. These were scattered all over the seabed and measured about three feet long and six inches square in shape. Altogether we located ten cannon of a pretty uniform size which later proved to be 32-pounder and 22-pounder. All were iron and looked to be almost cemented to the hard gravel on which they lay. We made several attempts using diving knives to separate the 'pigs' from the cannon, but quickly realized we were wasting our time. More substantial tools would be needed to break them away.

"Next we inspected every single cannon in some detail. The majority had gaping open muzzles, but they only went back a foot or so before being blocked with sand. However, at least two appeared either to have a tampion fitted or to have become completely overgrown at the muzzle. One particular cannon caught our interest—it lay in four neat sections. It looked just as though someone had cut it up with an underwater oxy-acetylene torch, the breaks were so neat. We found out later that it was the result of underwater blasting on the site by previous salvage attempts. The shock waves had broken a three-and-a-half-ton cannon as easily as cutting cheese. Naturally we had hoped to find some small items of interest, but on the first dive we were unfortunate and found nothing like that.

"But during the last few minutes of our first dive that evening, we sighted a large piece of brass protruding from the seabed. It appeared to be part of a narrow half-rounded plate and was embedded firmly in the shingle. We scrabbled at the bottom and removed a quantity of material from around its shape, and found that by standing up on the bottom we could rock it backwards and forwards. A rope was run out from it to the beach, and with one diver rocking and the others pulling on the beach it was slowly wrenched out. The shape still gave no clue as to its purpose until it was clear of the surf line on the beach.

(a) SKETCH OF PINTLE AND RUDDER OF "ANSON."

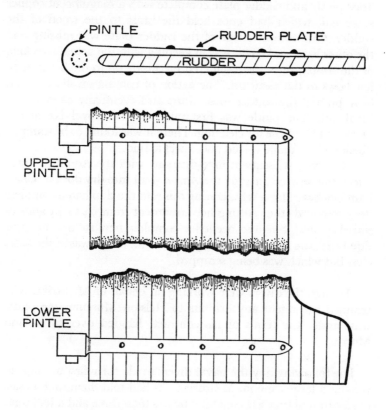

(b) PROBABLE REASON FOR BENDING OF PINTLE RECOVERED

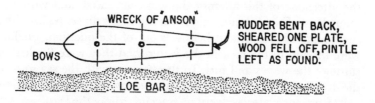

Why the *Anson*'s pintle was bent
drawing by R. Larn.

"When we examined it there it turned out to be an enormous brass pintle and rudder plate complete with a magnificent copper spike nail which had once held the brass to the wood of the rudder. One complete side of the rudder plate was missing and the other bent back. This was in keeping with the actual wrecking of the *Anson,* since she foundered broadside on to the beach with her bows to the eastward. The action of coming on shore would have pushed the rudder to seaward and eventually caused it to break off. The pintle was first taken to the Royal Naval Air Station at Culdrose for cleaning. There it was found to be stamped "Bellona"—a name we did not expect to find.

"However, subsequent investigations with the Admiralty produced the answer. In 1791 the *Anson* went into dry dock at Chatham Dockyard for a refit. During this refit the ship had a complete deck removed (thus cutting her armament from 64 to 44 guns as stated earlier). She also needed a complete new rudder and was fitted with the rudder of the frigate *Bellona*, which was of the same class but which was being scrapped."

(Though the divers were working on behalf of Mr Strike, who planned to present any exhibits to Helston Museum, the pintle was, under the terms of his contract, handed over to Roland Morris.)

The following day the naval divers made their first attempt to recover a large cannon. Measurements had told them that a mass of cast iron of that size could not be less than three and a half tons, not an easy recovery job on to a soft beach. Still, they went ahead. Wire strops were attached to the best specimen, and an attempt was made to lift the cannon, using five-ton lifting-bags. During the afternoon of this attempt the wind increased, and within an hour the surf was running high—so high that divers realized that swimming ashore without help was out of the question. Lifelines were thrown to the men in the water, and they were hauled out through the waves and surf. In the struggle with the sea some of the diving equipment was damaged, and eyewitnesses describe the exits from the water as "very ungraceful, to say the least".

The divers who were pulled out in this way thus had a good idea, even on a miniature scale, of the conditions that had faced the *Anson*'s crew.

It was a month before another attempt could be made to raise the cannon. Two air-bags of five-ton lifting capacity were attached to the cannon and filled from compressed-air cylinders. As the bags filled they strained against the cannon encrusted into the seabed. Finally the cannon broke free: the lift of the bags overcame the pull of the cannon's weight and its attachment to the bed. Once close to the shore, the ropes were attached to a truck, and the cannon was pulled up the beach. The largest recovered was in particularly good condition when cleaned up. The tampion of this one was still intact, and when removed the bore was still dry—and loaded! The *Anson,* like our modern warships, had been ready for trouble at any moment. This cannon had been loaded with grapeshot. Each iron ball was about the size of a golf-ball.

Both the cannon recovered will have spent some time at the Naval Air Station undergoing long preservation treatment to ensure their survival in the atmosphere. It is hoped that one will be mounted on a replica of its original gun-carriage and kept at the Naval Station. The other is due to be presented to Helston Museum.

While the divers worked on Loe Bar they were within sight of the small memorial cross on the cliffside to the *Anson* dead who were buried round about.

Visitors to the area can see other relics of the wreck of the *Anson.* Two cannon, which were recovered in 1961, are mounted outside the offices of Porthleven Fisheries. Two more, wrenched out in 1963, are rusting near harbour buildings in Porthleven. There are others at Gunwalloe, at Roland Morris's "Admiral Benbow", and one small one is used to tie up fishing-boats at Coverack.

There have not been a great number of attempts to salvage the remains of the *Anson,* the majority of the wreck ending up as driftwood on local beaches shortly after the sinking. The woodwork of her lower decks is probably still there, deep down in gravel, shingle, and sand. In 1909 an attempt was made by helmet divers after a huge tide had even uncovered part of a deck, but it disappeared overnight.

Will anyone find a fortune beneath the cannon? Were the stories believed by the *Anson*'s sailors about the hoard of money true? Nothing was mentioned about money in the evidence of the court-martial, but there is no reason why it should have been. Coins are found from time to time in the area of the wreck—so it could be true. Deep in the sand is the only place to find the answer.

It is interesting to note that while the wreck of the *Anson* was actually taking place a local man, Henry Trengrouse of Helston, watched many lives being lost. People on shore could do nothing to help, the sea was too great.

This unnecessary loss of life caused Mr Trengrouse great pain, and he became determined that such a thing should not happen again. He returned home to think up some device that could be used universally to assist sailors in distress. His ingenious mind hit upon an invention that is still in use to-day—the rocket lifeline apparatus.

The *Anson* was not the only shipwreck in Cornwall that year. It was a bad year for wrecks, and not the least to suffer was another branch of the armed forces.

The 9th Light Dragoons, a regiment of horse, had been looking after British interests in Montevideo, in Uruguay. Many of the regiment, some wounded, and all due for home leave, were placed on board the troopship *James and Rebecca*. She sailed from Montevideo with some two hundred cavalrymen on board and hurried back towards England.

Robert Rochester was the Master of the *James and Rebecca* (Transport No. 42), and, having made a good passage from America, he arrived in soundings during early November 1807.

As with the *Anson* some weeks later, the weather in the Channel was bad. Wind and heavy seas coupled with very poor visibility made the latter part of his voyage a continuous nightmare, and a most careful watch had to be kept at all times.

On November 6th the weather in Mounts Bay was appalling. Long, hurrying waves, their tops crowned with foam, raced by the ship; the wind rose to gale force, hissing through the rigging continuously; and for those on board the voyage that had so far been quite bearable was fast becoming a journey that all prayed to have ended quickly.

Their prayers were answered all too soon, and not in the manner that they desired.

Wolf Rock had been passed unseen, but Robert Rochester could tell by the action of the sea that currents were playing on his ship, and that no matter how he steered he could do little to arrest her onward rush. Nor could he alter her course away from the direction in which the wind was forcing him. The embracing arm of the Lizard was a danger he knew well, but he could not find out exactly where his ship was in relation to the land. As it was, all that he could do was to wait and watch and pray. If there had been today's Lizard light flashing away every three seconds, with its twenty-one-mile visibility, then he could have fixed his position and warned his passengers and crew, but there was no such light then, and no warning was given.

The feeling of unrest seemed to have spread down below decks from where Rochester stood. As he glanced from the water all about him to the main deck he saw groups of people moving about with little bags and parcels of personal belongings clutched in their arms.

Without being told, the passengers had realized that danger was imminent, and with a sixth sense had come out from the cramped below-decks to the open air.

Rochester, however, ordered all passengers to be kept below, and watched as the groups of Dragoons turned from the upper deck, many with a glance in his direction, and slowly went back down the steps to the darkness below.

For non-sailors they were behaving well, but Rochester felt that no matter how well behaved they were, they could not be allowed on the deck during this storm. They would only hinder the sailors, and an inexperienced soldier might well be caught out by the movement of the ship and disappear over the side for ever.

With the deck clear, he looked aloft to see how things were. Something was not right. His trained eye picked out the fault almost at once. A broken gasket on the main yard had allowed a small bag of sail to blow loose to add to the speed of the flying ship. He regarded it with some alarm, and a story told to him by an old sailor years before sprang into his mind.

The account concerned a little pinnace, the property of the sailor who told the tale. This vessel was in a gale of wind that was blowing from directly astern. The sailor had been going from Burgh Island in Bigbury Bay, Devon, to Salcombe, and having tacked out some way was met by a sudden and violent squall from the south-west which so unnerved him that he turned back the way he had come and headed for Bantham Sands and the mouth of the river Avon.

The squall passed, but within minutes the wind strengthened, and the sea got up so much that he found himself approaching the sands of Bantham at such a rate that nothing he could do would change the direction in which the boat was heading.

Large waves passed him by, hurrying on with white crests—he had never seen the like before—and as he glanced astern he saw two huge combers catch him up, which made him think that his end was very near. As the first wave reached him the stern of the pinnace raised up until it was at an angle of forty-five degrees to the surrounding water, but instead of the wave passing under him he found to his dismay that he was being carried on its front at what seemed to be a tremendous speed straight for the beach. The bow of the little ship was pushed farther down into the water until, with the decreasing depth, the top of the huge wave began to move faster than the trough, and his boat broached-to in an instant and was thrown stern over bow in the shallows.

He fell clear of the mast and found himself struggling in the water. As he came to the surface the second wave caught him like a cork and rushed him on to the beach like a piece of flotsam. He was able to touch bottom with his feet, and after a struggle against the ebb which roared out past him he staggered on to the dunes beyond the water-line, where he fell exhausted but safe from the waves.

Remembering this story, Rochester looked at the water about him, and the thought of broaching-to came into his mind. He noticed that although the waves still passed under the ship, their passage from stern to bow was taking longer than it had previously, and all the while the speed of the ship was increasing. The broken gasket had made enough difference to be very serious to the safety of the ship. He knew now that something had to be done at once to avert a calamity. To send a sailor aloft in this weather would be the height of foolishness, so some other means of slowing the ship had to be arranged.

The Carpenter was summoned, and within half an hour a mass of old sails, spars, and a spare anchor were streamed astern on the end of a cable to act as a sea-anchor. This trailing weight slowed the passage of the ship slightly, but not to the degree Rochester required. However, it was better than nothing, and he felt that the best had been done in the circumstances.

A new worry appeared in the shape of a seaman who shouted to him that the Chief Mate was dead. Some ten days before the Mate, unusually careless, had fallen and severely injured his head. Now the action of the ship in the storm had completed the damage.

A short while after this news the roar of water on land was heard ahead of the ship, and before those who heard it could turn to shout a warning the ship struck with a violent shock that brought the masts crashing down over the anchor-deck.

At once a succession of waves began to break over the stern, and with each blow the *James and Rebecca* was hammered against the bottom. Several planks were started at the bow, and water flooded in to bring chaos below deck among the struggling men and women.

Nothing could stop the might of the waves. Very soon bodies were being washed to the beach, and cries for help sounded thinly from the sea.

It was about half-past ten at night when the ship struck. Captain Rochester, his son, and all the officers of the Dragoons were able to come safely to shore, but some thirty of the Dragoons were sucked down to their deaths.

At Penzance the Custom House officials were alerted that a ship was ashore, and hurried to the scene to give what assistance they could. Little could be done for the ship as she was a total loss, but they were able to help the survivors away from the scene of death, and give them warm clothes and some food. . . . By the next morning the ship broke up, and at midday she disappeared from view. The beach near Gunwalloe was littered with parts of the ship, and horse harnesses and ship's stores were washed ashore all that day.

No diving expeditions have yet found out the last resting-place of the *James and Rebecca,* but the wreck did take place, and a party of divers searching the area have every chance of finding at the bottom the rusted remains of muskets, saddlery, and the occasional coin.

But no fortune will await the wreck hunters. The men of the Custom House returned to Penzance, and in due course a report was sent to the Board in London. The letter read:

CUSTOM HOUSE
TO BOARD OF CUSTOMS, LONDON
9th November, 1807

HONOURABLE SIRS,

We beg to acquaint your Honourable Board, that, on the night of the 6th instant was driven on shore near Gunwallow within the limits of this port, the Transport *James and Rebecca,* No. 42, Robt. Rochester master, from Montevideo, with 200 of the 9th Regiment of Dragoons dismounted, together with Military stores; the vessel went to pieces on Saturday last at 11 o'clock at noon, and melancholy to relate, 30 of the lives that were on board, have perished, and many of those who have escaped death, are dreadfully mangled; all the Officers and women are salved, and such of the stores that have been driven on shore, and carried to Helston and placed under the locks of this Revenue, they consist chiefly of Horse Accoutrements, and from the state they are in, they appear to be of little or no value.

CHAPTER
Eight

Soldiers in the Sea

A frosty January morning at Deal in 1816 found Major
Douglas and his men of the 59th Regiment paraded on
the quayside and ready to embark for Southern Ireland.
The *Seahorse*, which was to serve as transport, pulled gently at the
icy ropes which held her to the shore.

To a man in the ranks the wait to go on board seemed just
another example of standard Army procedure: you get somewhere, nobody is ready for you, you wait, then you find you're in
the wrong place . . . and it's always freezing cold! This time, however, though they had to wait, the troops were in the right place,
and slowly, file by file, they made their way aboard the *Seahorse*.
Once aboard they were directed to quarters amidships, and there
once again they settled themselves down to wait. At least they were
out of the worst of the cold.

James Gibb, Master, was impatient to be off, and soon the gang-
plank came crunching aboard and the voyage began. At the
Downs the *Seahorse* joined several other vessels to make up a
small convoy. As soon as she linked up the whole flotilla made sail
down Channel.

On board the troops relaxed and talked of battles past. The
veterans held some of the recruits enthralled with their war stories,
for Waterloo was not long past. Some had been in Ireland before,

and information, wildly distorted and slanderous to the Irish, was passed from man to man in the cramped space. Elsewhere in the ship were wives and forty children.

Two days later the *Seahorse* was south of the Lizard, bucking in a southerly breeze that freshened by the hour. As course was altered round the Wolf Rock, north-west for Cork Harbour, the breeze strengthened so that by the time the ship was half-way to Ireland and over the Nymph Bank she was off course. Instead of heading for Cork, she was now being blown farther to the east towards Waterford.

During the early evening of January 29th the Mate went aloft to study the coastline to see if he could fix their position. The ship swung, and in the strong wind he missed his footing and plunged down to the deck. He was nearly killed outright.

Gibb had realized that they were somewhere off Ballycotton and east of their destination. So he put his ship as close to the wind as possible and headed on the port tack for the Kinsale Light.

As the evening advanced the weather worsened, and the ship began making too much leeway for safety, so Gibb now wore his ship round on to the starboard tack to head south-east back into the St George's Channel and the greater safety of the open sea.

The other ships in the convoy were also in trouble, and they all began clawing out to sea, but the wind and sea were both against them. During the night the ships moved as much north-east as they hoped to sail south-east. By first light the *Seahorse* was off Mine Head. Now the Master could fix his position, and, noting the nearness of the lee shore, he shook out the reef from his topsails and again tried for the open sea.

By ten o'clock that morning he was near Newtown Head and no better off. Within minutes his mainsail would take no more punishment. It split from top to bottom, and the shock and noise sent waves of fear running through both troops and sailors. As the squall that did the damage passed through the mainsail it hit the canvas of the foremast with terrible force—more force than the mast could take. It snapped off short near the deck, hurling spars, rigging, and canvas clean over the bows.

Gibb was now almost powerless to steer his ship, dismasted, with her mainsail gone. Though he knew the *Seahorse* was doomed, he tried one last trick. Down came all the sail, and over went both anchors. But the poor holding-ground and the speed of the ship made the effort practically useless. With anchors bumping along behind her, the *Seahorse* moved on towards the shore.

The ship could now be seen clearly by the people from Tramore, who came out on to the strip of land known as the Rabbit Burrow to watch the stricken vessel. There was little, if anything, that they could do to help. At 2 P.M. she struck the bottom, and was held fast with waves hammering into the hull and bursting right over her in clouds of spray. The people on shore thought that the *Seahorse* had only the usual number on board, as only a few of the crew had been spied moving about on deck.

But on board the troops had been told that there was no help available—and the wives knew it too. The children, of course, did not understand that death was so near, and played about while husbands hugged their wives to them and pretended that there was still hope.

The iron, even brutal, discipline of those days now had its effect. The troops remained below decks even though common sense and the thunderous noise of the sea on the walls of their quarters told them that their best chance lay in the open air of the decks above.

The wife of the Quartermaster of the Regiment went into the main cabin and gathered her children about her. As she did so she said to one of the soldiers there, "It is the will of Heaven."

It was not long before the hull was completely smashed in and parts of the wreck started to come ashore. There were boxes. There were bales. There were muskets. And there were bodies. And bodies and bodies. To the horror of the onlookers what they had thought would have meant the death of a comparatively few sailors turned their beaches into one vast cemetery. Three hundred and sixty bodies of men, women, and little children were washed up on the shore.

But some were saved. James Gibb, the *Seahorse*'s Master, was one, and he was able to give expert evidence of the way in which his ship was lost. At the time that he came ashore he did not know what had happened to the other ships in the convoy. They had suffered too.

Two of the ships of the convoy were the *Boadicea* and the *Lord Melville*. The *Boadicea* had joined the convoy from Dover, and the *Lord Melville* from Ramsgate.

When the *Seahorse* was battling off the coast of Ireland east of Cork the *Boadicea* and the *Lord Melville* had broken from the flotilla and had headed west into the gale so that they would be blown in towards Cork Harbour as they neared the land.

It didn't work. When they sighted the land it was too late—and they were not near Cork Harbour, but were within the arm of the Old Head of Kinsale. They could well have taken Old Head as the entrance to Cork, thinking that it was Power Head near Gyleen, but once in the trap they realized their error and tried desperately to get out of the bay. However, once the sea had them between the Seven Heads and Old Head, it was not going to let them go. All points of sailing were tried, but each attempt only brought the ships nearer to the raging breakers of the shoreline.

The *Lord Melville*'s Master decided his best course was to run the ship ashore. With luck he thought the passengers and crew could then get on shore themselves.

He selected Garretstown Strand as the most suitable beach, and set the ship for it. His run started, he could do no more. The coast loomed nearer and nearer, and it looked as though he would manage to drive his ship right up on to the shore, but suddenly, when only three hundred yards from the breakers, the *Lord Melville* struck a hidden reef. She was firmly on, and began to break up almost immediately. Waves and spray whipped over the ship, and men on deck had to hang on to supports to keep themselves on board.

Despite the hammering of the seas, the Master still kept control of the situation. He ordered the fore- and main-masts cut away, and as soon as this was done a rope was got to the shore and made fast. Then the first attempt to reach the shore by boat was made. In the lee of the ship the boat was launched, and Captain Radford of the 62nd Regiment, who was desperately ill, two officers' wives and their servants, a sergeant's wife and child from the 59th Regiment, some soldiers of the 59th, and six of the ship's crew to man the oars were got aboard. They started for the shore. But the waves were too big, and they had hardly gone any distance before one swamped the boat and the occupants disappeared in the foam. Of the boatload only one sailor reached the shore alive.

No-one else on board wanted to try again in another of the ship's boats. Some made suggestions about other routes of escape, but all wanted someone else to try them first. Finally it was all left to the Master.

He struggled, dodging the walls of water that poured over the ship, to the forepeak of the vessel and looked carefully at the position of the ship. He could see that she had lodged nearly at the end of the reef, which extended to the shore, thickening as it did so, until finally it became part of the cliff itself. Near the bow of the ship was a large rock, and from there in to the shore were the tops of rocks which might be enough to form a 'path' to safety.

The *Lord Melville*'s Master now called on his crew to help. Under his guidance a long, strong spar was lashed out from the bow, and after several attempts finally fastened to the top of the nearest rock. Now that they were busy on something constructive, hope soared in those trapped aboard. And events started to turn in their favour. The sailor who had reached the shore from the capsized boat had contacted the local signal station. Lieutenant Harty, who was in charge of the Station, began organizing too.

Seeing the Master's plan, he started work from the shore end of the line of rocks. Soon men from the shore, carrying lighted sticks as torches, were stationed along the rocks, moving farther out as the tide dropped. The falling tide turned the balance between success and failure, for as it fell more rocks appeared to complete the path to safety. Even so it was a desperate struggle between ship and shore, especially for the women and children. Waves still broke over the rocks, and the sea sucked and tugged at them while they hung on to lines and groped for footholds on the weed-covered rocks. But it worked. Before first light all who had stayed on board were saved. Lieutenant Harty had arranged accommodation in near-by cottages, and as they were rescued each one found a bed waiting or a place near a fire.

During the morning of February 1st Edward Darley, the senior Army officer on board, sent soldiers back to the wreck to find any equipment that could be saved. The search-party even went between decks and dipped into the flooded holds. They recovered all they could, but the ship was none too safe to work in. When the work was done as best it could, Colonel Darley composed his report of the wreck of the ship to Lieutenant-General Forbes, telling of the loss of life.

He reported, too, that a quantity of guns and equipment had also been lost. As the Colonel wrote his letter the local Collector at the Customs House, John Meade, was also writing a report of the wreck, but his report went further than that of the Colonel. John Meade had also to report the loss of the brig *Boadicea*.

The *Boadicea* had tried another method when she found she was trapped in the same way as the *Lord Melville*. The Master of the *Boadicea* was perhaps less wise, but he decided that, as his ship was smaller, he would remain at anchor until the gale was over. At first he was successful, and his anchors took a firm grip on the seabed, but during the night the strain on the cables was too much for them. They parted, and the ship went aground and broke up quickly. Nobody on land—the rescue of the *Lord Melville* was in full swing—knew of the death of the *Boadicea*; nearly all on board were drowned. Meade, the Customs Collector, found many bodies on the beach, all from the *Boadicea,* the next day.

What remains today for divers to find of these two shallow-water wrecks it is hard to say—perhaps only the remains of a musket or two—but the heavier equipment of the *Lord Melville* would be worth searching for.

Not far from the remains of the *Boadicea* and the *Lord Melville* is the wreckage of yet another ship. She was lost some seventy-six years later than the first two, and is interesting because she had masts, yards, and sails, but also mechanical power. She was a mixture of sailing-ship and power-boat—a ship half of the past and half of the future.

The electric telegraph was also in existence, and the news that a liner was wrecked was soon sent to London by Reuter's News Agency. On Friday, July 1st 1892: "Intelligence has been received that the Inman and International Line steamer *City of Chicago,* from New York to Liverpool, via Queenstown, has run ashore half a mile inside Old Head of Kinsale, to the westward."

As with all ships on the North Atlantic run, speed was the test of success. The shipping line that could guarantee a crossing shorter than that of its rivals stood the greatest chance of a regular supply of fare-paying customers. As a result of this policy of speed, including a rapid turn-round in port, any vessel competing had to travel at full speed at sea and as fast as safety permitted in coastal waters.

The *City of Chicago* had been nine days at sea, had crossed the Atlantic, and had sighted Cape Clear over the port beam during the second dogwatch. Fourteen knots was maintained, and then the ship entered fog.

The 360 passengers knew that their sea passage was nearly over,

A fantastic wreck picture. The *Mohegan* still shows above the water after striking the Manacles during the night off the Lizard, Cornwall. (See p. 147.)

(*Below*) Battered, but apparently unholed, an empty steel lifeboat from the *Mohegan*. The wreck can just be seen in the background.

Diver Reg Dunton with a small brass cannon he found when searching the seabed off the Cornish coast. Many more such finds will be made, almost accidentally, as the number of amateur divers grows. (See p. 160.)

(*Right*) This stone marks the mass grave of the *Mohegan* victims in St Keverne Churchyard. (See p. 146.)

and were packing their belongings in readiness for entering Cork Harbour.

In the barber's shop Chief Engineer William Campbell heard the engine-room telegraph ring down "Full Astern" at 7.50 P.M., and then two minutes later he felt the shock which smashed through the length of the ship and brought the passengers running from their cabins with fear on their faces.

The *City of Chicago* had struck inside the Old Head, and in doing so had rammed her bows well into a cleft in the rocks. At first, with the engines still running astern, it was thought that she would get off, but after an immediate examination of the damage in the bow the engines were put to "Ahead" to hold the ship into the cleft and prevent her from dropping back into deeper water and sinking.

The Times report of this says that the passengers "at once became panic-stricken, although different narratives describe the excitement as varying much in degree of intensity". But the ship was not an immediate total loss, and soon after the collision with the cliff, passengers realized that all was not in fact lost.

The Master, Captain Redford, sent his Chief Engineer ashore over the bows. He scrambled up the cliff and went to Kinsale, where he reported what had happened. The agents for the shipping line, Cummins Brothers, were told of the disaster, and three tugs were summoned to steam at full speed to stand by. The Liverpool Screw Towing and Lighterage Company sent their famous tug the *Stormcock,* but all the aid they could render was not enough to get the *City of Chicago* back properly into the water and sailing again. The tide was ebbing, and the ship's bows settled deeper and deeper into the cleft.

Soon after the news had been passed to Kinsale the local coastguard team appeared at the cliff-top, and a rocket-line was fired over the ship. With contact now established, a rope-ladder was lowered. Up this the passengers and crew made their way to safety.

In daylight the next day many of the passengers came back to look down on their ship. When they saw the rope-ladder stretching down from the cliff-top some 200 feet, most of them could hardly believe that they had made such a climb in the dark. Some said that if they had known such a tremendous climb was ahead of them they would never have left the comparative safety of the deck. All the passengers were saved though, as were the mails and a great deal of the baggage.

The ship later broke in two. The remains are still there, and a woman diver was the first to find her again underwater. She has said that the wreck is very broken up now.

This part of Ireland has claimed many wrecks, and her waters cover many lost remains. The *Gelph*, the *City of Quebec*, the *Conchee*, and the *Falls of Garry* are all scattered round the Old Head, while a little farther out at sea the *Lusitania* went down. She lies on the bottom in 300 feet of water about twelve miles off. The local fishermen know her position well, despite the great depth. They fish the wreck when they can, as it is a great attraction as a home for fish. There have been diving expeditions on the *Lusitania*, sunk in 1915, but because of the depth she is rather out of reach of the amateur wreck hunter. Off Ireland too is the *Laurentic*, a 15,000-ton liner which was carrying £6,000,000 in gold bars when sunk by a mine in January 1917. Nearly £5,000,000 of the gold was recovered in an epic salvage operation.

A ship of about the same period as the *City of Chicago* is, however, within the reach of amateur divers, and owing to their efforts her last resting-place is now known.

She was found, as wrecks often are, by accident. What happened was this. During 1962 there were several diving expeditions to the area around Start Point in Devon. These were organized principally by the Start Bay Branch of the British Sub-Aqua Club, and in particular by George Tessyman, whose boat was invariably the means of transport. (You will have read about George in the chapter on the *San Pedro* at Hope.) While on one of these dives George swam over something that was remotely ship-shaped. As he swam he peered about him to try to fathom out what it was, and if it was a ship, then which ship it was.

What he saw was a mass of twisted metal with odd pipes sticking out of various places. He searched closely, probing among metal plates, pushing aside weed, and letting the sand filter through his fingers. As he did this he noticed on the sand a short distance away a separate piece of metal of an unusual shape. It was about nine inches long and one inch across.

On closer examination the metal appeared to be brass, and was designed as some sort of scroll. When the accumulation of verdigris had been removed and the plate properly cleaned letters could be seen impressed along the face of the scroll. They spelled out the word "MARANA".

From this beginning and clue to the ship's identity it was possible to build up all the background.

The night of March 9th 1891 is still remembered by Devon veterans. It was the night a tremendous blizzard struck the West Country. In Devon, Cornwall, and West Somerset chimneys were blown from houses. Sleet and heavy snow filled the narrow lanes to the hedgetops, and immense drifts shifted like sandbanks across the countryside. At sea things were worse, and there was no shelter. Waves piled up to colossal heights, and all shipping near harbours ran for shelter. But not all were able to reach it.

One of these ships was the iron steamer *Marana*. She was en route for Colombo, Ceylon, with a cargo of railway sleepers. She was caught in the Channel by the gale which came howling in from the south-east, her route to Ceylon being via Swansea, where she was to pick up coal. As she passed by Berry Head, Torbay, the gale enveloped her in driving snow, and blotted out the coastline. The ship steamed on towards the Start, and was noted by the Coastguard Station at Hallsands as behaving in a strange manner, a manner indicting that her steering-gear was out of action. She was within the Skerries Bank, and then headed out to sea again towards the Start Light. She then went out of sight of the coastguards, and they hoped she would be able to clear the dangerous rocks.

At the lighthouse Mrs Briggs, wife of a lighthouse-keeper, was looking out of her window at the storm. Suddenly out of the whiteness came the *Marana*. She just scraped past the rocks on the eastern side of the Start. It was obvious to Mrs Briggs that the ship was in grave danger of running on to the rocks below, so she raced to the head lighthouse-keeper, Mr Jones, and told him what she had seen.

Mr Jones at once hurried out to do what he could, but the *Marana* struck on the Blackstone and quickly broke in two.

The stern half sank at the Blackstone, while the forepart drifted away and soon sank a short distance away to the west of Start Point. A messenger was sent to Prawle to ask for life-saving apparatus, but by the time he returned all signs of the ship had disappeared.

It looked as though all the crew were lost, but in fact there were some survivors. Four men had clung to an upturned lifeboat until they were washed ashore on the Mal Rock, east of Prawle Point. Once they had managed to scramble over the rocks to shore, they still had to climb the cliff. This they somehow managed in their frozen, semi-conscious state, but after reaching the cliff-top they could do little more than take cover in a brake. Even there they were still exposed to the pitiless weather, and were near death when some coastguards found them five or six hours later. Ramossen, one of the survivors, died from exposure and the hurts he had received when the lifeboat crashed on the rocks. Two boats had been launched from the wreck, but these four men were the only survivors. The other twenty-four died in the raging sea. Of the 1682-ton *Marana* only the battered wreckage that George Tessyman found remains: the cargo of railway sleepers presumably floated away.

Storm caused the loss of the *Marana*, and the blizzard was well remembered in the West Country. But rough though the sea was then, it could not compare with the storm that had burst in the West some years earlier. This wild outbreak of weather was to become known as the *Royal Charter* storm—one of the few such meteorological displays to be called after a ship.

But then the loss of the *Royal Charter* was no ordinary shipwreck, nor was the storm that caused it. On October 25th 1859 winds gusting to over 100 miles per hour shrieked across the West Country and up the coast towards Liverpool. Many small ships were lost in the first few minutes of such winds and the colossal seas that sped along with them.

The *Royal Charter* was homeward bound to Liverpool from Australia. A 2719-tonner, she was the pride of the Australia run —a run she could manage in under two months with her huge sails and big auxiliary steam engine. Not the sort of ship with her iron sides to give way to a storm at sea of any ordinary power.

But this storm was different. In Liverpool Bay, just off the coast of Anglesey, the storm hit the *Royal Charter*.

Despite the power of the auxiliary engine, the *Royal Charter* could make no headway against the storm. In fact, she was losing ground and being pushed steadily towards the shore. The Captain ordered away both anchors. They bit, held, and then suddenly snapped. In she drove towards Moelfre Bay, and finally hit the shore stern first. Perhaps it would have been all right if it had really been the shore she struck, but the part of the land she drove on was a rock reef.

Dawn on October 26th showed the hundreds of passengers that the shore was a mere thirty yards away. But it might as well have been thirty miles. One seaman managed to claw his way ashore through a wild froth of sea with a line. Some thirty men escaped down that line, but it snapped as the seas lifted the ship and smashed her down, broke her back, and then proceeded to destroy ship and passengers, men, women, and children, on the savage, barnacled rocks.

Over 400 people died. Down with the ship went over £300,000 in gold bullion from the Australian goldfields—and who knows how many small private hoards of gold from those miners among the passengers.

The disaster was, of course, front-page news, and among the journalists who came to the little fishing village of Moelfre was Charles Dickens. His description of the scene can be found in *The Uncommercial Traveller*.

Salvage divers recovered much of the bullion from the wreck. But wreck hunters are still sometimes on the scene in the hope of finding any overlooked pocket of gold.

In 1959, in December, the late Peter Small, one of the founders of the British Sub-Aqua Club, who was later to die establishing a world-record dive to 1000 feet with Hannes Keller, who survived, dived on the site of the *Royal Charter* wreck.

In thirty feet of water he and Mike Taylor, of the Derby Branch of the Sub-Aqua Club, found some rusted ship's plates. Later Mike Taylor found more wreckage—in two-feet visibility—and was able to swim some distance over two lines of iron ribs. The keel was presumably still attached and buried deep in sand. But they found no gold.

More recently other attempts have been made, but without great success.

Course for Disaster

THEY have the bloodiest record of any group of rocks around the coasts of Britain. Their score-card of ships sunk runs into hundreds, and their death-roll into thousands. They are the Manacles, a scattered tangle of rocks just a mile out from the end of the Lizard, in Cornwall.

Seen from the shore or a boat well outside the danger area, they are insignificant. But their strength is that of icebergs: only a fraction of what lies underneath can be seen from shore or ship.

Only when you are in a diving-boat anchored out among them can you know what the Manacles are really like. The surface of the sea around you changes pattern every few moments. Wallowing pits appear as some underwater rip swirls round one of the hidden rocks, bumps into another just below the surface, and drops away. Short, sharp seas form around other hidden obstacles. If you have any great imagination it is not a happy place to be—especially when suddenly your anchor-rope snaps like a piece of twine! (The Manacles under water seem to have special saw-edges for dealing with anchor-ropes.)

To the diving wreck hunter the Manacles hold many prizes, but they are not for the inexperienced—either underwater or on the surface.

The depth of the hidden rocks is in many places only ten feet or so, but this falls away to depths of more than 140 feet. The dense underwater jungle of weed disappears in these Cornish waters at about 50 feet; below this the diver finds sandy bottoms, big purple-and-blue spiked sea-urchins, and sometimes huge turbot, which are inquisitive enough at 140 feet to nuzzle the diver's air-bottles in search of food. The diver also finds odd currents, an intensely strong tide, and rapid changes of surface weather conditions. This last reason makes it absolutely essential for the diver to have as the skipper of the boat from which he goes down a local man who knows and respects the Manacles. There is no doubt that diving on these rocks is difficult. Imagine what chance then has someone flung into the sea from a ship which crashes on to them in foul weather! Records over the years show how low the survival rate really is.

The lists of ships that have perished there are long and grim. And the list of which there is no record may be even longer. Many ships have disappeared without trace, and some of them owe their silence to the Manacles. In 1620 Sir John Killigrew wrote: "Nether is yt possibell to get parfitt notice of the whence and what the Ships ar that yearly do suffer on and near the Lizard for yt is sildom that any man escapes and the ships split in small pieces."

Local divers have collected lists of hundreds of identified ships, but every now and then they come across evidence of some disaster without name. In the 1800's, however, even the Manacles surpassed themselves. In only three of the annual wrecks on these deadly rocks more than 500 people died.

January 1809 was unusually bitter all over the country. Birds and animals were frozen to death in the fields, and the ground was rock-hard. On January 21st it started to snow, and in the night the wind grew until it was reaching near hurricane force. Out at sea the Army transport *Dispatch,* which had left Corunna on January 14th laden with men and horses of the 7th Dragoons, was blinded by the blizzard and being driven on shore. Aboard were three officers, headed by Major George Henry Compton Cavendish, son of Lord Burlington. Under their command were 72 N.C.O.'s and privates and 36 horses.

At half-past three in the morning the *Dispatch* struck on the rocks near Lowland Point. Seven Dragoons reached the shore alive. That was all. An hour and a half later, at 5 A.M., another ship hit the other end of the Manacles. This was the *Primrose,* a brig-of-war, carrying 120 officers and men and six passengers. The *Primrose* was outward bound. Fishermen managed to save a boy. That was all. As a result of these appalling losses the beaches of the little coves round about were lined with bodies, while their luckier regimental friends moved among them identifying the dead.

In 1855, on the 3rd of May, the same grim job was done on exactly the same beaches. This time the immigrant ship the *John,* bound for Quebec, went straight on to the Manacles, and 196 men, women, and children were drowned. Most of the casualties were from among the passengers, who were washed off the deck during the night, while many of the saved were found clinging to the rigging. The Captain was tried for manslaughter, but was acquitted.

Then on Friday, October 14th 1898, came another disaster —perhaps the most puzzling of all—when the passenger and cargo liner *Mohegan* went on to the rocks at nearly full speed. As she sank, 106 people drowned.

The story of the *Mohegan* is all the more amazing because had she not hit the Manacles her course was such that she would have run straight into the cliffs of the Lizard itself.

The *Mohegan* was no old hulk worth more in insurance money under the water than on top. She was, in fact, brand new and in the luxury class. All her passengers travelled first class.

She had been launched at Hull that same year, and was the largest ship built by Earle's Shipbuilding Company. She was originally designed for the Wilson Line of Hull, to run between London and New York. But when the usual launching ceremony, complete with champagne, was carried out the name that had the whole yard cheering was not *Mohegan,* but *Cleopatra*—8500 tons, length 482 feet, breadth 52 feet, and depth 34 feet 6 inches.

Whether it was because the Wilson Line were tired of waiting for the ship—she should have been completed the previous year, but was delayed for months by an engineers' strike—or whether they thought it better to take the profit offered them at once, no-one now knows. But they sold her as soon as the final touches of paint were dry. She sailed to London from Hull in July, and made a trial trip to New York for her new owners soon afterwards. They had renamed her the *Mohegan,* which means 'a good canoe man'.

They had named her, but not too well. *Mohegan* may mean

'a good canoe man', but this *Mohegan* gave her new owners a good deal of trouble. They had paid £140,000 for her, and on insuring the ship they took £38,000 of the risk themselves and let Lloyd's carry the other £102,000.

Some of the owners found out quickly that their investment might cause them some bother. Despite her very modern layout and the fact that she was fitted with "steam steering engines and hand steering gear," and despite the fact that the Board of Trade examined her carefully, her maiden voyage to New York—with some of the owners on board—was not exactly plain sailing.

The *Mohegan* was temperamental. She gave a great deal of trouble both with her engines and her boilers, so that her quick trip home lengthened into twenty-one days at sea. Those directors who were on the trip made sure that matters were quickly put right. The ship was overhauled, her compasses were adjusted, she was inspected once more by the Board of Trade, and then she was ready for the New York trip again.

On Thursday, October 13th, the *Mohegan* sailed from Gravesend. One or two of her fifty-three first-class passengers mentioned afterwards that they didn't like the idea of sailing on the 13th, but apparently none of them mentioned it at the time.

Her crew of ninety-seven and the six cattlemen on board to look after any livestock had no time to think about the date, for Captain R. Griffiths was a Merionethshire man who didn't like to see his crew idle. He was the commodore of the Atlantic Transport Line, the *Mohegan*'s new owners, and had had a great deal of experience. This was his third big steamship command.

A stiff breeze met the *Mohegan* as she came into the Channel. The wind veering between south-east and east had more than a hint of winter in it, so the passengers, who were gingerly trying out their sea-legs, found it necessary to wrap up well.

The *Mohegan* had 150 tons of cargo—jute, tin, and rolls of linoleum—in her holds, and was carrying 2000 to 3000 tons of water ballast. Her passengers found that she rode the sea well, and their confidence in the *Mohegan* rose even higher. What more could they ask? The food was good, the crew seemed efficient, the Captain looked, and, indeed, was, a man of great experience, and if the worst came to the worst, look at those eight large lifeboats which, said the plaques at the lifeboat stations, could carry 234 people between them! Those who were not seasick settled down to enjoy a most pleasant voyage.

As a result of such happy thoughts the celebrations of sailing went on in the saloon far into the night.

The next day the *Mohegan* was well on her way. The only untoward thing that passed unnoticed by everyone except Engineer Officer Ferguson, who was in charge of *Mohegan*'s engines, was that the lifeboat stations were not allocated. This was normally done on the company's ships on the second day out. This time it wasn't, and Ferguson, with his ten years of experience with the company, noticed it—but he didn't worry. He had enough to care for with his engines.

At ten o'clock Quartermaster Juddery took over the wheel. "West-threequarters-north," said the man as he handed over to him, and the watching officer made no comment. Having an officer present when the wheel was handed over was a check that the correct course was being handed on. So west-threequarters-north it was, and Juddery found his spell at the wheel quite pleasant. The weather was fine, and the ship was within sight of land. The Isle of Wight dropped back, and Portland started to come up. The *Mohegan* was making an easy fourteen knots, and the ebb tide was with her. As the ship drew level with Portland Juddery handed over the wheel sharp on noon.

As he went below Juddery put out a steadying hand to one of the women passengers who was caught off balance by a sudden motion of the ship. She was, he thought, a fine-looking woman, but probably recovering from some illness and taking a cruise to put some colour back into her cheeks. He based this final observation on the looks of the man with the woman, Mrs Compton Swift. The man looked to Juddery like a doctor. He was right. The man was her physician, Dr Fallows.

Luncheon was served in the saloon, and by all accounts was an excellent meal. More of the seasick passengers were about now, and the voyage looked well settled in. In fact, "All well" was the signal passed by the *Mohegan* to Prawle Point at 2.50 P.M.

Quartermaster Butt took the wheel from 4 P.M. to 6 P.M. "West-by-north" was the course he was given by Quartermaster Blake, and as there was no word of interruption from Chief Officer Couch at the handing over, that was the course Butt steered.

Only a minute or two after Butt took the wheel the Eddystone

Lighthouse was sighted at an angle of 45 degrees to the ship's course. And Juddery, who had been resting on his bunk after lunch, came up on deck for a breath of air. As he came up he saw the lighthouse at once. "She's close," he thought to himself, and mentally put the lighthouse's distance from the starboard bow at about three miles.

Seeing him apparently unemployed, Chief Officer Couch interrupted Juddery's ponderings on the Eddystone's nearness, and ordered him to help with observations and the entries in the log. Juddery noted carefully that the calculations showed the Eddystone to be passed at a little less than three miles and the ship's speed to be eleven knots.

Mrs Compton Swift was another person who noticed how close the ship was to the Eddystone. In fact, she commented that the ship had been very close in most of the way down the Channel.

Not many of the other passengers cared, though a young American singer, Miss Rodenbusch, going home with her stepmother, thought it a fine sight.

The thoughts of most people were turning towards dinner. George Maule, the leader of the six cattlemen in the ship's company, had little to do except think about the next meal. His job was the care of the horses which the line brought regularly to England from America for sale. His job would start in earnest when the horses were loaded in America. . . . Until then he was determined to eat well and rest as much as possible. Now, he decided, was the time for a nice cup of tea.

Quartermaster Butt held firmly to the course which he had been given. The wind had freshened now and was blowing strongly from the south-east.

Chief Officer Couch kept looking at the binnacle, and Butt was determined not to be caught off course for one second. He'd show him how a real quartermaster should steer!

At 5 P.M. Captain Griffiths appeared suddenly from behind Butt and stared at the course in silence. But soon to Butt's relief he moved away satisfied, and stood talking to Mr Couch.

At 6 P.M., with a feeling of a job well done, Butt handed over the wheel to Quartermaster August in the presence of the Second Officer.

"West-by-north," said Butt. "West-by-north it is," said Quartermaster August. The course for disaster was set. Only a new order could save the *Mohegan* from the Manacles. It never came.

As Butt handed over the wheel, Huntley in the crow's nest thankfully gave up his position to the ship's boy, Daniels. A little while later one of the deckhands, Seaman Wood, saw a light two points off the starboard bow. It was about three miles away, and he thought it was a shore light. As he saw it he heard the warning bell from the crow's nest. What the boy Daniels said he could not hear, but he heard the bridge reply clearly enough. "All right," said the bridge.

At 6.30 dinner was served in the saloon. Miss Rodenbusch and her stepmother, Mrs Grandin, were among the first to take their places. Mrs Compton Swift was rearranging her dress in her cabin, and Dr Fallows was waiting patiently outside to take her to dinner. He noted that the ship was much more lively now. The wind had increased to a moderate gale, and the sea was becoming much rougher. They were going to be late for dinner if Mrs Swift didn't hurry up. . . .

In the dining saloon Mr Pemberton looked round the table at his wife, his two children, and the maid, and made a mental note to see that the children had something to eat in their cabin in future. By the time the meal was over they would be nearly asleep. At a near-by table the measurer for the New York Yacht Club, Mr John Hyslop, started to eat his soup. Miss Katharine Noble, seeing that nobody was waiting for her to start, decided to eat her soup anyway.

The minutes were ticking by. And still the *Mohegan* continued on disaster course. By now she had been seen from the shore. Rockets were fired to warn her. Blue fire—an early type of flare— was let off to show the ship that she was heading straight for the shore.

James Hill, the lifeboat coxswain, of Porthoustock village, near the Manacles, was standing at the door of his stable when he first spotted her. He could do little except stand and gape. "She's coming right in," he yelled, and started running to the lifeboat station. He estimated that she was a quarter of a mile away, and still coming on with all lights blazing "just like a London street". But he didn't then know that it was the *Mohegan*. He thought it was the Irish steamer from Falmouth. Nothing else indeed—no ship— should be in the position that the *Mohegan* was in now.

At last the Captain, who had not been dining with his passengers, seemed to have realized his danger. The *Mohegan* turned slowly, but at the speed she was travelling she had no chance. Whether it was the Manacle Bell, put there in 1838 to warn ships of the rocks, or whether he saw the flares and rockets, we shall never know, but the *Mohegan* turned in towards one of the main groups of the Manacle Rocks. She would have done better to go straight on shore.

At 6.50 precisely the engines were signalled to stop, and half a minute later the *Mohegan* struck.

Miss Rodenbusch was just finishing the "soup and fish". Mrs Compton Swift was just about to sit down. Miss Noble had finished her soup.

Mr Ferguson—the man who had noticed that no lifeboat stations had been allocated—got the "Stop" signal very suddenly. Quick as he was, the engines had barely stopped turning when he heard, rather than felt, the ship strike. It was a scraping noise like a cable running out of a chain-locker. Then the water spurted through from the engineers' store cupboard on the starboard side, and within seconds was pouring in. It began to rise rapidly. Ferguson yelled orders to open the valves on the boilers, and finally followed the other engine-room men to the deck. As he came up on deck the ship took a list to port, and all the electric lights went out as the water reached the dynamos.

In the dining saloon the shock of striking had been felt more clearly. A steward hurried down the stairs and shouted, "All up on deck to save yourselves." The dining saloon erupted into confusion, but most people made their way with little trouble to the deck and fresh air. After the bright lights of the saloon they were blinded for a few moments.

Mrs Compton Swift and Dr Fallows were surprised to realize after a few seconds that the darkness was not so dense. In fact, it was only just dark. Mrs Swift said to Dr Fallows, "We'll need lifebelts most." Dr Fallows went to get them, and came back in addition with his coat and Mrs Swift's sealskin bag. By now Mrs Swift did not feel so frightened.

So she asked the Doctor if he had her jewel-case too. "No," said Dr Fallows, "but I can easily get it." "Don't worry about it," said Mrs Swift, regretting having mentioned it, but he had rushed off. He didn't come back, so Mrs Swift set off down the cabin stairs in complete darkness to find him. He was at the foot of the stairs, waist-deep in water—the ship was filling rapidly—and together they managed to get up to the deck again.

By now the deck was tilting well to port. The port lifeboats were in a difficult position. The Captain on the bridge shouted the traditional order—"Women and children first." The seamen struggled with the first of the port lifeboats, but it swung inboard, owing to the list, and jammed. The seas around the ship were now looming up over the passengers as the ship settled lower in the water. She was going fast. The seamen abandoned the jammed boat and moved to the second. This was successfully lowered into the water. Twenty-seven of the passengers were safely in, but there was no officer in charge. Two seamen plunged into the sea and swam out to her. With a struggle they were got safely aboard. Within seconds the boat was gone from sight into the night.

It was hopeless to get the other port-side lifeboats away, and Miss Noble, who had taken a place in one of them, got out again. She heard the Captain cry, "Hurry up with the boats," and order people over to the starboard side. The seamen struggled desperately with the starboard lifeboats. But Miss Noble could not find a place in any of them. One of the stewards gave her a lifebelt, and the Fourth Officer tried to help her get into one of the boats, but it was impossible. Finally, seeing that it was no use, he found her a place above the railing, where she should be able to swim clear when the water reached her, and went off to try to help other people. Miss Noble sat there trying to keep calm while the ship sank beneath her.

Mrs Compton Swift had been more fortunate—or so she thought at first. She found a place in one of the boats on the starboard side, with twenty-five other people. She heard the Captain cry out, "Men! Aren't you men? Can't you launch those lifeboats?" But though they struggled hard, only one seemed to get into the water. This was the boat in which were Mrs Compton Swift and Miss Rodenbusch, her stepmother, Mrs Grandin, and some children.

At this moment there was an explosion—probably the water reaching the boilers. The ship shuddered.

Chief Officer Couch gave orders to cut free all the lifeboats and let them float off when the ship went down—which seemed only seconds away.

Stunned by the explosion as she was, Mrs Compton Swift, safely in a lifeboat, realized that they were once again in deadly peril. It says much for her that she was still able to react to fresh dangers. Many of the passengers were fixed in terror, clinging to railings or huddled together on any part of the ship that would keep them above the fast-advancing waves.

But Mrs Swift had spotted that the lifeboat in which they were seated was still fastened by ropes to the ship at both ends and would be dragged under at any moment. She screamed to the man next to her in the bows to cut the rope. He did so, and started the knife on a perilous journey from hand to hand along the boat to the man in the stern. The man suddenly panicked, shouted that he couldn't cut it, and dropped the knife into the water in the bottom of the boat. There was no time to recover it. A huge wave came out of the darkness and clicked the boat over as though it were a child's toy. Most of the passengers spilled out into the spume and wreckage around the *Mohegan*.

On the bridge, Captain Griffiths looked round in despair. His once fine ship was a shambles. The screams and cries in the water around told him that most of his crew and passengers were now struggling in the cold Cornish waters. He had managed to get some rockets fired, and from the others exploding in the sky along the darker line that must be the coast he knew that help could not be far away. The trouble was that from the feel of the ship he knew that the *Mohegan* would not be there to meet the rescuers. She lurched again. He had one more command to give. "Get as many women as you can into the jigger rigging," he yelled—at least the water might not be too deep for the rigging to stand out from the sea.

Captain Griffiths took a firmer grip on the bridge-rail. He was going down with his ship. It was now four minutes past seven. The soup-tureens chinkled together in the swirling water of the dining-saloon, and the rest of the plates for the meal that was never finished slid out through a hole that the boiler explosion had blown in the side of the galley.

The *Mohegan* was going. Mr John Hyslop, the yachtsman from New York, watched the Manacle Rocks start to rear up beside the ship. He sized up the situation quickly, and decided that no more boats were going to get away—or if any did they should

Diving on the Manacles, Cornwall. In the foreground is Roy Davis, one of the divers who relocated the wreck of the *Mohegan*. He is wearing a wet suit to protect him from the cold Cornish sea. The suit has been torn on his right arm during a previous dive, but general body warmth will not be affected by this. (See p. 147.)

A great steel ship, the *Preussen*, under full sail. She died under the White Cliffs of Dover in November 1910. (See p. 149.)

be filled with women and children. So he decided to take his chance in the mizzen rigging. He was only just in time.

At exactly 7.5 P.M. the *Mohegan* settled, stern first. The waves overtook Hyslop in his climb. But he struggled up through it, fearing every second that he would be entangled and drowned. Finally he was clear of the water. Just below him in the rigging he found the Assistant Stewardess, and Quartermaster Juddery and another seaman. Hyslop shifted from one foot to another to ease the strain. Over and over again in the darkness he pictured the last moment of the *Mohegan*—and saw First Officer Couch dive away from the stern just as the water closed over it.

George Maule, the chief stockman, who had been having tea in a cabin between decks at the time of the strike, thought at first that the *Mohegan* had collided with another vessel. He rushed up on deck and met Chief Officer Couch. Couch too kept his head, and shouting, "Keep cool, boys, and we'll get the ladies and children off first", made sure that all the women were fitted with lifebelts. Maule stuck with him until the end, and when finally Couch dived away Maule jumped over after him.

William Ferguson, the Engineer Officer, who had injured his left hand badly in efforts to launch the lifeboats, was one of many who were flung into the water as the ship gave the final lurch. After swimming for half an hour he climbed on to the ship's funnel, which, together with the mainmast, was the only part he could discover above water. The screams and cries around him soon died away as the strong seas pounded on to the rocks.

Katharine Noble found herself in the water very suddenly. She swam to a plank and drifted with it. Then a larger piece of wreckage floated near by, and she changed over to that.

Mrs Compton Swift found herself in darkness, utter and complete. She believed that she had been drawn down under the *Mohegan*. She was quite conscious. A body bumped against her, and it cried out with a child's voice. Mrs Swift tried to hold the body up, but it drifted from her reach. Then a man's voice spoke something unintelligible in the darkness. Then it stopped. Only gradually did it dawn on Mrs Swift that she was underneath the upturned lifeboat. She struggled desperately to get free, but found herself trapped fast by her foot. Somebody else bumped into her, and Mrs Swift struggled to hold her up. After what seemed a long, long time the woman she was holding started to scream and scream.

Mrs Swift found herself thinking quite calmly that the voice which went on screaming was a trained voice—she was right; it was Miss Rodenbusch—and said to herself, "That's good, that sort of voice will save us because it will carry well."

By 7.20 P.M. James Hill, the coxswain of the Porthoustock lifeboat, had got his boat launched and was heading for the Manacles and the scene of the wreck. He burnt a white light, but received no reply. The wind was freshening even more, and the sea rising. Suddenly they spotted a ship's lifeboat upside down. He heard Miss Rodenbusch's screams, and they righted it. Miss Rodenbusch was quite clearly alive, but, looking at the other figure, with its head jammed between the side of the boat and the seat, one of the lifeboat men said, "It's no good taking this one, she's dead." Mrs Compton Swift heard the words with horror. "I'm not dead!" she shrieked. "I'm not dead! You must save me!" To get her free, lifeboatman Francis Trip climbed into the ship's boat and with an axe chopped away the wood that pinioned her leg. Finally Mrs Swift, bruised and battered, lay beside Miss Rodenbusch in the bottom of the lifeboat as it resumed its search for survivors.

Within minutes the Porthoustock boat linked up with the one lifeboat that had got away nearly full. On board was Mr Pemberton, his wife, two children, and the maid. James Hill, the lifeboat coxswain, burnt three white flares to show he needed help, and returned to shore with the survivors. Then he set out again for the wreck. Coming right up as close as he dared, he heard cries from the rigging.

Quartermaster Juddery timed his dive from the rigging just right. With a rope tied around him the slightly built man swam to the lifeboat. Then to safety also along the line came all those who had taken refuge with him, including Mr Hyslop.

Lifeboats from the stations along the coast were now arriving. George Maule, the stockman, was picked up by the Falmouth boat after seven hours in the water.

Engineer Ferguson was taken off the funnel after clinging there for hours. Miss Noble was found holding on to her piece of wreckage after hours in the water.

Gradually the survivors moved back to their homes, the bodies of the drowned were collected, and many were buried in a mass grave in St Keverne Churchyard, near tablets marking earlier disasters on the Manacles.

The Board of Trade inquiry opened, and during most of it the red funnel and four masts of the *Mohegan* stayed above water, marking the Manacles more clearly than any buoy or bell. The work of salvage went on. And the inquiry in London dragged on, checking whether the *Mohegan*'s compasses had been properly adjusted, or whether some other reason could be found for her suicide course. The inquiry was hampered a great deal by the fact that practically every officer, including the Captain, was dead.

Finally, on November the 26th, the inquiry closed with the verdict that "the cause of the stranding of the vessel was that a wrong course was steered of west-by-north after the vessel left the Eddystone." But the inquiry failed to find out why such a course was steered. It was left like that. The court warmly commended Hill of the Porthoustock lifeboat and Engineer Juddery for their bravery. And there for most people the matter closed.

But the *Mohegan* remained on the rocks after they started blasting to salvage more metal. And then—no-one seems to know exactly when—one morning she was gone.

Where she went to nobody knew either. The confusion grew worse over the years, until nobody was quite sure where she had been, despite the existence of some photographs of her on the rocks.

In 1961, however, two local divers, Roy Davis and Bernard Rogers, relocated her. They used an aquaplane to find the ship. This method is interesting because, though it is often used for such a search in the calm, clear Mediterranean, this is the first reported use of such a method of wreck location in this country.

The aquaplane can be anything from a simple board with handles for the diver to hold, to a much more sophisticated craft, complete with windscreen and movable 'wings'. But the principle remains the same. The board, aquaplane, or underwater sledge is tied on behind a powered boat at the end of a long length of rope. By moving controls or tilting the board downward the diver is able to dive below the surface and, like a glider, follow the boat's path on the surface but over the seabed below.

And this is how the two divers found the *Mohegan* again. Roy Davis tilted the board downward and headed towards the bottom. Above him the fishing-boat's diesel was hardly turning over, but below surface it was fast enough. The water was cold, but visibility was about 40 feet. Suddenly, out of the gloom at 60 feet the unmistakable shape of a ship's boilers loomed up. It was the *Mohegan*.

Her bow is in 50 feet of water, and her stern in 70. The boilers are fairly central with the wreck, running bow to stern, south to north. From the boilers northward is the prop-shaft. On each side of this large plates and shallow compartments rising to about 15 feet from the seabed are still there. In these compartments it is usual to find large angler fish on every dive. Finally the shaft peters out, and the wreck is scattered among outcrops of rock. Just as this happens there is a sandy gully slightly to the north-west, and it is here that most of the ship's plates, crockery, and cutlery lie in the sand.

From the boilers southward the wreck is not so clearly defined, as large rocks rise to within 15 feet of the surface and break up the line. Here there are masses of kelp to add to the confusion, but farther on are unmistakable bow-plates flat on the seabed. There too are three sets of bollards.

The twisted and bent lifeboat davits are there, but much of the steel plate is so corroded that an anchor goes right through it. For a comparatively new ship she is very broken up. But then the Manacles have a reputation for being unkind to any ship.

Last of the Sails

THOUGH steam was obviously the driving force of the future, the great sailing-ships did not give up easily. But they did die one by one, until now only the odd example is left and used as a training-ship for young sailors of the future.

In their day these were the giants and greyhounds of the seas; these were the ships that raced over the world's oceans, sometimes beating steam-powered vessels, and always making a fight of it.

Their names were the names of clippers and four-masted barques and five-masted full-rigged ships—names like *Sovereign of the Seas*, like *Parma*, *Viking*, *Penang*, *Herzogin Cecilie*, *Preussen*, and *Padua*. They travelled at speeds that today hardly seem credible. The Yankee clipper *James Baines* is credited with a top speed of twenty-one knots, and many of the others were only a fraction slower.

Some continued well into the thirties, and some survived the War, but the largest of them all, the German giant five-master *Preussen*, lived nothing like so long. She died within sight of the white cliffs of Dover, on the not-so-white rocks at the foot of those huge ramparts.

The *Preussen*, registered port Hamburg (owner Ferdinand Laeisz), was full-rigged, and the only one of her class built in 1902.

She was, at the time she went down, the largest sailing-ship afloat, with a length of 407 ft. 9 ins. and a beam of 53 ft. 7 ins. Her tonnage was 4768 register, and she was described as a steel ship in that she was steel-plated.

The German people, already searching for status symbols at the time of her launching, were rightly proud of this fine ship. For eight years the *Preussen* queened it among the world's sailing-ships, and her tall silhouette became well known to most of the larger ports.

Her last voyage, from Hamburg to Valparaiso with 5000 tons of general cargo worth £22,000, started well enough. On November 6th 1910, just before midnight, she was about eight miles off Newhaven. There was a light breeze, north by west, which, despite the haze, was threatening to become stronger. Captain Heinrich Nissen, her Master, though watchful, had no cause for alarm. Most of the crew of forty-eight were men skilled in the use of sail.

Captain Nissen exchanged a few words with his passengers, both of whom were taking a breath of air before turning in. They joked about the pianos—100 of them—in the holds as part of the general cargo. One of the passengers was a painter of seascapes, who considered himself fortunate to be in such a fine ship.

The other passenger was not so much interested in the beauty of swelling sails as in the actual handling of the ship. He was a navigation instructor. What he was about to see made a mockery of navigation.

Captain Nissen had seen the lights of a steamship approaching him, but felt no anxiety. He glanced automatically at his own lights. It seemed to him then that the ships would soon be well clear of each other. He continued to give routine orders as the *Preussen* dipped easily to a sea that was becoming perceptibly rougher.

The seconds ticked by, and Captain Nissen was suddenly aware that the steamship was very close—much too close. He took another careful look at her, and decided that she must be going astern. Now he recognized her as the Channel steamer *Brighton,* plying between Newhaven and Dieppe on the Paris–London service.

But the *Brighton* was not going astern. On she came as Captain Nissen watched helplessly. Then with a grinding crunch the two ships met.

Captain Nissen watched in horror as, almost in slow motion, his foremast snapped and crashed downward with the topmast still rigged. The *Brighton* ploughed on into his bow, and the bowsprit and jib-boom cracked into matchwood.

It was still misty, and getting darker minute by minute. In the *Brighton* it seemed that the *Preussen* had loomed up out of the murk from nowhere. Her Captain could be forgiven for thinking that his ship and the ninety passengers on board were doomed. At the time of the collision the seas were rising rapidly, but the lurch of the *Brighton* when she struck was like no sea she had yet encountered.

For a moment it looked as though her entire deck was going to be swept away by the high rigging and bows of the *Preussen*. Over the side went her forward funnel. Her mainmast snapped at the base and joined the funnel in the sea. Her port-side lifeboats were crushed, and much of her port side was damaged. Fortunately no-one was in the officers' quarters on the port side near the engine-room, for these appeared to take the brunt of the collision. As the *Brighton* swept on, her after funnel took a severe blow, but still remained on board.

There was hardly time for confusion, and on both ships everyone kept their heads. The *Preussen* from the point of view of seaworthiness was in the worse state. To add to her troubles it was clear that a gale was coming up out of the darkness and blowing directly on shore.

Once the Captain of the *Brighton* realized that he was in no danger of sinking, he stood by the disabled sailing-ship for as long as he could. But the safety of his passengers, endangered by the growing seas, was his first concern. He turned back for Newhaven.

The *Brighton* reached Newhaven at about 3 A.M., and immediately the London and Brighton Railway Company's tug *Alert* was sent to the assistance of the *Preussen*—if she could find her.

Those of the somewhat shaken passengers who wanted to continue their journey to France were transferred, together with the mails and baggage, to the French passenger steamer *France* as soon as she completed her night trip from the Continent. The *Brighton*'s Captain reported simply to his employers that he had been steering north-north-west off Newhaven when he came into collision with the five-masted sailing-ship *Preussen*. To this brief report he added a provisional estimate of the damage to both ships. Even today it is not clear who was responsible for the accident. Both Captains were cleared in their respective countries.

At the time most concern was for the *Preussen,* which, it was felt, was probably leaking badly and adrift in the darkness of the Channel. Captain Nissen had good cause to be alarmed. The *Preussen* was now making water in the forepeak, and was unable to use her head-sails. She was hove-to, and the Captain's first concern was to clear away the wreckage and to try to stop the forward leak, while waiting for the tug.

When the tug did not appear he decided to try to make for Portsmouth, but the wind increased and backed more to the westward, so he then decided to try for Dover. The weather continued to turn against him: the wind increased so much that when passing Dungeness he decided to try to seek shelter in East Bay.

At that moment Captain Nissen saw a very comforting sight— the tug *Albatross.* Working on the principle that there was nothing like local knowledge, he asked the Master of the *Albatross* for advice on where to anchor in safety. Once he had that information, Captain Nissen could justly think that most of his troubles were over.

Away went the starboard anchor, and no sooner had the chain started to run out than a sudden squall hit the ship. Now the chain shot out in jerks, and within seconds ninety fathoms of chain had shrilled out. Out went the port anchor at Captain Nissen's command, but it was too late. The strain on the starboard chain was too much, and it parted.

Realizing that he was now in danger of losing both anchors, Captain Nissen ordered the port anchor up, but it was impossible to stop it now. Helplessly, he felt, rather than saw, the chain race out on his second anchor, and within moments the port chain parted too.

Nissen now put the *Preussen* on to the starboard tack and hove-to as best he could. The tug *Albatross* came alongside, and Heinrich Nissen decided to run for his home port. Would the tug tow him there? *Albatross*'s Master pondered. He didn't like the look of the weather at all. But his decision was shelved, for at that moment the pilot cutter *Pathfinder,* with John Dickson, Trinity House pilot, aboard, also came alongside the *Preussen.* John Dickson had no doubt of the right course to take. The glass was falling rapidly, and he thought it too dangerous to try to take the ship across the North Sea. At the end of a short discussion it was decided to engage tugs and make for Dover.

More tugs arrived—they almost scented work for themselves—and three took the *Preussen* in hand. The weather was worsening all the time, but finally the *Alert* was made fast on the starboard side amidships. The *John Bull* took the starboard bow, and the *Albatross* the port. Then they got under way once again—this time for Dover.

At first things went well, despite the increase in sea and wind. From being Force Four when Nissen had tried to anchor, the squalls had now turned into a continuous blow of about Force Six, and still increasing. Nissen had only one shred of comfort in this stage of his fight against the sea—that in the collision no-one had been hurt. He had found this out from the Master of the *Alert*. "Thank God for that," said Nissen, and turned back to his charts.

Studying the German chart of the Channel and the chart of the Straits of Dover, Captain Nissen began to think that safety was at least within striking distance. They were making a good seven knots, though at times he almost lost sight of the *John Bull* at the end of 60 fathoms of four-inch wire and the *Albatross* even farther away at the end of 120 fathoms of five-inch wire. At last they rounded towards Dover Harbour, and the wind seemed determined to make their task more difficult. It was now blowing Force Eight to Nine, and sudden squalls ripped in from Dungeness. The seas were huge, and suddenly the tugs were making no headway. The wind and tide had them.

It was now 4 A.M. and still dark, so Captain Nissen was glad to have John Dickson at his side. Though Dickson was now giving the orders as pilot, they were working together well. The cross-sea was making steering difficult, but slowly the tugs won their way towards the eastern entrance to the harbour.

By now Nissen knew that provided he could get into harbour the damage to the *Preussen* could be repaired. The water was being held by the pumps, and all the wreckage had been cleared away. The *Preussen*'s 80-foot-long steel bowsprit, however, was bent to port like a banana.

But his luck changed again. The tugs could not make it. The only thing that they might have been able to do was to pull the

Preussen's head out to sea, where she might stand a better chance. Both Nissen and Dickson agreed that the best thing for the *Preussen* was to make sail. The command had no sooner been given than the *John Bull*'s tow-wire snapped.

Captain Nissen saw what was going to happen. He yelled for the lower topsails to be set in a forlorn effort to back her off, but the *Preussen*, hit by yet another giant squall loaded with rain, in John Dickson's words, "walked away from the tugs". Wires snapped, and the *Preussen* was free and helpless.

Two tugs were soon lying to seaward of her, and another two moved out from the shelter of Dover Harbour. Comforting sight though it was, Captain Nissen felt that they would have little chance of saving him before he went aground under those savage bare cliffs. As he fought with every trick he knew to edge out just a little from the perilous position under the cliffs, first one tug and then another tried to get lines to him, but each attempt failed.

In Dover itself lookouts, hampered by the rain-squalls, at first thought that one or other of the tugs would get a hawser to the *Preussen* before she struck the rocks of Crab or Fan Bay. But at 4.50 the first maroon exploded over the town, calling the lifeboatmen and rocket-apparatus crews to their stations, and telling all who knew of the *Preussen*'s danger that in the lookouts' experienced eyes she was due to strike soon.

Through glasses at least it was clear from the sea breaking in at the point where the *Preussen* lay that she had not long to live. But even in her death-throes the big *Preussen* did not look like a little plaything of the sea. To the watchers on shore she still seemed a giant, with her four remaining masts towering up through the rain-belts as they passed her to smash on the gaunt cliffs.

More maroons soared skyward, and boatmen and seamen came hurrying to the lifeboat station on the marine promenade. The lifeboat *Mary Hamar Hoyle* was ready almost at once, and Coxswain Brockman picked his sixteen men carefully. It was obvious that once clear of the harbour's shelter the lifeboat would meet enormous seas. Even so one of the men who took a seat was James Driscoll, who was over sixty. Brockman thought that his experience was worth more than the brawn of some younger man.

Dozens of willing hands seized the hauling-off rope and heaved, but the lifeboat stuck. A more concerted heave, and the boat slid forward and plunged into the sea. Soon she was rolling and bobbing on her way, and another maroon was fired to tell the *Preussen* that help was coming. The maroon performed a dual purpose, for one of the Dover Harbour tugs came back into the bay and took the lifeboat in tow.

Up on the cliffs above the *Preussen* the wind made standing up difficult, but the St Margaret's rocket-apparatus crew had somehow got into position. Two hundred feet below them the *Preussen* had still not struck, but it was clear that this was only a matter of minutes.

Coastguard Arthur Hughes, of the St Margaret's team, had no difficulty in making the ship out—a black blob in a white patch of foam. He had his doubts about the chances of getting a line across her in face of the wind which was blowing dead onshore. He knew that the tide was rising and that nothing now could save the *Preussen*, but even if a line could be dropped across the ship, hauling the crew up the cliff in the breeches-buoy would be a dangerous job. He heard the maroon signalling the lifeboat's launch, but didn't fancy the lifeboat's chances much either. Any attempt to go along the exposed side of the ship would result in the lifeboat being dashed against her, and as for moving inside the ship . . . well, the gap was narrowing every five minutes between the ship and the foam-line where the waves struck the cliff.

In the lifeboat, now under tow by the Dover tug *Lady Vita*, Coxswain Brockman was having rather similar thoughts. As soon as the boat had left the shelter of the harbour huge seas swept down on them and tossed them around like a cork. His crew cursed and swore as the sea hit them. More than one slipped from his seat and had great difficulty in regaining position. Then the *Lady Vita* had them under tow, and things were better, but only a little. Communication between tower and towed was minimal. Shouting had no effect, as the wind whipped the words away.

Gradually both tug and lifeboat drew near the *Preussen*, and Brockman saw that she had now struck. Though each giant wave lifted her, there was no doubt that her keel was hitting the seabed.

Somehow Brockman and the tug skipper worked together. While the tug held station off the stricken ship, the lifeboat, carried by wind and tide, was 'lowered' on the end of a long hawser towards the ship's quarter. As they neared the *Preussen* the lifeboat crew shouted in unison, but there was no reply from the great ship that alternately towered over them and then, as they were lifted by giant waves, was almost below them. The lack of movement on the ship struck Brockman as eerie. Lights were burning in the deckhouses and other parts of the ship, but there was no sign of anyone, nor any reply to their shouts.

A larger wave even than the others broke against the *Preussen*, and despite the wind the lifeboatmen heard the crunch as she bottomed hard. The same wave half swamped the lifeboat, and Brockman, seeing his crew half sitting in water, knew it was time to go. The tug towed them off, and after fighting hard right into the eye of the gale they got back safely to harbour.

By 10.30 that night a second rocket team was in position. This was the Dover Coastguards, and they had made their way along the foot of the cliffs. Arthur Hughes with the St Margaret's team knew that communications must be set up between the two rocket crews, or one could spoil the work of the other. There was only one way to do this. A flimsy-looking rope-ladder was tossed over the cliff-top, and, discarding his oilskins as too cumbersome, Arthur Hughes started down. Within seconds he was drenched through. Twice he lost his footing and spun round with the ladder, clinging only by his hands. The gale dashed him against the cliff, and his hands were cut. Worse was to come. Half-way down he found the ladder had twisted. Finally he managed to clear this obstacle, only to discover that the ladder ended thirty feet above the ground. His lifeline was the only way down, and he cast himself off from the ladder and pushed himself away from the cliff as best he could with his injured hands.

On the foreshore the *Preussen* could be heard grinding heavily on the rocks with every wave. She was now only 200 yards out and broadside on. Some lights were still there amidships, but the rest of the ship was in darkness. But the rocket crews could see her clearly—every sweeping flash of the South Foreland Lighthouse, a mile away along the cliffs, lit her up like a ghost ship.

Ghost ship she looked, for despite the lights there was no other sign of life aboard. But there was life all right. Captain Nissen, his passengers, and crew were so far all safe and sound. All hands were taking a turn at the pumps, and they sang softly as they worked. The bumping and grinding from beneath their feet was the worst. That is why they sang softly, each man straining his ears for the next message from the rocks of Crab Bay, and then when it came trying to judge how much damage it had done.

Food and hot drinks were available, and so high were the sides of the *Preussen* that not all that much sea came aboard. In fact, except for the strain on their nerves, the men on board were more comfortable than the men outside trying to save them. But within half an hour the position changed dramatically—or so it seemed. There was a sudden rush of water into the forward hold. Despite the pumps Captain Nissen saw the water mount to fourteen feet. On this evidence he judged that some other part of the ship was giving way, and ordered distress signals to be fired.

At 11 P.M. the watching rescue teams saw the distress rockets— the first sign of life on the *Preussen* for some while. The lifeboat was launched again, and at last the wind seemed to be less.

By the early hours of Monday morning the rising tide had lifted the ship and carried her closer under the cliff. Now she lay on her side, with breakers tumbling over parts of her deck.

The Dover lifeboat was standing by again, with two tugs in attendance. A rocket-line was fired across the ship at the sight of the distress signals, but the German sailors would not use the breeches-buoy.

During the rest of the night the wind dropped steadily, and when the lifeboat was within range a few shouted sentences told the tired crew that the *Preussen*'s men intended to stand by the ship as long as there was a chance of her being saved. The lifeboat-men took all this with only a few muttered obscenities. They could understand the crew's feelings, but doubted if the Germans could understand theirs in the open boat for hours at a stretch.

At dawn the *Preussen* was still firmly fixed on a rock-ledge in Crab Bay, but the German crew were still singing, louder now, as though they wanted to drown the incessant hammering of the sea. At first the watchers on shore had difficulty with the song, then with the wind came a full-blooded chorus of the sea-shanty *Away Rio*. Presently the mood changed, and the concertina accompaniment was clearly that of a hymn.

With scarcely a pause the singing went on until the light spread out from the east and the lifeboat crept back through the teeth of the seas to harbour. There were now two rocket-lines aboard the ship, but the crew still refused to leave.

The day showed the damage. The bowsprit, with all its gear, was gone. The fore topmast wasn't there either. The lee scuppers spouted white as the sea swept on, but the boats in the davits appeared undamaged, and the bulwarks still stood. Now figures moved, scrambling over the decks, and some attempts were made to tidy the mass of loose cordage.

Tugs came and went. At one time there were ten in attendance, but the *Preussen* was too hard on to be moved. At nine the lifeboat with its tired crew took station once more, but again could not persuade the German sailors to leave and come ashore. In the *Preussen* they just pointed to the ship and indicated that they were staying aboard. They were not unappreciative of all the efforts made on their behalf—as the bottle of brandy lowered into the lifeboat showed—but they were staying put.

In the afternoon the lifeboat came back into harbour. She had been swept by seas time and time again, and the men were so cold that no-one could throw a coiled rope to the quayside.

They were so cold indeed that when they did come ashore they could hardly walk, yet sixty-year-old James Driscoll, the oldest man in the boat, said, "We're ready to go out again if they want us."

But one man did leave the *Preussen* in another small boat. It was Captain Nissen, who came ashore to talk to the owner's agents. Once ashore, he could not get back, but planned to return to his ship the next day.

By now most of the Kent countryside knew of the *Preussen*'s fight, and crowds of sightseers made their way into Dover. The Press had taken a keen interest in the story, and the *Daily Mail* reporter managed to get a short interview with Captain Nissen. Said Nissen: "When I sighted the *Brighton* I thought she was going astern, but somehow we collided. . . .

"I am proud of my men. When the lifeboat came to us they said to me, 'Capt, we will stick by you. At worst, we can swim ashore and we have lifebelts.' They were cheerful, and they sang the night through at the pumps as they worked. They did not mind, and we were fairly comfortable, although she lifted and bumped heavily, but not much sea came aboard, for my ship is high. Even the passengers did not mind, and when I came off they decided to remain in the ship. They are brave fellows.

"I want to be back with them tonight," continued Nissen, "but no boat can put me aboard. Tomorrow I go back, and I hope then to get my ship off and have her pumped clear."

The last part of his statement seemed very much wishful thinking, for it was now common knowledge that there was fourteen feet of water in the hold, held back only by constant pumping; the bows had been partly torn from the hull, and there was a great hole there. The only thing on Captain Nissen's side was the wind, which, having done the damage, was now moderating fast.

That night the hull of the *Preussen* was a black shape on an ocean of foam, lit by the beam of an Admiralty searchlight installed on the cliff. A tiny shadow that reared and ducked in the lee of the ship was the Dover lifeboat—out again—finding little shelter there. Out to sea the tugs' red and green lights danced in the darkness, but most of them had given the *Preussen* up for lost.

And the *Preussen* was finished. November the 9th dawned fine and clear, and in the afternoon the ship's two passengers and eighteen of the crew came ashore. They had been forty-eight hours in danger on the ship, and their accounts completed the gloomy picture of the *Preussen*'s future. She was now hull-pierced in two places, as well as being damaged in her bows.

But before his crew started to split up Captain Nissen had one last duty to perform. At the office of the agents he had received a telegram from Germany.

He mustered his entire crew on the sloping deck of the great ship and read to them the following telegram from the Kaiser:

'DEEPLY MOVED BY THE NEWS OF THE DISASTER TO THE PROUD FIVE-MASTER PREUSSEN, I DESIRE TO EXPRESS TO THE OWNERS MY WARMEST SYMPATHY. I SHOULD LIKE A DIRECT REPORT REGARDING THE RESULT OF THE CATASTROPHE AND ESPECIALLY ABOUT THE FATE OF THE BRAVE CREW, WHICH CAUSES ME MUCH ANXIETY"

When he had read the telegram Captain Nissen looked over his crew, all together for the last time. Then, taking off his cap, he called for "Three cheers for the Emperor." And, leaving only a skeleton watch on board, he joined the men in the boats. Salvage work on her cargo started immediately. First to go were the 100 pianos! . . .

A year later the *Preussen* was in the news again. On March 4th 1911 Mr Justice Bargrave Deane, sitting with two of the Elder

Brethren of Trinity House, was called on to decide a damage action brought by the *Preussen*'s owner, Ferdinand Laeisz, against the London, Brighton, and South Coast Railway Company, who admitted that the collision was caused by the negligent navigation of the *Brighton,* but denied that the later stranding was a result of the collision.

On April the 12th Mr Justice Bargrave Deane gave judgment for Laeisz, and found that the stranding was a direct result of the collision, and that the Railway Company were responsible for the whole loss.

On November the 20th the claims came before the Admiralty Registrar. The claim for the *Preussen* herself was £52,000, and the cargo was valued at £22,000. The dividend to all interests was not great, for the Railway Company had paid into court £8761 as the limit of their liability for all claims.

Fifty years later the skin divers returned to the *Preussen.* Now even the local boatmen cannot always find her first time. This time it took the diving-boat two exploratory stops with divers down to locate her main wreckage. She lies under those towering cliffs in thirty feet of water, and on very low tides one rib may break the surface.

The diving team from Bromley Branch of the British Sub-Aqua Club was headed by Mr Reg Dunton and Mr Malcolm Todd. Visibility, says "Mike" Todd, was down to eight feet, but even so there was no doubt underwater that the *Preussen* was a big ship. She lies as she died, broadside on to the cliff, and the tide that the divers encountered, not yet on the flood, gave some idea of the force that had moved the *Preussen* in over the rock-strewn bottom.

Some of the ribs still have great strength in them, mussel-covered and encrusted, but still standing upright along part of her length. Steel plates litter the bottom, providing some cover for lobsters of small size. Small crabs too hide in the weed-covered bottom plates. The steel is in surprisingly good condition.

Safety-lines had to be trailed from the diving-boat overhead, for if a diver lost his hold on some part of the wreck he was liable to surface some distance away from the boat. Diving was conducted more on a 'crawling' system. A diver would descend the shot-rope and before leaving go make sure of a good grip on a steel plate. By swimming and grabbing at handy plates it is pos-

Malcolm Todd, one of the first divers to revisit the *Preussen*, shows a crayfish he took by hand during a dive in Cornwall. (See p. 160.)

(*Below*) The *Preussen*, battered, with bowsprit gone and fore top-mast broken, lies trapped under the Dover cliffs. (See p. 149.)

THREE STAGES IN THE
DEATH OF A SHIP
(1) (*Left*) The *Herzogin
Cecilie* aground under Bolt
Head after hitting the
Hamstone. (See p. 161.)

(2) (*Right*) Trapped and being stripped.

(3) (*Left*) She could take
no more. The waves broke
her back.

sible to cover most of the ship's length. The sea and the salvage workers have done their job well. There is little of any value left on the *Preussen*'s remains.

The divers left the *Preussen* with only one unanswered question in their minds. Along a great part of her length are what appear to be barrels, but when these 'barrels' are closely examined they are found to be solid concrete or cement. Was she carrying cement in barrels as part of her general cargo? Or were these her ballast to counteract the weight of five great masts? If they were barrels the wood has long since gone.[1]

After forty minutes below the Bromley divers left her, a sad, broken, shattered thing, unrecognizable as what she once was— the largest sailing-ship of her time.

Another of the great sailing-ships was to meet her end on the coast of Britain. This was the 3111-ton four-master *Herzogin Cecilie,* which was also built in Germany, at Bremerhaven, and launched in April 1902. She took part in the grain races to Australia and back, and was very fast. Her top speed was 20¾ knots —only just short of the record clipper *James Baines.*

The *Herzogin Cecilie* carried over an acre of sail when fully spread, and was 336 feet long, with a beam of 46 feet. On January 28th 1936 she took on her cargo of wheat at Port Lincoln, South Australia, and sailed for England. Eighty-six days later she dropped anchor in Falmouth Harbour. It was her fastest run home, and it was to be her last. On the evening of April 24th the *Herzogin Cecilie* sailed once again, this time for Ipswich. During the night she ran into fog, and at dawn, with the fog still around her, she ran on to the Hamstone just off Bolt Head, in Devon. (This treacherous though charted rock claimed the clipper *Halloween* in 1887 as well.)

But though the Hamstone had holed the *Herzogin Cecilie*, it could not hold her, and she drifted off to ground under Bolt Head itself. Fortunately the weather stayed fine, and the ship was soon linked with the cliff-top by breeches-buoy. The crew stayed aboard, and the job of salvage commenced.

---

[1] Later inquiries at the National Maritime Museum gave the divers the answer to the cement question. Listed in the general cargo was cement—so what they were in fact examining was the damaged, un-salvageable part of the *Preussen*'s last cargo.

It was slow work even when small coasters were used, and after some days there was talk of an attempt to tow the *Herzogin Cecilie* into Salcombe. There the rest of the cargo could be removed, and temporary repairs made to the hull before towing her to a major refit in Plymouth.

The first part of the operation worked well. Two tugs strained at the tow-ropes on a high spring tide, and with pumps working to cope with the water in the forehold she moved—moved so well that they towed her into Starehole Bay, near the mouth of the Salcombe Estuary. There they let her settle on to the flat bottom and worked to remove the rest of the wheat. It seemed that the *Herzogin Cecilie* might be saved after all.

But the weather broke, and a gale sent huge waves crashing into the bay. The great sailing-ship could take no more. She lifted and thudded down again and again. For a while the sand cushioned her, but then it slid away, and the hull was crashing on to rock. No ship could take that sort of treatment. Her back broke, and she was finished.

They ripped everything out of her that was salvageable, and then left her.

There she stayed, upright, a shell of a ship. Holidaymakers gazed down on her from the cliff-tops, and the braver spirits swam out to her. Eleven months after her wrecking the sea came back to end the work she had started. The storm sent a swine of a swell into the bay once again. But this time it was worse. The ship broke up. Her masts crashed down, and overnight she went out of sight, to die shattered on the bottom in thirty feet of water.

One of the first Aqualung divers to see her again was author Bob Matkin. She was very broken up even then, says Matkin. What the diver can see today depends on what the winter storms have done to the sand around her. Each year the picture is different. Fronds of sea-kelp sprawl all over her, no matter what the winter has been like.

"Generally always visible," reports Matkin, "is one of the masts and the forward chain locker-room. Nearest the shore is what I suspect to be the stern-post sticking upright to the surface. It is from the chain locker-room that most of the small items recovered by divers have been found—such as pitch-forks (used in last attempts to shift the cargo), tiles, and wooden blocks. These are now in the Overbecks Museum at the Youth Hostel in Salcombe."

A few fish seem to have made their home around the wreckage, and glide idly from kelp-cover to kelp-cover as the diver approaches. Visibility varies considerably, but when conditions are good it is around forty feet. Little, if anything, of value was left in her when she was finally abandoned; even the greater part of the superstructure was salvaged.

Some of the salvaged parts were used in a bar in Salcombe, and the figurehead is believed to have been shipped back to a museum in Stockholm.

Nowadays the *Herzogin Cecilie* still gives pleasure. Youngsters on Youth Hostel courses get a great thrill from aquaplaning across what remains. To them this is "The Wreck".

The area is rich in wrecks, and divers are finding them one by one. The superb divers of Torbay Branch are well in the lead in most cases (see Chapter One), but visiting divers on holiday are making finds too.

In Salcombe Estuary, for example, is the 136-ton *Placidas Farroult*. She lies inside the Blackstone Rocks on sand in thirty feet of water. Built in France in 1927, this small coaster was one of the ones that got away when France fell in 1940.

The Resident Naval Officer in Salcombe from 1940 to 1945 was Lieutenant-Commander F. Murch, now retired. He says that about twenty of the French and Belgian craft which escaped from France were brought to Salcombe. Commander Murch was instructed by the Admiralty to construct a boom defence across the entrance to Salcombe Harbour, using any local material available.

The *Placidas Farroult* and a French lifeboat were used as gate vessels. Buoys and beacons marking the harbour entrance were removed. One of these, the Wolf Buoy, together with some cable, was stored in the hold of the *Placidas Farroult*. Both gate vessels were securely moored, but in a strong south-westerly gale on November 1st 1940 the coaster broke away and drifted on to the Blackstone Rocks. She was badly holed and her sides corrugated. She lay on the rocks with her stem pointing seaward, but on the next tide the waves drove her off, and she sank broadside to the Blackstone, with her funnel at first showing at low tide. Since then she has settled down in the sand. For a long time her mast was used as a datum pole for the minefields.

Today she is regarded by local divers as a good dive for beginners at low water. Care must be taken, however, of the tide which races through a gap in the Blackstone Rocks.

The Wolf Buoy—a large wooden conical one—is still in her hold. She is standing on an even keel, and is visited by divers quite often. Recently the port hand-lamp was found intact—still filled with paraffin!

Mystery of Pudding Pans

THOUGH you will have seen from previous chapters that the Aqualung diver has been very active around our coasts, you will also have noticed that most wrecks that have been found and investigated date from the Armada. So far there has been no major discovery of any of the really early ships. This is due partly to chance, but also to the fact that such a ship may well be almost completely concealed by natural growth and features of the seabed. Yet, it is surprising that no such discovery has been made. It must come—for the history of our islands is one with the history of shipping.

At the end of the British Neolithic period—around 2000 B.C. —ships, probably flat-bottomed with some sort of leather sail, were travelling hundreds, even thousands of miles from Southern Spain, via the West of England, up to Scotland and on to Sweden. These people were undoubtedly sea-going, for all their elaborate tombs are on the western sea-route. They came from South-west Spain and Portugal, and they certainly reached Ireland—something that would have been impossible without a boat much larger than the dug-out canoes of which we have some examples.

There were other types of tomb-builders. They too sailed along similar routes, but from the Pyrenees and Southern France. Up the Irish Sea or round the West of England they sailed, and settled in South-west Scotland, Ulster, and Man. Throughout the years these islands were constantly absorbing invaders, all of whom must have come by boat.

Then there are references in early writings to the British tin trade. Every indication would point to a good number of ships being employed in this. Diodorus writes in about 10 B.C. of the trade in tin, and describes an island called Ictis, off the main coast-line of Britain. The island, he says, is left dry at low tides, and the tin was brought from the shore in carts. Here the traders bought it from the natives and carried it to Gaul.

Timaeus too mentions the island, but he calls it Mictis, and says that the traders sailed to it in coracles. There would appear to be good reason for supposing that Ictis was in fact today's St Michael's Mount.

Diodorus went further. He told us that the natives who produced the tin dealt with it in a special way. He said that they melted it into the form of astragali, or knuckle-bones, but unfortunately he either didn't know or forgot to mention why. This would seem to be a far cry from an early wreck, but in 1812 a peculiarly shaped block of tin was dredged up from Falmouth Harbour between St Mawes and Pendinath.

The block of tin, which is now in the Royal Institution of Cornwall County Museum, weighs 158 lb. It is 2 feet 11 inches long, 11 inches wide, and 3 inches thick at the centre. Perfectly flat on one side, it is curved on the other, and has four 'prongs', one at each corner. Each of the 'prongs' is one foot long.

Learned archaeologists of the time who examined it had no doubt that this was a block of tin shaped in the form of an astragalus, and that the mark stamped on it was also an astragalus, and probably the 'trademark' of some ancient trader. It appears that Diadorus was right.

Fifty years after the block was raised Major-General Sir Henry James also had no doubt. He pointed out—and it is a good point—that the block of tin was perfectly shaped for transport by boat. In a little booklet he produced on the subject (the booklet is in the care of the Public Library at Falmouth), he wrote:

But we are naturally led to inquire why this peculiar form was selected for the blocks.

We are told (by Diodorus) that the traders resorting to Ictis there buy the tin from the natives and carry it to Gaul, over which it travels on horseback in about thirty days. It was therefore necessary that the blocks of tin should be cast in such a form, and be of such a weight, as to be conveniently carried both in boats for transport to Gaul, and then on horseback for the journey overland; and it is impossible to look at this block of tin without being struck with the admirable adaptation of the form and weight for this double purpose, and also for the purpose of being easily carried by hand by two men, or slung for lifting it either into or from a boat, or on and off a horse.

This is seen at a glance: the curved surface of one side of the block exactly fits the curve of the bottom of a boat, whilst the flat plane surface of the other sides would form a continuous level floor to the boat, which being covered with bottom boards would entirely conceal the valuable cargo beneath. Again the ribs of the boat, coming up through the divided ends of the block, would prevent the possibility of any shifting of the cargo when the boat was pitching or rolling in the sea, and the blocks resting on the keel and ribs of the boat would prevent any strain upon the planking when the boat was run ashore and grounded. As ballast to the boat when under sail, the blocks are in the lowest and best possible position.

Though the General, who was Director-General of the Ordnance Survey at the time, has assumed a great deal about boat construction in those early days, it would be a bold archaeologist even today who would deny absolutely that the General was wrong in all his surmise. It is true that the block is a good shape for a boat, which could well have been moving coastways to Boulogne, or just seeking shelter in St Mawes Inlet from a storm, when she sank with her cargo of tin.

Here we may have a clue to a shipwreck of very early times. Against this, however, is the fact that though a Bronze Age sword was found in Falmouth Harbour, no other blocks of tin have been found in the area. Yet the block is undoubtedly of great age. Its shape is fascinating, and not a far cry from that of the almost pure copper ingots raised by George Bass, of the University of Pennsylvania, in his underwater excavation of a Bronze Age wreck in ninety feet of water off Cape Gelidonya, Turkey. These ingots have been called ox-hide ingots because they are shaped more or less in the form of dried cow-skins, and each was supposed to have equalled the price of one cow or ox.

In a report to the World Congress of Underwater Activities in London, George Bass said, "Our ingots, however, seem to disprove the ox-hide theory; the weights vary considerably, making their use as currency unlikely. . . . And the legs, which did not appear on similar but earlier ingots found in Sardinia, Crete, Cyprus, and Greece, simply evolved to ease the burden of porterage." It would seem that for both General Sir Henry James and George Bass, despite the years between them, the legs have it!

Recently local divers have searched the area where the Cornish block of tin was discovered. They found nothing but a bare bottom where the tide rips smartly through the narrowing channel. Yet the fact that the block was dredged up might still indicate a wreck, though by now it may be many feet down under hard-packed sediment.

As time passed the pace of shipping to these islands increased. Julius Caesar brought his fleet. Trade grew. In Roman days a large Channel fleet stood by to deal with the Saxon pirates from North-west Europe. Shipping and more shipping poured around our shores. Yet where are the ancient wrecks?

In the clear, calm Mediterranean, books and films would lead you to believe, scarcely a day goes by without some Aqualung diver finding (and possibly looting) an ancient Roman wreck. While it is obviously not quite like that, most regular Mediterranean divers do discover some trace of the ancient shipping routes, even if it is only a few broken shards of a wine amphora—the jerrican of olden days.

Why there and not around our coasts? Surely even if the volume of shipping was not so great as that in the Mediterranean our more violent weather would have taken an even greater toll? Against this, however, must be set two important facts. One, the English Channel is not so clear as the Mediterranean, and a diver would need a great deal of luck to land right on top of an ancient wreck when visibility is only a few feet, compared with the normal hundred feet in the warmer sea. And, two, when an ancient ship sank in British waters it was far more liable to be disastrously broken up in a short while. Therefore, instead of getting the neat amphora mound, the British diver is more likely to swim over tiny pieces of wine-jars covered with heavy marine growth, which is also missing in many areas of the Mediterranean.

But British divers will discover a sunken Roman ship one day.

They may even be doing it as you read this book. As the number of sport divers increases, so the chances increase.

The hopes of those who believe that this will happen soon were given a boost very recently when reports of the recovery in fishermen's nets of amphora came from Brittany.

Before we go on to cover the most likely wreck sites of these ancient ships in Britain it would be a good thing to recall very briefly what we do know about the ships that plied around our coasts in olden times.

Probably the first form of water transport was the dugout, and many of these have been found. They were not confined to small, two-man affairs. One discovered very recently in Poole Harbour was at least thirty-three feet long, and they seem to vary in length from about six to fifty feet. There is a difficulty here in dating such finds precisely. A strongly built dugout could survive for centuries of service after its maiden voyage. Five or six dugouts were found in the river Arun, and here divers were able to help in the work of recovery. Speaking generally, the dugouts were confined to river and sheltered waters.

In about 1500–1200 B.C. we have the appearance of the North Ferriby boat. Named after the place where it was discovered—in fact, only a section was unearthed—it appears to have been designed for estuary work on the Tyne, and could have been Britain's first inshore fishing-boat.

It is the superb workmanship of the Ferriby boat that makes it such a step forward. It was carvel-built, with the planks lashed together with withies.

Then a jump in time to A.D. 1190–1430. This is the period given by radio-carbon tests on an oak-pinned frame which had been wooden-pegged on to a dugout-canoe shell. It was found at Kentmere, near Kendal, and was clinker-built.

The Roman boats we know were carvel-built, as were most Mediterranean-inspired craft. The planks were held together with dowelled tongue and wooden pins.

At the same time as these Roman ships were trying to contend with British seas, full-sized boats of wicker and hide coverings, complete with keel, stern, and stem, were also sailing about like huge coracles.

The keel slowly developed around Britain, but in A.D. 900 the Viking ships were eighty feet long and had full keels. This style continued until many centuries later. You can see similar ships on the Bayeux Tapestry, and some sources say that the invasion fleet depicted there consisted of 3000 ships.

Remembering all these different kinds of ships, remembering the Viking raiders, and keeping in mind the fact that the Romans had a Channel fleet to deal with Saxon pirates from North-west Europe, one can just begin to realize how many ships, perhaps now only tiny fragments, are left for the British divers to find.

Is there no sign of an ancient wreck other than the solitary block of Cornish tin we mentioned earlier? Yes, there is. Many divers believe that there is a wreck of about A.D. 160 on Pudding Pan shoal, off Herne Bay.

Edward G. Goldring, Borough Engineer and Surveyor of Chelsea, who is a first-class diver of the British Sub-Aqua Club, is the acknowledged expert on the subject of this site. He used to live at Whitstable in a house which looked out to sea at the group of shoals, two of which bear the odd names of Pan Sand and Pudding Pan. So perhaps it is only natural that he should have delved so deeply into the history of this underwater area. The following passage is based on the results of his research on land and under-water.

In about 1780 Thomas Pownal, a former Governor of Massachusetts, wrote an article for *Archaeologia* about red earthenware Roman pottery that was used by fishermen on the north-east Kent coast. These ancient pots were used for ordinary domestic chores in the cottages of the fishermen, who said that they had been dragged up by their nets from a shoal some four miles off Herne Bay. So a special search was organized, and the first three hauls are recorded as having produced three complete pans or pots.

The fishermen told Pownal that they believed the pots and pans were from a wreck of many centuries ago, but Pownal was more inclined to believe that a Roman pottery factory had existed on Pudding Pan rock and had in the course of time been swallowed up by the sea.

Pownal's theory is heavily damaged by the fact that though hundreds of pieces have been recovered over a period of time, there is no record at all of the appearance of moulds or potters' tools.

There the matter seemed to rest for about twenty years. Then Reginald A. Smith presented a paper to the Society of Antiquaries of London on "The Wreck on Pudding Pan Rock" (*Proc. Soc. Ant.*, Vol. XXI, No. II). He tabulated a total of 238 specimens in the collection to which they then belonged, together with a record of more than thirty potters' names. And finds of moulds and potters' debris at Lezoux, in the Allier district of France, led to the identification of Lezoux as the site of the factory which produced the pots that ended up on Pudding Pan. It was quite clearly a mass-production job, and now it was possible to add a date—about A.D. 160.

It would seem to us, therefore, as it did to Smith, that the pots must have been in transport from France to England, and were lost in the Pudding Pan area. It is also fair to assume that either a wreck or a complete abandonment of deck cargo in a storm took place.

The Society of Antiquaries was certainly interested in Smith's paper. Some of them might even be described as excited about the whole affair. Several of the Fellows of the Society got together and organized a search of the seabed around the Pudding Pan rock. They went further than Pownal, and hired a diver.

Hugh Pollard, a certified diver, was commissioned to do the job. The time he chose was not the best—conditions in the area are usually poor for diving—but he worked for a week diving and dredging. He reported that the last pot dredged up had been "in a water lane in the direct line of the Girdler light on Reculver, about a mile north of the rock as charted". But this did not seem to have helped him much. In his week he worked over a wide area from Swalecliffe to the Pan Sands, and he recovered three pieces of pottery.

Pollard referred to the scour of the tides which would roll the pottery over a wide area, probably far from the wreck site itself. He suggested that the finding of large tiles from time to time would be more likely to indicate the wreck spot, as they were heavy and would not move far. Pollard, it would appear, was not just any old diver. His powers of observation were good, and he noted that when a south wind blew, the seabed in the area was soft, but when a north or east wind was in force it set hard. This is confirmed today by local fishermen.

Edward Goldring says: "Anyone who has handled this Samian ware—for that is what it is—cannot but be amazed by the beauty and delicacy of the designs, the amazing clarity of the potters' marks and the remarkable state of preservation of a large number of the specimens. Even today after more than 1800 years under the sea, off a coast which has suffered considerable erosion by the scour of tides and where they have been crossed and recrossed thousands of times by heavy fishing gear, many of the pieces would enhance the tables of today.

"In fact Councillor Wallace Harvey, one of the trustees of the Whitstable Museum, told me that he remembers them being used by local people for making Lent Pies—a Kentish farmers' dish of pastry lining filled with ground rice and custard and topped with currants."

The pots recovered appear to have rested in an upside-down position on the seabed. The insides and rims are almost untouched, but in many cases the bases have been broken off or rubbed by shingle or oyster dredges. It is amazing that any have survived, for dredges of that kind can smash up stronger things than pottery.

The tiles mentioned by Diver Pollard have been dredged up from time to time off this part of the Kent coast, and it was the finding of these and the recovery of pieces of what was thought to be cemented brickwork that first gave strength to the belief that there had been a pottery factory at the spot.

Actually the cement-stone boulders on the seabed there can be found at other places in the Thames Estuary, and, although it would seem that no rock ever existed there—there is certainly not one today—they may well have been the cause of the misleading use of the name Pudding Pan rock.

Since Smith's paper and Pollard's diving some pottery has been brought up by dredge from the area around the Pudding Pan, but Goldring, who has spoken to some of the few surviving dredgermen of Whitstable and retired sailors, feels sure that the finds are now very few and far between. Two skippers of the Seasalter and Ham Oyster Fishery Company told him that, in forty years of dredging, they had between them picked up about six pieces of pottery. One skipper gave the area where finds have mostly been made as "immediately east of the intersection of a line through Herne Bay Clock Tower to Herne Mill and a line through West Pan Sand Buoy and the Pan Sand Beacon [see plan]".

Another fisherman with thirty years of trawling and dredging experience has done better. He has averaged about one piece a

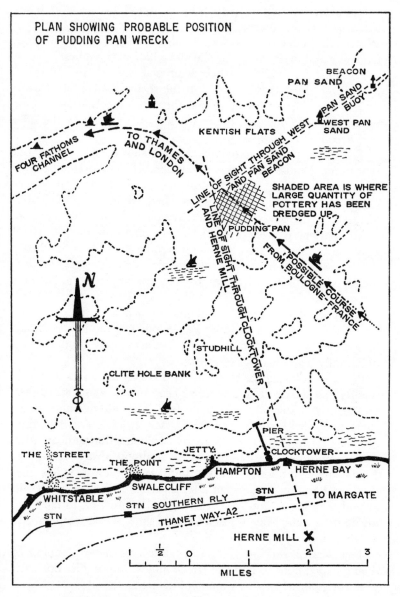

PLAN SHOWING PROBABLE POSITION
OF PUDDING PAN WRECK

BEACON
PAN SAND

PAN SAND
BUOY

KENTISH FLATS

WEST PAN
SAND

FOUR FATHOMS
CHANNEL

TO THAMES
AND LONDON

LINE OF SIGHT THROUGH WEST
AND PAN SAND BEACON

SHADED AREA IS WHERE
LARGE QUANTITY OF
POTTERY HAS BEEN
DREDGED UP

PUDDING PAN

LINE OF SIGHT THROUGH CLOCKTOWER
AND HERNE MILL

POSSIBLE COURSE
FROM BOULOGNE-FRANCE

N

STUDHILL

CLITE HOLE BANK

PIER

CLOCKTOWER

THE STREET

THE POINT

JETTY

HAMPTON

HERNE BAY

SWALECLIFF

WHITSTABLE

STN SOUTHERN RLY

STN

TO MARGATE

STN

THANET WAY-A2

HERNE MILL

1   ½   0   1   2   3

MILES

Edward Goldring's plan of the Pudding Pan site

year, but stresses that the pottery he has found has not been in any one area. "It is scattered," he said, "over a very large area from Whitstable Street Buoy to Pan Sand Buoy—a distance of about five miles and over a width of one and a half to two miles."

Local fishermen all have their theories about the wreck, if wreck it is. Some think that it sank into the seabed and is silted over. Others think that it broke up and the cargo was scattered, some remaining near the spot, the rest being rolled away by the tides or shifted by the dredges.

The list of pottery recovered in 1909 showed 282 pieces, but that number must have grown considerably. The original collections have been split up and added to, and Pudding Pan pottery can be seen at Whitstable, Herne Bay, Maidstone, Rochester, Canterbury, Leicester, Kingston, Liverpool, Bristol, and London.

The pottery recovered could have formed only part—a small part—of the ship's cargo, which gives some strength to the theory that the ship never sank—that the pieces found were, in fact, merely the jettisoned deck cargo when the ship was caught in a severe storm.

But it could, of course, be true that the whole of the rest of the ship is down there in Pudding Pan Sands waiting for an Aqualung diver to find the mother lode. Unfortunately conditions do not usually help the diver out there.

Edward Goldring has made many dives on the wreck area. He reports that the depth at low-water neap tides is about seven feet, and at high water about eighteen feet. The tide averages about three knots, with about one hour slack at high and low tide, ordinary springs extending to nearly two hours during neap tides.

"Visibility below water," he says, "is almost always very poor. I have known it about eight feet, but it is almost always less than that number of inches, except after a period of calm, when it will extend. For this reason winter diving in the area, or, in fact, any diving before late May, is just a waste of time. Water temperatures are then about 53-55 degrees F."

This sort of varying visibility makes long-range planning of diving expeditions to find the wreck almost impossible. But each year attempts are made by amateur divers on the site.

Goldring himself, however, believes that a diver might have a chance of finding one of the heavier pieces. He draws attention to this type in the museum collections.

What he has in mind are the large and heavy shallow dishes with spouts in the form of mortaria. Goldring thinks if these were partially buried upside down on the seabed it is possible that dredges have passed over them without pulling them up.

A disadvantage is that there are several areas not far from the Pudding Pan where the bottom is dotted with the cement-stone boulders mentioned earlier, and though these areas are not so heavily dredged by fishermen as other spots, it is here that the diver might well pass over a buried dish and think it just another boulder.

Another experienced diver in the area is Hugh Singer, a Whitstable dentist and keen local British Sub-Aqua Club member. He stresses that the diving area is not for beginners, even though on one occasion he has found visibility up to twenty feet. "The tides are tricky," he says, "and what is a calm sea suddenly turns into a nasty chop. In my dives on the estimated site of the wreck I have never found anything, nor have I heard of any diver who has. The bottom is mostly granular sand, with some patches of shingle of round pebble form. There is some green and brown weed with holdfasts on to these pebbles."

There, for the moment, the mystery of the Pudding Pan remains. Soon, however, there may be more news. Talks are now going on with marine electronic-equipment experts. If divers can be assured of accurate seabed 'fixes', then a proper, systematic search of the area, foot by foot, can be carried out.

A Roman wreck has been discovered in home 'waters'. In September 1962, during excavations on the Blackfriars Bridge traffic improvements, workmen found the grab biting into ancient timbers. Archaeologists were later able to remove a major portion of some sort of ancient ship. These old timbers, many pinned together with foot-long nails, were then taken to the Guildhall Museum for preservation treatment. Broken pottery showed that the barge was in use during the second and third centuries A.D., and lying in the mast step was a worn Roman coin of the Emperor Domitian, minted in about A.D. 89.

Archaeologists who worked on the ship, under Mr Peter Marsden, believe that she was a river and estuary sailing-barge (her cargo was Kentish ragstone) about 55 feet long and with a beam of about 22 feet.

She is just further evidence of the amount of shipping that was afloat around Britain in early days.

Coming forward again in time to one of the known sites of an old ship, we move into the river Hamble.

Here, three-quarters of a mile above Bursledon Bridge, is the wreckage of the *Grâce Dieu,* built by Henry V in 1418. She was laid up in the Hamble river, but was accidentally burnt in 1439. Timbers that have been measured give her length as over 135 feet and her beam as about 37 feet. The rest of the ship lies buried in the mud. Though there have been many arguments about whether this is indeed the *Grâce Dieu*—one theory put forward was that it is a Viking ship—there seems little room for doubt. What is amazing is that no proper excavation of the site seems to have been made. The mud makes this a difficult site for divers, but it is possible that they could be of help.

But British divers have many sites to investigate. There is, for example, the *Marye Rose*. King Henry VIII stood at Portsmouth in July 1545 and watched in horror as this great ship of his heeled over and sank with the loss of nearly 700 lives.

The story of the sinking of the *Marye Rose* is almost unbelievable. The English fleet was in harbour at Portsmouth, where Henry VIII had come to visit them. The beacons warning of the sighting of the French fleet were already burning, and orders had gone out to all the King's ships within range to make all speed and join the fleet at Portsmouth. There Henry appointed Sir George Carewe on H.M.S. *Marye Rose* to be his Vice-Admiral. While the King was dining with his officers on board the *Greate Henry* the French fleet was sighted, and he gave orders for his fleet to sail.

In manuscripts of the time is this description of what happened then:

> And first he hath secret talks with the Lord Admiral, and then he hath the like with Sir George Carewe, and at his departure from him, took his chain from his neck, with a great wistle of gold pendant to the same, and did put it about the neck of the said Sir George Carewe, giving him also therewith many good and comfortable words.

The King then took his boat, and rowed to the land, and

The loss of the *Royal George*. A watercolour of the scene by Buttersworth, now in the National Maritime Museum, Greenwich. (See p. 179.)

(*Left*) A diver and his equipment. This is Alexander McKee, who has done important work on the wrecks of the *Boyne*, *Impregnable*, *Royal George* and *Marye Rose*. Note the camera. Photography in British waters is very difficult due to usually poor visibility. His face-mask has 'side ports' to increase viewing arc underwater. (See pp. 85, 90, 179, and 180.)

(*Below*) Possible evidence of the oldest known shipwreck. This block of tin may date back to the earliest times. It was dredged up from Falmouth Harbour. (See p. 166.)

every other captain went to his ship appointed unto him. Sir George Carewe being entered into his ship, commanded every man to take his place, and the sails to be hoysted; but the same was no sooner done, but that the *Marye Rose* began to heel, that is, to lean on the one side. Sir Gawen Garewe being then in his own ship, and seeing the same called for the master of his ship, and told him thereof, and asked him what it meant, who answered, that if she did heel, she was like to be cast away. Then the said Sir Gawen, passing by the *Marye Rose,* called out to Sir George Carewe, asking him how he did? who answered, that he had a sort of knaves, whom he could not rule.

And it was not long after, but that the said *Marye Rose,* thus heeling more and more, was drowned, with 700 men which were in her; whereof very few escaped. It chanced unto this gentleman, as the common proverb is 'the more cooks, the worst potage'. He had in his ship a hundred mariners, the worst of them being able to be a master in the best ship within the realm, and these so maligned and disdained one the other, that refusing to do that which they should do, were careless to do that that they ought to do; and so contending in envy, perished in frowardness.

The King this meanwhile stood on the land, and saw this tragedy, as also the lady the wife to Sir George Carewe, who with that sight fell into a swooning. The King being oppressed with sorrow of every side, comforted her, and thanked God for the other, hoping that of a hard beginning there would follow a better ending. And notwithstanding this loss, the service appointed went forward, as soon as wind and weather would serve; and the residue of the fleet, being about the number of one hundred and five sails, took the seas. The Frenchmen perceiving the same, like as a sort of sheep running into the fold, they shifted away, and got them into their harbours; thinking it better to lie there in a safe skin, than to encounter with them of whom they should little win.

It was not, of course, long before the French were claiming the sinking of the *Marye Rose* as a result of their cannon-fire, but there is little doubt that this was just propaganda, for there is no record of any engagement at the time. It is interesting to note that a contemporary painting, which formerly hung at Cowdray House in Sussex (there is a copy in the offices of the Corporation of Portsmouth), shows the *Marye Rose* sinking before the battle, if you can call it that, had been joined.

Within a few days of her sinking there were plans to raise her, and on August 1st 1545 the Duke of Suffolk wrote to Sir William Paget a letter which contained this wildly optimistic sentence: "I trust by Monday or Tuesday at the farthest the *Marye Rose* shall be weighed up and saved." It was not to be, and in 1552 another letter to Sir William, this time from Viscount Lisle, made it clear that the Admiral of the Fleet had great doubts of the possibility of even stripping the ship completely.

So the *Marye Rose* was almost forgotten until the 1840's, when divers of the Royal Engineers, who were working on another wreck—that of the *Royal George*—misread their bearings and arrived on top of the *Marye Rose*. Divers being what divers are, they immediately went to work on this new find. Up came five brass cannon, all dated 1535, and twenty others of iron. The iron cannon were of great interest, as they were breech-loaders, a style that was not to be really in general use in the Royal Navy until Victorian times (see Appendix Two).

Present plans for expeditions to the site of the *Marye Rose* include a team of archaeologist divers of the British Nautical Archaeological Research Committee and the Scientific and Technical Group of the B.S.-A.C. (see Appendix Three). The divers include Peter Choulman, a member of the committee. A number of exploratory dives have already been made.

Choulman looks upon the present expedition and diving work as nothing more than a probe to test for a firm position, and to see if it would be possible to carry out a full-scale archaeological underwater excavation of the sunken ship, the first to be done in British waters. It would be of great archaeological importance if this work could be carried out. It would then be possible to say that anything found in the wreck was in use or being carried in ships during July 1545.

The search for the *Marye Rose* was brought dramatically nearer to a successful conclusion by the recent rediscovery of the *Royal George*. Now we know that the *Marye Rose* lies only a short way from the *Royal George,* and it may be that the first relic from the *Marye Rose* has already been brought to the surface.

This is what happened. Alexander McKee of Hayling Island, whom you will have read about in the chapter on the *Impregnable,* was also interested in diving on the site of the loss of the *Royal George*. While working in his dark-room one Christmas he wondered if it would be possible to transfer old chart bearings on to a modern sea chart if certain corrections were made. This he did with the position of the sinking of the *Royal George*.

In April 1965, together with other divers of the Southsea Branch of the British Sub-Aqua Club—John Baldry, Roger Hale, Alan Lee, and John Towse—McKee dived on the site position he had worked out. This, he hoped, would put the divers right on to the wreckage of Admiral Kempenfelt's flagship *Royal George*, which capsized at Spithead on August 29th 1782 with the loss of nearly 900 lives, including women and children. McKee's plan worked like a dream.

From a depth of eighty feet the divers brought up a 32-pounder cannon-ball, a piece of carving, rigging, and bones. Says McKee: "The seabed there is an archaeologist's paradise. There was a relic of some kind to every square yard of it. The oldest was a stone cannon-ball, which might have come from the *Marye Rose*."

Spithead has been a man-of-war and convoy anchorage for many hundreds of years. It is also the place where modern diving gear of the helmet type was first tried out by the Deane Brothers of Gosport on the wrecks of the *Marye Rose* and the *Royal George*. Even though Spithead is no stranger to ships and wrecks, the sinking of the *Royal George*, a great battleship of 108 guns, was the greatest tragedy Portsmouth had ever known.

The *Royal George* was about to sail with a British fleet to the relief of besieged Gibraltar when it happened. The last stores were being loaded, and many relatives and friends were on board saying goodbye to the crew. But the hull of the old ship was rotten. She had been hurriedly patched together in the hope that she would last one more summer—a decision taken only because of the Gibraltar crisis.

As the final batch of rum-casks was lowered with a thump on to her decks and trundled below there was a "bodily crack", according to one seaman. He was quick and managed to jump out of a stern window as the huge three-decker rolled on to her side. In ten seconds the great mass of people on board tumbled down the decks, together with guns, cannon-balls, and loose gear. The ship remained flat on her side for one minute, and then was gone. The Admiral had no chance even to get out of his cabin before the water closed over him.

So swiftly did it happen that a lady writing a letter by a window of her Southsea home looked out one moment to see the flagship at anchor on a calm and windless sea, wrote one sentence, and looked again. The ship was gone!

It had all happened so quickly that there were dark murmurings ashore later that this was divine retribution for the horrible scenes that had taken place on Southsea Common only two weeks before. A traitor, David Tyrie, convicted of selling naval secrets to the French, had been ritually hanged, drawn, and quartered there. As the blood spurted the crowd had burst through the cordon of soldiers and fought for possession of parts of the body. Men and women cut the fingers off the corpse, steeped handkerchiefs in the blood, and a certain "Buck" Adams obtained the best trophy of all—the head, which he pickled and charged fees to all who wanted to see it.

Divine retribution or not, of the 1200 people thought to be in the *Royal George* that day, only 300 were saved. Only 300, even though every ship in the anchorage sent boats, including the *Victory*. One of the rescuers was a Lieutenant Bligh, later to gain fame or infamy in the *Bounty* mutiny. For weeks after the tragedy bodies floated to and fro at Spithead, many locked together in the groups that they seemed to have been in at the moment of their deaths. And when in the 1840's the Royal Engineers divers blew part of the hull apart they discovered two cloaks wrapped together—one of a woman, the other of a little girl, who had died in each other's arms. After the Engineers left no-one visited the wreckage for 122 years, until Alexander McKee's recent dive.

McKee's report on conditions encountered reads: "No sophisticated instruments being available, location was by modern marks worked out on basis of old chart positions. These proved exact and accurate, the boat being actually anchored on to the wreck. Team One dived first, found artifacts almost instantly and the mother lode of the *Royal George* after about ten minutes.

"They returned to surface with a cannon-ball, rigging (shrouds) etc. Team Two set off in the direction that the *Marye Rose* is believed to lie, found many artifacts and a heavy piece of wreck, which was buoyed and lifted. Probably *Royal George,* but could be *Marye Rose.*

"Visibility varied between six and ten feet. Rather cold. Not an easy site. Four frigates passed in line ahead above Team Two, and one member of Team One was convinced he heard Asdic transmissions." (Divers have been warned by the Admiralty that Asdic transmissions close to could be dangerous.)

A month later another team, led by McKee and including Maurice Harknett and Jim Dipnell, dived on the *Royal George* site.

Dipnell located small mounds of shingle dotted over the seabed, and thought these significant and possibly built up by the currents over artifacts from the ship. McKee too found these mounds among barren patches of flat, muddy clay. They were shingle, about six to eight inches above the normal seabed level and irregularly shaped. They were marked by small weedy growth and the presence of marine life, crabs and anemones in particular. In one of them he found something deeply buried. When he pulled it out he found that he was holding an encrusted bowl of some kind.

The bowl was later dated by archaeologists as pewter of the late eighteenth century, which fits the dating of the wreck perfectly. McKee believes that these shingle mounds will be the main clues to many artifacts from the *Royal George,* as the blowing up of the ship has dispersed portions of her over a wide area.

There are reports of doubloons found on the beaches of the Isle of Wight. Doubloons again are reported from Whitstable. There are few places, as we have said before, around the British Isles that have not got their story of wrecks and wreckage. Every fisherman knows areas which are profitable to him for fish, but which are difficult to trawl because of obstructions. Of course, all obstructions are not wrecks, but many are. And from time to time divers go down on these sites.

Normal survey work in the Thames Estuary recently uncovered a sunken-ship mystery. The Port of London Authority's Hydrographic Service were carrying out the survey between Number 4 and Number 5 Sea Reach Buoys. Suddenly they got a 'peak' on their echo-sounder, and there just shouldn't have been one there.

It was decided to investigate, and divers of the Wreck Raising Service were called upon to do so. Under the command of Captain G. R. Rees, the Mooring and Wreck Raising Officer, the divers went down.

Telling what happened then, Captain Rees said: "On a bright sunny day in the Estuary at about this point a diver has about three-feet visibility. This was such a day. When the diver surfaced he reported finding a lot of timber ribs of an old wooden vessel sticking up out of the sand. He moved along it for a 100 feet or more before being forced up by the tide. That was all we could do that day.

"The next day when we put down a sweep wire on the spot it snagged. When we hauled it in up came a beautiful bronze cannon. We didn't find anything else. Looking back through the old charts afterwards, we found there was a wreck there marked at one time with a light. But that was in the 1800's."

Further work on records and the cannon only deepened the mystery, for the chart-marked wreck was about 1820 and the cannon is engraved with the year 1636. Two wrecks, it would seem, were one on top of the other at the same spot.

The cannon is vastly interesting. It is cast entirely in bronze, and a Latin inscription on the rim at the breech end says that it was made by a Belgian, Johannes de Guindertal, at "Havre de Grâce" (now Le Havre).

The Port of London Authority, with their usual efficiency, have supplied us with more details of the cannon's markings.

The French anchor is marked on the breech, together with the name "Cardinal de Richelieu" and the date 1636. (Richelieu was Grand Admiral of France from 1624 to 1642.) A large cartouche bears the arms of France and Navarre, which were united in 1247. A French royal crown and the collars of two French Orders of Chivalry, the Order of St Esprit and the Order of St Michel, surround the design. Near the muzzle is a French crown and the letter "L", the Royal Cipher of Louis XIII.

The cannon fired a 9-lb. shot. The bore is four and a half inches in diameter, but is not central, and shows that it was formed in the casting by means of a core, not bored after the casting (see Appendix Two). You can see this cannon now in the Tower Armouries. It is a fine specimen.

Another cannon mystery developed off Black Rock, Brighton, in 1963, when antique-dealer Dave Berry was spearfishing for plaice and sole on a summer's evening. He was in fifteen to twenty feet of water when he suddenly saw a cannon. He says that there was no doubt in his mind what he had seen from the surface through his face-mask—there among the rock and weed was a cannon! It was not heavily corroded, and diving down and measuring it against his hand-spear Berry estimated its length at about seven feet and saw that it was made of bronze.

"Obviously I could not add it to my evening catch," he says, "but I made certain that I could find it again by landmarks. I let myself drift away from the spot, and then, guided by my landmarks, succeeded in finding it again. I did this several times, just to make sure, before heading for home."

With his friend Mike O'Brian, a Brighton lifeguard, Dave Berry made several dives to the cannon to clear it for lifting. Three attempts were made, using small boats, but the gun was too heavy. George Wheeler, chairman of the Brighton area of the Fishermen's Association, was approached for help. The Association made a trawler available, but bad weather held up operations.

When the weather settled, divers attached the trawler's lifting-gear to the cannon, and it was raised in position under the hull and towed to Brighton fish-market beach. There a winch was used to haul it up the beach. The cannon, or rather minion (see Appendix Two), was taken to Brighton Museum. Then came long declarations to the Receiver of Wrecks and communication with the Ministry of Transport (see Appendix One).

The Brighton minion is nearly 8 feet long, weighs 15 cwt., and bears a faint coat-of-arms, which appears to be indecipherable. Barely readable too are the letters AE or AG, which might indicate Dutch origin.

Dave Berry finally received a letter from the Minister of Transport (Mr Marples) valuing the gun at £270 scrap value, plus £30 historic value. Of the £300 Dave Berry received one-third, which he shared with his helpers.

The minion is now in the Tower of London Armouries. But the Brighton mystery does not end there. Since that discovery Dave Berry has located another cannon, this time of cast iron, which is too corroded to lift at the moment. And farther down the coast at Rottingdean two more cast-iron cannon have been found by members of the Brighton Branch of the British Sub-Aqua Club.

The bronze minion is dated by experts as being around the middle of the sixteenth century, but there is no trace in local records of any shipwreck involving a ship of that date—or, indeed, of any large shipwreck in that area at all. Yet the site of the discovery is within swimming distance of the shore, and such a major event as the wreck of a big ship seems unlikely to have gone un-noted by local historians.

There are rumours of other cannon in the sea at Brighton—farther out to sea, say the rumours, and larger, more like three tons, and bronze. Soon a diver may prove the rumours right or wrong.

Farther along the coast Swanage is a very active diving centre. Not only do Bob and Dennis Wright run their excellent diving training-centre there, but the area is a popular one with other amateur divers.

One of the keenest divers locally is Bob Campbell, a development engineer, who describes himself as "an inveterate beach-comber above and below the surface".

When diving in Swanage Bay Bob Campbell found himself over a rocky outcrop on the seabed about a mile due north of Peveril Point. The depth of water at this point is about thirty feet. There is little marine growth in the area, and the sand around the outcrop is flat and barren. The rock-ledges of the outcrop rise to about ten feet off the seabed. Visibility is usually good.

It was here that Bob Campbell made a discovery that set an underwater puzzle for quite a time. He noticed among the flattish rocks of the ledge just in front of him a spherical, if knobbly, shape. It didn't fit in with the rock formation. It was firmly cemented to the rock, but when dealt a smart blow a cloud of inky fluid filled the water around the diver. It was enough to tell Bob Campbell that he had probably found an iron cannon-ball.

He brought his find to the surface, and regained the diving-boat—only to be told by his companion diver, who had been a little distance away from him, that he too had found a cannon-ball.

Since then Campbell has found several, and believes that in all about twenty-four have been recovered. He says: "When found the balls are encased in a thick cement-like crust of sand and rust about one inch thick. The general outline of the ball is still spherical, though rather knobbly. The shape does show up (to the experienced eye) against the flatter rocks of the ledge. The first one is always the most difficult to spot—after that it is easier to recognize the tell-tale shape. The crust can be broken away readily, although in so doing the visibility disappears in a cloud of inky black. This is the real clue to the hidden iron.

"After breaking away the crust the ball may be lifted out, and this is the easiest way to retrieve a ball, though I do not recommend it. I prefer to bring them up complete with their shells. The snag here is that they are firmly cemented to the rock-ledges by this crust, and a crowbar and considerable effort is needed to prise them loose."

On their removal from their shells Bob Campbell found that the cannon-balls were still spherical, with little mishaping except for the small area where the ball was in direct contact with the rock. They are six inches in diameter and weigh twenty-four pounds. How true to the original size and weight these figures are is open to doubt.

Which ship could these cannon-balls have come from? A search in local records produced only one likely suspect.

On Sunday, January 1st 1786, the East Indiaman *Halsewell* set sail from the Downs, outward bound for Bengal. All went well at first, but on the Tuesday, when she was off the Isle of Wight, a southerly gale caught her, and the gigantic seas that followed so pounded the ship that she sprang a leak. Soon the holds were flooded to a depth of seven feet. The crew fought hard, but by dawn on Wednesday the ship was dismasted and almost helpless. For a while the wind dropped, but on the Thursday it came back. Still blowing from the south, it drove the *Halsewell* on to the lee shore. There was no escape.

For a while they managed to hold the ship off the rocks by anchoring, but soon the cables snapped and the drift towards the cliffs began again.

At 2 A.M. on Friday the *Halsewell* struck broadside on to the shore. She was half a mile to the west of Seacombe Quarry. The cliffs here are high, but at sea-level there is a 'cavern' ten or twelve yards deep and wide enough to take a large ship broadside on. The *Halsewell* lay opposite this cavern and broadside, so that her whole length stretched from side to side of it.

A number of men from the ship managed to reach the back of the cave, where they were fairly safe. Many others reached the rocks forming the shore, but were either washed off or fell trying to climb the cliffs.

Soon the *Halsewell* broke in two, and the forepart moved slightly farther out to sea. Before daybreak both halves of the ship sank.

The ship's Quartermaster finally succeeded in climbing the cliffs and raising the alarm. When help came 82 men were rescued from the cavern. But 182 died in the darkness of the icy sea.

Little was ever recovered from the *Halsewell,* except a few of the ship's guns and some timbers. There are good diving conditions at Seacombe, although it is not easily accessible.

All gear has to be carried for the last mile down a path which drops some 300 feet on the way. Entry at the water's edge is good. Carrying the diving equipment down is not too bad, but it is crippling on the way back even for the really fit. The tides in the area are of moderate strength, but there is the chance of swimming ashore at Winspit if carried too far to the west or at Dancing Ledge to the east. The depth of water varies from twenty to thirty feet.

Bob Campbell's latest theory is that the cannon-balls did not come from a ship at all—that they were fired from a battery mounted on Peveril Point since the reign of Elizabeth I! In his researches he found references to 18-pounder carronades, a 32-pounder cannon, and a mortar mounted there at various times. And some of the few guns saved from the wreck of the *Halsewell* were mounted there after their recovery.

Where is the wreckage of the *Halsewell* now? It seems likely that the spot has been found. Swanage divers Bob and Dennis Wright and Barry Edgington have certainly found the grave of an old ship at about the right place. On the bottom are cannon-balls and at least one cannon about seven feet long. Regular dives are being made on the site.

Bob Campbell has two other wrecks as well as the *Halsewell* to investigate in the area. They are of later date. The *Wild Wave* and the *Alexandrovna* are worth Aqualung divers looking for, he believes.

The *Wild Wave* was a brigantine loaded with coal and bound for Poole from Exeter. It was about 3 A.M. on January 23rd 1875 when the Captain of the *Wild Wave* sighted Durlston Head, but in the darkness thought it was Handfast Point. So he turned as he thought into Studland Bay, and, shortening sail, ran in heavy seas in towards the shore. The ship was borne swiftly to its doom. Peveril Point loomed ahead, and she struck the hidden Peveril Ledge a hundred yards offshore.

Rescue attempts with two small four-oared gigs in gale-force winds went on for an hour and a half. But they could not reach the wreck, over which the seas were now breaking. Three rocket-lines were fired. One reached the ship—on which there was no sign of life—but became entangled as the ship shifted on the ledge.

As day broke five sailors were spotted clinging together amid-ships, but every now and then they disappeared in foaming water. A message was sent for the Poole lifeboat and steam tug. Procedure in those days was for the tug to tow the lifeboat as near to the wreck as possible, and the lifeboatmen would then try to row to the stricken vessel.

The wind now swung from south to south-west, and the survivors gained some protection in the lee of the cliffs. At the same time the tide slackened on high water, and the two little boats of the coastguards were again launched. This time they reached the wreck and took off four men and a boy, before the Poole lifeboat could arrive.

The *Wild Wave* now broke up and sank between the twin ledges of Peveril Point. An account of the rescue and shipwreck appeared in *The Times,* and the report was largely instrumental in establishing a lifeboat station at Swanage.

Peveril Point is a tricky, dangerous spot to dive, only possible in slack water. Low water would be best, as the oncoming flood tide would be less violent than the ebb.

The *Alexandrovna* was wrecked seven years later—on Saturday April 29th 1882. She was a 1250-ton sailing-ship registered at Liverpool, and was caught by a gale which increased in force during the day until it was reaching hurricane force by the afternoon. At 4 P.M. the disabled *Alexandrovna* was sighted from Anvil Point, being driven towards the cliffs. Before any rescue attempts by rocket could be made she was driven full force into a solid cliff-face.

She sank in ten minutes half a mile west of Anvil Point. There were no survivors. A portion of her topmast was found on the top of the cliff, where it had been thrown by the impact. Over twenty men were lost. Her Captain and eight seamen are buried in Swanage Cemetery.

Those are three ships for which the divers are now searching.

Off St Abbs, Berwickshire, in fifty-five feet of water, three members of the Edinburgh Branch of the British Sub-Aqua Club, discovered another sign of tragedy. The divers—Roger Bruce,

Ian Leslie, and Bill Peacock—found the iron steering-wheel of a ship. After ten minutes' work they succeeded in freeing it and bringing it to the surface. The Harbourmaster there, Mr James Colvin, told them the story of what they had found. The wheel came from the *Alfred Earlson,* which sank on a strange night of thick fog, huge seas but no wind, in October 1907. Mr Colvin, who was twelve years old at the time, said, "We heard the boat strike and the men calling for help, but their cries gradually faded away."

The Arbroath lifeboat searched for hours without finding a survivor. In the morning the shore was covered with the ship's cargo of pit-props.

But there was one survivor—the ship's dog—safe on a rock. A tablet in the crew's memory—from donations, including those of schoolchildren—is in St Abbs Church. The divers presented the five-and-a-half-foot-diameter wheel to the harbour authorities, who planned to erect it on a building in the fishing village.

One of the many victims of mines in the First World War lies on the sand in fifty feet of water near Dawlish. She is the *Gallicia,* a 5922-ton cargo-vessel. She struck the mine on May 12th 1917, one and a half miles from Parson and Clerk Rocks, and sank almost immediately. The wreck is greatly dispersed, but seems to be a central meeting-point for all the marine life in the neighbourhood.

Another First World War casualty of a most unusual kind lies right out in the middle of Lyme Bay in 138 feet of water on a sandy bottom. She is the *Empress of India,* 14,300 tons, which was sunk "by accident" in November 1917 while being used by the Royal Navy as a target ship!

A Second World War accident has produced a wreck on which diving is strictly forbidden—in fact, the result of doing so could be one of the greatest disasters in British history. For this ship is loaded with 3000 tons of high explosives, which some experts say could be set off by a jolt, collision, or even spontaneous detonation.

The ship is the United States Liberty ship *Richard Montgomery,* which sank in the Thames Estuary after running aground less than 4000 yards off Sheerness in 1944. The area of the wreck is prohibited owing to the danger to surrounding land of her cargo of war bombs. Questions have been asked about this danger in the House of Commons, and two amateur divers who planned to have a look at the ship as she is now were warned off in the strongest terms.

No book about wrecks would be complete without reference to the *Empire Politician,* which went aground in the Sound of Eriskay, South Uist, in 1940. The ship carried a cargo of thousands of crates of export whisky. This wreck was the inspiration for Sir Compton Mackenzie's novel and the film *Whisky Galore.* The bow section of the ship, complete with whisky, was successfully salvaged and towed away—though no-one ever knew exactly how much evaded the Customs on shore!

Whisky-drinkers will be appalled to learn that the aft section of the ship was blown up once the authorities had—so they thought —removed all recoverable whisky.

However, over twenty years later a naval diving team, led by Lieutenant George Wookey, was attached to the guided-weapons range at South Uist to locate any missiles which landed in the sea.

Lieutenant Wookey, the Navy's top diver, and already a legend in the diving world, was the man who established a world-record descent in a standard diving-suit using an oxygen-helium mixture. He went down to over 600 feet in a Norwegian fiord.

While in *Whisky Galore* country it does not seem surprising that the naval divers did their diving exercises, when not needed for missile location, in the Sound of Eriskay.

Wookey, writing in the British Sub-Aqua Club magazine *Triton,* tells what happened:

"After many hours and days of fruitless search, towing divers back and forth between Eriskay and Barra, during which we found thousands of the largest scallops I have ever seen ... the tumbled remains, quite unrecognizable as a ship, were at last located, completely grown over with thick kelp seaweed. An interesting find, of course, but divers, though of temperate habits, are reluctant to leave even the smallest piece of wreckage without completely exploring the remains.

"When the first bottle of whisky was unearthed from somewhere deep in part of what seemed to be the bilges—can you imagine the excitement? Our endurance underwater suddenly showed a remarkable increase. When the second and subsequent bottles were found our enthusiasm knew no bounds, in spite of torn suits from the jagged wreckage and icily cold water.

"After the first frenzy of indiscriminate searching, we began systematically groping in complete blackness, the bottles passing in turn from diver to diver to a level where the shallowest diver could hold each bottle up to the light; if it appeared quite clear it was placed in a flour-sack kept for such an emergency, later to be hauled to the surface. Bottles containing sediment were discarded."

A high proportion of the whisky appeared unaffected by its long immersion. Some, however, after the cork was pulled, turned from a pale amber colour to a pale chartreuse green!

The moral of this story to every wreck hunter must surely be —look hard at everything, leave no piece of wreckage unturned, and if you find a golden treasure it may not be quite the kind of gold you expected!

Silver from the Sea

SINCE the very first raft was built by man there have been shipwrecks, and as long as the sea is the sea we know today there will be more. Many of the earliest wrecks are of great historical value, and their contents, once raised and preserved, would provide information and proof of happenings and customs throughout the ages of which we now know practically nothing.

For example, there is a story that is mainly legend, but which would seem to be based on fact, that tells of the loss of the *Drakkar* (the *Serpent*), a Viking ship, in the Thames during the year 851. Her remains would be worth a great deal to any museum in the world.

Up in the Shetland Islands, on the south side of Gulberwick Bay, the wrecks of the *Fifa* and *Hialf* occurred in the sixteenth century. Towards the end of that same century—about 1590—the *Santa Catarina* went down in a small bay near Colliestown, Aberdeenshire.

This bay is known as St Catherine's Dub after the wreck, and cannons have been raised from the site. One of these, the property of Lord Aberdeen, was brought up by the parish minister of Slain, Mr Rust, in 1855. It was last heard of at Hadds House, and being quite bulky—seven feet nine inches long, with a four-inch bore—it is still there to this day. The diving in the area is not good, the best underwater visibility is about six feet, and the bottom at ten fathoms is of fine concealing sand and mud.

Off Pembroke, in Wales, the *Santa Cruz,* a reputed treasure-ship, went down on January 11th 1679. Her remains have yet to be found. The local branch of the British Sub-Aqua Club have searched, but so far have found nothing.

In the south, inside the Isle of Wight, the ordnance transport *Guernsey Lily* went down during November 1799 at the entrance to the Solent. *The Times* of November 5th 1799 reported: "We are sorry to state the loss of the *Guernsey Lily* ordnance transport. She foundered in Yarmouth Roads on Friday, but it is with pleasure we can inform the public from authority, that all troops on board, together with the whole of the crew, were saved by the exertions of the Navy."

These vessels, and thousands like them, remain on the bottom, some covered with murky ooze, some with growing seaweed. All await the visit of the wreck hunter.

But what a wreck looks like now depends a great deal, of course, on the date of sinking, the method of construction—whether wood or iron—and where she sank. One thing you can be sure of is that she will not look like the Hollywood film-maker's idea of a sunken ship. In some films all the sunken ship—guarded, of course, by a huge octopus—needs is fresh canvas, and she'd be as good as new. On the other hand, even while laughing at this, you cannot be dogmatic and say she would be a mouldering heap of rubbish. That might be going too far. Strange things happen to wrecks at the bottom of the sea.

When a ship sinks, from one cause or another, either the bow or stern will usually strike the sea-floor first. This simple fact determines how she will lie. If her last resting-place is flat the bow or stern strikes first, the opposite end follows, and then the whole ship keels over to port or starboard. Some ships when seen on the sea-bed have very little heel, but there is usually some.

Anything that will float usually breaks free at the first strike. These pieces are soon gone to join the wreckage on some beach. It will take as little as six months or as long as thirty years for the ropes to rot and release other objects. These by then are probably so waterlogged that they do not travel far from the wreck before sinking to the seabed in their turn. Modern synthetic ropes

Green glaze pottery bowl from the area of the wreck of the *Royal George*. (See p. 181.)

(*Left*) John Baldry with a 32-pounder cannon-ball recovered from the *Royal George* site. The ball was heavily encrusted. Note the special underwater watch, worn by divers to help them calculate decompression times and so avoid the crippling divers' disease aptly called the 'bends' because of its twisting effect on muscles and joints. (See p. 180.)

A beautiful bronze cannon recovered from the Thames by the Port of London Authority's Wreck Raising Service. It is now in the Tower Armouries. (See p. 182.)

(*Below*) Cannon-balls which may be from the East Indiaman *Halsewell*, sunk near Swanage. On the right is the encrusted, almost unrecognizable, ball. Foreground, the inch-thick crust of rust and sand is broken away to show the ball inside. Top centre, a ball is lifted clear of the crust. (See p. 184.)

will have a much longer life, and this must be taken into account in any future calculations.

That first strike on the seabed may release some heavy objects that fall some distance from the wreck. Explosions in boilers can also fling large objects some distance from the main wreck. In one case that we have seen the boilers themselves are some distance from the ship, something that could not have been caused by any fouling unless the surface ship was in the aircraft-carrier class.

If our wreck has landed on mud, or a mud and sand mixture, it may well be only a few years before the sheer weight of the ship does half the covering work itself. It will sink in, and further disturbances of the water will slowly move the rest of the mud over the remains of the ship.

Such a wreck is, of course, the most difficult to find, but if it is found the mud may well have been a blessing. For a wooden ship will be preserved by such a mud covering: it helped a great deal with the *Vasa*. A wooden ship, on the other hand, that lands on rocky ground will not last long. Though here again it is unwise to be dogmatic. Armada ships' timbers have been found in quite a tough state, though it is generally sand, shingle, or mud which has protected them.

Iron and steel die hard—especially when the ship falls into a valley in the rocks. Support from rocks around and a normal position do not put such strains on vital parts as would a more exposed resting-place.

It is extremely difficult to say how long an iron or steel ship will last. The *Preussen* (Chapter Ten) has its main ribs remarkably intact, but the *Mohegan* (Chapter Nine) has parts where the plating has worn so thin that the wreck hunter can almost push his finger through.

Wood too varies in its reaction. A fishing-boat in Wales was rotten in fifteen years, but the *Lady Dalhousie*'s wooden block tackle worked underwater off the Lizard, and her ship's wheel was still recognizable. She sank in 1870.

In addition to the wood-eaters and worms in the area where she sank and the rate of rusting of the various metals in sea-water, our sunken ship has many other enemies to fight. Water movement will do as much damage as anything. If every ship sank in quiet waters sheltered from the direct action of the sea, what a feast of wrecks we should have!

Unfortunately, it has been calculated that the wave action of water below the surface is directly in relation to the height the wave reaches above normal sea-level. And many ships sink in what must be considered shallow water—less than sixty feet deep. Therefore many of them are affected badly by underwater wave action in storms. Even if they sink down clear of such a surface disturbance the tide will not leave them alone. Vast masses of water are constantly pushing first this way and then that. And, as many sinkings take place at water-disturbance points like headlands, there are new hazards to the sunken ship. Special rip currents and tidal movements swirl around her.

Closer in to shore, storms will move tons of shingle and pour it over your wreck, sandbanks will move overnight, and what was once a completely exposed wreck can disappear by the morning after high winds and heavy seas. Such is the case with the *Anson*. Anyone who has felt the ground shake beneath his feet and heard the thunder of waves on Loe Bar, in Cornwall, will realize the power that can make this happen.

Strangely enough, it is overcoming some of these difficulties that gives wreck hunting something of its fascination. Derek Cockbill, whom you will have read about in Chapter One with the Torbay divers' fantastic exploits on the *Maine*, divides wrecks into two categories.

The first category contains those ships which have been wrecked by going ashore and end up lying in shallow water. Such vessels are quickly broken up and dispersed, often in a matter of days, by gales. Even a wreck sheltered from heavy seas, if lying in tidal waters, will, owing to the wetting-and-drying action of the tides, break up quicker than another which is totally submerged.

On-shore wrecks, as opposed to inshore wrecks, are often an easy salvage proposition, so what is left after the sea and salvage work is done is usually little more than a few scattered plates, ribs, and boilers. Nevertheless these have their interest points, and they are very suitable for novice divers to get their first sight of a wreck.

The *Louis Shied* is a good example of this type. A 5945-ton Belgian cargo-vessel, she was torpedoed and ran aground 100 yards from the Links Hotel, Thurlestone, South Devon, on December 8th 1939. She is no distance at all from the Thurlestone Golf Clubhouse for those who like to mix their sports! The remains lie in thirty feet of water on a rocky, weed-covered bottom, and the boilers used to house some magnificent specimen wrasse. Parts still show slightly at low water.

The second category of wrecks is more interesting to the wreck hunter. These are the ships that lie in deep water. They are usually victims of the unusual—collision, bombing, torpedo, or foundering—and though charted are often forgotten and usually untouched by divers since the sinking.

But even with the charted wreck—clearly marked on the Admiralty charts—finding her is not so easy. There are exceptions, of course. Those wrecks buoyed by Trinity House as a possible danger to navigation are the easiest. A quick dive down the line of the buoy-cable should produce results.

One of the best examples of this kind of wreck is the *James Eagan Layne,* a 7176-ton Liberty ship built in 1944. On March 21st 1945 she was six and three quarter miles from Plymouth Breakwater on her way from Barry, Wales, to Ghent loaded with United States Army engineers' stores. At 2.35 P.M. a torpedo ripped into her. Number Four and Five holds flooded, and the engine-room was making water. She was beached at 10.30 P.M. the same day, half a mile from Rame Head Elbow. There were no casualties.

This ship is one of the favourite dives of Britain's amateur wreck hunters. She is in seventy feet of water on an even keel on a shingle bed, and part of the superstructure is often showing. Large pollack, wrasse, conger, crab, and lobster have made the ship their home. Salvage operations on the cargo began in 1953, and were carried out by an Icelandic firm.

With other ships, however, the actual locating of the wreck underwater is the big problem for the amateur, as he usually has only limited time at his disposal. Some time can be saved by working out from the charted position some marks or bearings that can be used to establish the same position at sea. But no-one knows better than the diver that the sea is a big place—and in our often limited visibility a miss of a few yards is as good as the proverbial mile.

Once having found your wreck, it is most important to check your marks from the anchored position over the sunken ship. Torbay Branch of the British Sub-Aqua Club claim that their marks for the *Maine* (see Chapter One) are now so good that they can even select a particular part of the wreck to anchor over.

We have mentioned before that the obstructions known

196 *The Wreck Hunters*

to fishermen are often wrecks, but it is worth bearing in mind that the 'wreck-marks' used by trawlermen are often for trawling on a line to *miss* the wreck. But local knowledge is vastly important, and only the foolish diver would ignore advice given by local fishermen.

An echo-sounder is often used by wreck hunters with considerable success, but if this equipment is not available the area can be searched systematically with a weighted anchor on a length of chain towed behind the boat. It is amazing how much you can feel of the progress of the anchor and the type of bottom by pressing with your hand on the tow-line. Supposing that the search succeeds and a solid obstacle is found to be a wreck, the best way of being able to return to the exact spot is by buoying your discovery.

Some care must be taken over this. Use wire rather than rope. And to avoid trouble with the coastguards do not use a metal buoy, but rather the large orange plastic type which will do no harm to a craft which runs it down. It is also good sense to fix a small non-collapsible buoy to the wire at a position that will always be underwater, no matter what the state of the tide. This will hold up the lower end of the wire and stop it from becoming entangled at low tide and out of sight at high.

So much for finding the wreck. Diving in the area demands some additional precautions to those normal safety rules observed by every sensible diver. Every wreck hunter should wear a knife on every dive, because science in helping the fisherman has added a new danger to the diver. Many local wrecks are good fishing-marks and well known to boatmen taking out parties of anglers. As a result the wreck may become festooned with snagged and broken angling gear. Nylon line is sometimes invisible, and can easily wind round the diver's equipment. Should this happen the diver should not attempt to pull himself free: a likely result is that the hook will be drawn up and into him! The simple remedy is the use of a knife, or in more complicated tangles the help of your companion diver.

Another hazard of a similar kind is the trawl or long net lost by fishermen. Some time ago these could be relied on to rot away in time, but the new fibres make net and rope almost a permanent feature of the part of the sea in which they were lost. A sharp lookout must be kept for these hazards, particularly in known trawling areas.

Wreck divers usually wear gloves and carry a 'crabbing-hook' —a rod about two feet long with handle at one end and open-hook shape at the other. This hook, apart from its obvious use for easing out crabs and lobsters, is an ideal method of pulling oneself along over rusted plates and frayed wires. A serious cut underwater from rusting plates reduced to razor edges may hardly be noticed until the surface is reached. Unprotected hands can take a lot of damage during the course of one wreck dive.

However, the experienced wreck diver knows that there is no greater thrill than seeing the shape of a ship loom up from the surrounding green or grey gloom as you move down on to her. This thrill comes even if the wreck has been so badly damaged that, as one diver put it, "she looked like two overturned Nissen huts that an elephant had sat on".

Such a thrill may come quite unexpectedly, as it did to Richard Larn, who took part in the *Anson* diving work. He says: "The sinking of the little *Italia,* a steel-screwed schooner of some 2790 tons gross, was not witnessed by anyone except her crew. And she might have gone undiscovered for ever had I not found her on a 'crawfish dive' from *MFV 1031.* This dive was part of the annual diving week of the Naval Air Command Sub-Aqua Club, of which I am Diving Officer. We had already been in the Isles of Scilly for four days, generally exploring underwater.

"As I slipped down the steep rock-ledges offshore from St Agnes, a wreck was far from my mind. I was concentrating on the wavering antenna of crawfish. I went deeper into the gloom, and visibility decreased rapidly as I passed 75 feet. Round a large rock, deeper, and suddenly . . . there on the bottom was a wreck. Not intact by any means, but obviously quite old.

"For the next few days we scoured the wreck from end to end to find some clue to her identity, but nothing came to light. Among the finds which were all returned to the wreck were both her engine-room telegraphs, portholes, mainmast steering light, and bathroom tiles."

On the last day available Larn's search provided a clue. And this gives a good illustration of the difficulty there is in tracing a wreck's history. The clue was a ship's log, detached from the stern, but on a rock-ledge near by. The log was in excellent condition and bore a serial number and maker's name. The instrument firm who made it in Birmingham found the serial number in their records. Yes, they had made the instrument in September 1911, and had sold it to a Cardiff ship's chandlers in December 1911. Richard Larn pressed on with his inquiries.

The Cardiff firm wrote to say that they had a record of the purchase and had sold it the following year to a ship called the s.s. *Italia*. Now Larn had something concrete to go on. Step by step he traced the ship's history. The *Italia* had started life as Contract No. 300 by Hawthorn Leslie of Newcastle-on-Tyne on May 5th 1890. Launched on November 27th 1890, she was named the *Gulf of Florida*. She was delivered to the Greenock Steamship Company on February 10th 1891, and was driven by a combination of steam and sail. She was fitted with two double-ended boilers and a triple-cylinder steam engine of 286 h.p. She also had two masts with three yards for sail on each. Built for a crew of sixty-three and six passengers, she journeyed to the Mediterranean, and later to the United States.

In about 1910 she was sold to an Italian firm at Spezia and renamed the *Italia*. She continued to haul mixed cargoes, including coal from the United Kingdom to Italy. When the First World War was declared she was fitted with a gun to discourage submarines (Larn found several rounds of ammunition in the wreck).

Finally she sailed from Cardiff on May 9th 1917 with a full cargo of coal. Going down the Bristol Channel, she ran into dense fog. Making for the safe anchorages in the Scillies, her Master took her close inshore. Hearing noises and seeing lights ahead, he stopped her engines and allowed her to drift. The lights and noises were in fact attempts to rescue the crew of the *Plympton*, which sank in the same area on the same night. The *Italia* drifted too far. She hit the rock-ledges and holed her bows badly. As she went astern the propeller and rudder hit as well, and she foundered on the edge of a steep underwater cliff. There she stayed until May 11th 1917, when at 9 P.M. she slipped off the rock with the tide and sank down into 120 feet of water.

There she lies now. Her coal cargo is spilled across the seabed, her engine standing out proud from the wreckage. And all that information was gained from the clue of a ship's log!

But now she is not as complete as she was. Richard Larn holds the salvor's warrant for the *Italia*, and recently was able to lead an expedition to salvage the 40-mm. Italian-manufactured stern-chaser gun. It was safely raised, and will be presented to the local museum.

Larn's research and knowledge of the ship's construction will help him immensely in future dives. This sort of advance information will give divers some idea of what to expect as they explore. For unless a real effort is made to remember the point of departure in relation to the rest of the wreck, it may be very difficult to return to the anchor-rope and so surface close to the diving-boat.

If this is a first dive on a newly discovered wreck particular care should be taken when rounding the bow or stern, for it is easy to be taken off guard by the full force of the tide, from which the ship's side may have protected you.

Currents and tide can never be taken lightly. Brighton Branch of the British Sub-Aqua Club, who have considerable experience of wreck diving and have many of the most experienced divers in the country in their go-ahead club, stress this when giving information about wrecks in their home waters. For example, six miles south of Beachy Head is the wreck of the 6000-ton Swiss freighter *Nyon,* which sank as recently as June 1962. She lies in 185 feet of water, and is subjected to considerable currents which may lead to difficulty with decompression stops for the foolish or unwary.

Not too far away is a casualty of World War I—the *City of Brisbane.* She was torpedoed, and is now in eighty-four feet of water with her superstructure flattened. Once again, say the Brighton divers, care must be taken with tides.

Another Brighton area wreck is the *Miown,* sunk in 1911 about a mile south-west of Shoreham Harbour. The wreck has been demolished by explosives, but is still interesting to divers. Another wreck in Sussex waters is the *Indiana,* sunk in 1901, and now a popular fishing-mark about a mile south of Worthing Pier.

With all wrecks great care must be taken. With the wrecks that are only slightly damaged a new temptation presents itself —to go inside.

Exploration of the interior of any wreck is something to be thought about very seriously before entering. Guide-lines must be rigged, and any wreck in very fragile condition should not be entered. The interior of a wreck can become an extremely ghostly place when visibility is obscured by disturbed silt, and panic could overcome even those who scoff at such stories when safe on the surface.

When exploring a wreck the job of identification should always be borne in mind. During a dive the sort of thing to be looked for are items which might bear the manufacturer's or company's name. Crockery, cutlery, brass fittings, and, of course, the ship's bell are worth looking for.

Derek Cockbill told us of the difficulty of positively identifying a ship the Torbay divers now own—the *Riversdale* of 2850 tons, a cargo-vessel which sank during salvage attempts to refloat her after she went aground close to Prawle Point in 1917. She is virtually intact on an even keel on a sandy bottom at 150 feet.

One day the divers raised a small bronze wheel. On cleaning it they found the letters "H G M R" amateurishly centre-punched on one of the spokes.

At first they assumed the letters to be the initials of some seaman, but on checking found they were the *Riversdale*'s signal letters. "A very lucky long-shot," comments Derek Cockbill.

But it is the long-shot, the unexpected underwater meeting between diver and a ship that no-one else has seen for maybe hundreds of years, that makes wreck hunting so exciting for those who take part.

The Lamorna Cove wreck is a good example of this. Ten members of the Southsea Branch of the British Sub-Aqua Club were on a diving holiday in the Penzance area. The year before one of them, Adrian Worley, had heard rumours of guns "at Buck Rocks" near Lamorna Cove, and had a good idea of where they might be. So they decided to try to find them. Anthony Bye, another member of the party, says: "All the possible sites had been explored one after the other without result, and we were getting rather fed-up. It was decided to have one more try.

"John Powell and I went down first, reaching the bottom at 90 feet. Almost immediately we found an anchor, very corroded and obviously very old. A couple of yards past it was the first gun.

"John pointed it out to me, but I didn't recognize it as a gun at first, as it was about five feet long and of a uniform thickness, instead of being tapered in the way most illustrations show guns. It had very prominent bands round it.

"There were about five guns scattered among the rocks, one of them still on the remains of its carriage. I took a few pictures of

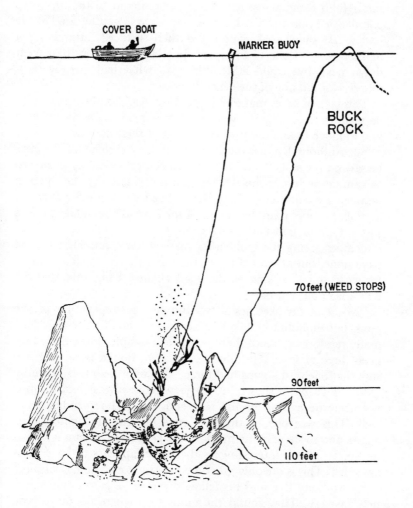

COVER BOAT

MARKER BUOY

BUCK
ROCK

70 feet (WEED STOPS)

90 feet

110 feet

Anthony Bye's drawing of the Buck Rock discovery

the guns (or thought I did, because they didn't come out), and then had a look round for anything small enough to take up to the boat, but all I found was a piece of pottery half buried in the sand. John came across another anchor similar to the first; this one had a broken shaft. By now our air was getting low, so we had a last quick look round and then surfaced, after tying a marker-buoy to one of the guns. Jim Dipnall and Adrian went down next, but could add nothing to what had already been found. Nor did any of the other divers."

This lack of other material is puzzling. And, as always seems to happen, the next day the weather turned against the divers, who had to move to another site for the rest of their holiday.

But Anthony Bye has made some excellent sketches of the guns he saw on the seabed, and they have been provisionally identified as cannon-periers, a short-range gun much used by the Spanish between 1550 and 1650. Says Bye: "The guns at the Bucks are of a smaller calibre than the periers of the Armada period, but it was just a type of gun and could come in various calibres. I don't remember seeing the gun on its carriage now, although I must have done, but at least three of the other divers do. It's unusual for wood to last so long, so there is a chance, a slim one, that the wreck isn't all that old.

"No. 2 of my sketches shows the general appearance of the guns, but shouldn't be taken as accurate. I don't remember how many reinforcing bands there were, for example; there may have been three or four. The pivots are shown dotted because I feel sure that one of the guns had them, although the others certainly didn't. This gun is shown in No. 3. (without pivots), and again is not accurate except for the rear end, which I remember quite well. This was one of the two guns instantly recognizable as a gun, and so stuck in my memory better. The other gun is shown in No. 1. This is interesting as the barrel appears to have been extended. This is the only gun on which the touch-hole is visible."

So Anthony Bye and his fellow divers have a triumph and a new mystery. They found the guns—but where do they come from—what ship? Or was there any ship at all?

Bye continues: "A thing that really puzzled us was the total absence of ballast and cannon-balls. There should literally have been tons of them about. John Baldry swam over the area at forty feet above the bottom, so that he would be able to see the

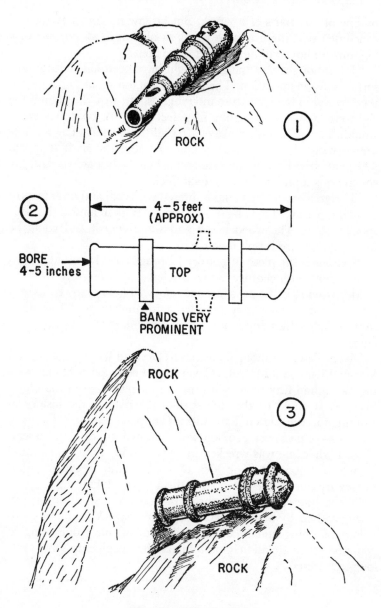

① ROCK

② 4 – 5 feet (APPROX)

BORE 4–5 inches → TOP

BANDS VERY PROMINENT

③ ROCK

ROCK

The Buck Rock guns

outline of any parts of a wreck. But he saw no traces at all, and concluded that there was no wreck at all—at least, not one of a big ship. So how did the guns get there then?

"John thought that the guns might have been lost during some sort of salvage operation. The anchors are too small to have been used by a ship big enough to mount guns, but would be about the right size for a boat about fifty feet long. A boat this small wouldn't leave much wreckage after all those years. The anchors are very old. I hit one with a hammer, and the shaft snapped. The shaft had been about one and a half inches across, and the concretions round it about an inch thick.

"The area around the guns is littered with coal and fragments of planking. The coal may be from a trawler sunk in almost the same spot in 1922. The wood is old and waterlogged, and could be from anything, so it isn't much help.

"Neither is the piece of pottery I brought up. It was identified as late eighteenth century. So we are left with a mystery."

More diving in the days to come may well help to solve this one. Just as more diving may produce a fortune in gold and silver from a Dutch East Indiaman which sank in 1711 near the Shetlands.

Divers Peter Bannon, Lieutenant-Commander Alan Bax, and Marine Lieutenant Malcolm Cavan have been reported as recovering more than fifty silver coins from the wreck area in the Outer Skerries. It could be the richest diving 'strike' in the history of Britain, for the Dutch East India Company ship *De Liefde* is said to have had over 220,000 newly minted guilders and ducats aboard when she was wrecked in 1711. Today those coins could be worth £500,000. The idea of such wealth is exciting. But sunken treasure is the exceptional thrill in wreck hunting.

Wreck hunters get their thrills in many ways—some by just diving; others by the unexpected sight of a wreck; some by meticulous planning and final discovery. But all have one thing in common: they are all helping to make the sea give up some of its long-lost secrets.

1 Wreck Hunting and the Law

It is sad but true that the wreck hunter, once having found his wreck, will soon be in contact with a mass of laws and regulations regarding salvage, wreck, and treasure trove. Whole books have been written on the subject, so all we can do here is to give general guidance. This, if followed, should keep the wreck hunter on the right side of the law, and also give him a basic knowledge of what he must do on finding his wreck.

The first point to bear in mind is that all wrecks belong to someone. The first thing to do, therefore, is to trace who that person is—before taking anything from the wreck.

Secondly, anything found on a wreck or in the sea must be reported to the Receiver of Wrecks at the nearest local Custom House. Don't think that this doesn't include small things from a wreck of any age—it does.

Let us suppose that you have found a wreck. Well, it is possible —indeed, probable—that the ship and cargo were covered by insurance, and when it sank claims for a total loss may well have been paid. Now, the rights in this particular ship probably belong to the underwriters.

The underwriters can, if they want to, sell the rights to someone else. So you could conclude a salvage contract with them or buy the wreck from them. Lloyd's, Leadenhall Street, London, E.C.3, might be able to help you in tracing the owners or underwriters. If you write to them, do try to give as much information as possible—position, name, date of sinking, and so on. The Salvage Association may be able to help too. War casualties—Allied shipping sunk during either of the two World Wars—can often be traced through the War Risks Insurance Office of the Ministry of Transport.

If your wreck is shown on an Admiralty Chart it is sometimes possible to get more information from the Hydrographer to the Admiralty, Hydrographic Department, Oxgate Lane, Cricklewood, London N.W.2.

If you decide to salvage anything from your wreck, and conclude an agreement with the underwriters, you should still write to the General Lighthouse Authority concerned in case your salvage operation can be classified as an obstruction or danger to navigation. The addresses are as follows: The Secretary, Trinity House, London, E.C.3; The Secretary, Commissioners of Irish Lights, Irish Lights Office, 16 Lower Pembroke Street, Box 73, Dublin 2; The General Manager and Secretary, Northern Lighthouse Board, 84 George Street, Edinburgh.

The Merchant Shipping Act of 1894 has something to say concerning wrecks that should also be borne in mind. Section 518 provides:

> Where any person finds or takes possession of any wreck within the limits of the United Kingdom he shall—(a) if he is the owner thereof, give notice to the receiver of the district stating that he has found or taken possession of the same and describing the marks by which the same may be recognized; (b) if he is not the owner thereof, as soon as possible deliver the same to the receiver of the district: and if any person fails, without reasonable cause, to comply with this section, he shall, for each offence, be liable to a fine not exceeding one hundred pounds, and shall in addition, if he is not the owner, forfeit any claim to salvage, and shall be liable to pay to the owner of the wreck if it is claimed, or, if it is unclaimed to the person entitled to the same, double the value thereof, to be recovered in the same way as a fine or a like amount under this Act.

It is foolish, to say the least, to remove any wreck without prior permission. The word 'wreck' perhaps should be explained in the legal sense. The definition given in the same Shipping Act says that the term 'wreck' includes jetsam, flotsam, lagan, and derelict found in or on the shores of the sea or any tidal water.

'Jetsam' covers all objects that have been thrown overboard from a ship that has later sunk, 'flotsam' covers the objects that remain afloat after a ship has sunk, 'lagan' covers the objects that have been thrown overboard attached to a buoy or marker, and a 'derelict' is a vessel that has been abandoned without hope of return.

Section 525 of the same Act provides for the disposal of unclaimed wrecks, and for wreck hunters this is the crux of the matter. It states:

Where no owner establishes a claim to any wreck, found in the United Kingdom and in the possession of a receiver, within one year after it came into his possession, the wreck shall be dealt with as follows:

(1) If the wreck is claimed by any admiral, vice-admiral, lord of a manor, heritable proprietor, or other person who has delivered such a statement to the receiver as hereinbefore provided, and has proved to the satisfaction of the receiver his title to receive unclaimed wreck found at the place where that wreck was found, the wreck after payment of all expenses, costs, fees, and salvage due in respect thereof, shall be delivered to him;

(2) If the wreck is not claimed by any admiral, vice-admiral, lord of a manor, heritable proprietor, or other person as aforesaid, the receiver shall sell the same and shall pay the proceeds of the sale (after deducting therefrom the expenses of the sale, and any other expenses incurred by him, and his fees, and paying thereout to the salvors such amounts of salvage as the Board of Trade may in each case, or by general rule, determine) for the benefit of the Crown, as follows; (that is to say),

(*a*) the wreck is claimed in right of Her Majesty's duchy of Lancaster, to the Receiver-General of that duchy or his deputies as part of the revenues of the duchy;

(*b*) If the wreck is claimed in right of the duchy of Cornwall, to the Receiver-General of the duchy or his deputies as part of the revenues of the duchy; and

(*c*) If the wreck is not so claimed, the receiver shall pay the proceeds of sale after the decease of Her present Majesty to her heirs and successors.

You will see from the above that it is possible to claim the wreck after a year, or if it is not claimed you can be granted salvage. But all these legal matters are rather overwhelming to the amateur, and to avoid them it is possible to purchase a wreck on the bottom, and then, as legal owner, set about taking it apart piece by piece to your heart's content. However, you are not out of the wood yet, as the law regards wreck with a very careful eye, and it becomes an offence to salve only part of a wreck and leave the remains behind, for as an owner you are responsible for your wreck and should another vessel be damaged or sunk by it, then you would be liable for the damage done. A rather worrying thought if you happened to be responsible for the loss of the *Queen Mary* or an aircraft-carrier.

Although there are these responsibilities, it is quite pleasant to be the owner of a ship, even though that ship is, at present, on the bottom of the sea.

From time to time the Admiralty offer ships for sale, and it is possible to tender for them. Here again rules and regulations are produced to distress the prospective buyer, but these are not quite so bad. However, the Admiralty always retain the right of inspection of the wreck, and will at all times have access to the wreck as Licensees of the Purchaser. Also, no cash, or notes, or personal effects, or fittings of a confidential nature, are included in the sale. So should you discover a chest of Navy Pay in your recently acquired hulk, then you are, regrettably, bound to hand it over to their Lordships.

A final legal note is of interest. Should you discover a wreck within three miles of the coast, and take it to a foreign port and sell it, then you will be liable to serve five years of penal servitude. So be warned—take any wreck, or advise any wreck, to the local Receiver of the district.

Every now and then rumours go round among the divers that someone has struck it rich—that one of the Armada galleons or some such treasure-ship has been found by divers. Most of these stories are just rumours, but if you as a wreck hunter did come across large quantities of silver plate, how do you stand then?

Well, once again there are heavy and complicated laws regarding this sort of discovery, and once again here is some simple guidance.

The Law of Treasure Trove is as old a law as any, and in

The Brighton minion, affectionately called "Berry's Banger" after Dave Berry, who located it in the sea off Brighton. (See p. 183.)

(*Left*) The 'breech' end of the eight-foot-long bronze minion.

(*Right*) The coat of arms on minion is too worn for tive identification.

An unusual underwater photograph. The hook of a grapnel is in the empty fuse-hole of a huge explosive cannon-ball as it is hauled up to the surface. This type of ball was designed for super-heavy fortress artillery of about 1860.

(*Below*) The cannon-ball shown underwater (*above*) is safely in the boat. Maurice Harknett found the ball in shallow water near a Hampshire fort.

Halsbury's *Laws of England* reference is made to Chitty's Prerogatives of the Crown concerning trove:

> Treasure Trove is where any gold or silver in coin, plate or bullion, is found concealed in a house, or in the earth, or other private place, the owner thereof being unknown, in which case the Treasure belongs to the Queen, or the grantee, having the franchise of Treasure Trove; but if he that laid it be known or afterwards discovered, the owner and not the Queen is entitled to it, this prerogative right only applying in the absence of an owner to claim the property.
>
> If the owner, instead of hiding the treasure, casually lost it, or purposely parted with it, in such a manner that it is evident he intended to abandon the property altogether, and did not purpose to resume it on another occasion, as if he threw it on the ground, or other public place, or in the sea, the first finder is entitled to the property, as against everyone but the owner, and the Queen's prerogative does not in this respect obtain.
>
> So that it is the hiding, and not the abandonment, of the property that entitled the Queen to it.

It will be seen from the foregoing that a court will have to decide whether or not the treasure was hidden or casually lost, and this decision is rather a hard one to make where the true owner is unknown. It could be argued that a ship had been deliberately sunk to protect its cargo of gold, and therefore the treasure was 'hidden' and by law belonged to the Crown; and then, again, the argument could be that where a ship is lost the contents of that ship are lost also, and that the intention was to abandon the cargo as the ship was abandoned when the Captain and the crew left the ship to preserve their lives.

However, these arguments are pointless, and it is only necessary to remember that where treasure trove is discovered, then ownership will have to be decided by a court of law.

Basically the same thing holds true throughout these rules and regulations: report your find whether it be cannon, a complete ship, a few lengths of brass piping, or even an old bottle of whisky. The Receiver of Wreck, will advise you on the procedure then. It is better to do this than find out later that you have laid yourself open to heavy fines.

2 Cannons

WRECK-HUNTING divers are the most likely people to come face to face with a piece of ancient ordnance, so a brief résumé of cannons and some of their identifying peculiarities will be of assistance to them.

The history of cannoneering stretches back into the ages, and Chinese 'thunder of the Earth', or gunpowder, had been known and used for years before Christ. Firearms appear in the tenth century, and from that time their improvement in strength and accuracy has progressed until the present-day rockets to the moon have become possible. From early mortar-type missile-discharging pieces that tossed iron and lead balls at the enemy, cannons improved so much by the 1400's that they were then able to produce 700-lb. stone projectiles and hurl them nearly a mile at enemy troops or entrenchments. The ancient bombard type of cannon was fabricated from strips of metal held together by iron hoops in the manner of a barrel. This method of manufacture was not completely satisfactory, as poor metal-work resulted in imperfect seals, so that much of the power was lost before the projectile actually left the muzzle. However, cast guns had appeared by the fifteenth century, and from then on the weight of cannon increased tremendously, while size seemed to be the ruling factor when cannons were fabricated. About 1525 the Great Mortar of

Moscow appeared. This immense creation was eighteen feet long and had a bore of thirty-six inches. Its projectile was of stone and weighed a ton.

It soon became apparent to cannoneers that although these huge cannon could inflict terrible losses on a stationary enemy and could be used with success against castles and walled cities in siege, they nevertheless were most awkward to move from place to place. They were extremely difficult to train from left to right and back again when in actual use in battle. The Great Mortar was obsolete almost before it had begun to fire, and throughout the world the manufacture of cannon was concentrated on castings that were smaller and lighter in weight. The placing of cannon on gun-carriages and the inclusion of trunnions in the casting of the gun made transportation and firing simpler.

As various terms possibly confusing to the layman have already appeared in the above paragraphs, it might be well to list the main terms used in cannon description:

Bore. The inside of the barrel along which the cannon-ball is shot.

Bore diameter is the distance across the bore, and can be taken at the muzzle.

The bore length is the distance along the inside of the cannon from the muzzle to where the bore finishes just behind the touch-holes.

Breech. The rear end of the cannon between the cascabel and the touch-hole.

Calibre. The internal diameter of the bore. A three-inch gun would have a bore three inches across. Also used as a ratio of bore to bore length—*i.e.* 30-calibre cannon would be a cannon whose bore length was thirty times its bore diameter. So a three-inch 30-calibre gun would have a bore length of 90 inches (30 x 3).

Cannon. A general term to denote a muzzle-loading gun. However, a cannon was also a particular type of ordnance, as opposed to, say, a culverin, during the sixteenth century.

Cascabel. The handle-like protuberance at the back end of the cannon rather like a door-knob, occasionally pierced with a hole to enable the cannon to be fired with a hot iron, or decorated with iron loops to enable training-ropes to be fixed.

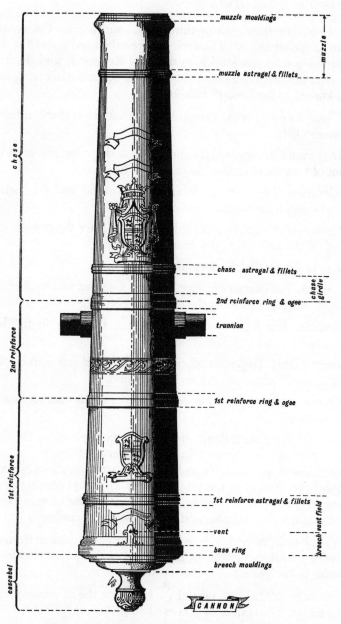

The parts of a cannon—drawing by "Gus"

Chase. The front half or third of the gun-barrel. The part in front of the trunnions. The area between the breech and the first reinforcing ring was known as the First Reinforce, and the area between the first reinforcing ring and the second reinforcing ring was known as the Second Reinforce.

Chase diameter is the diameter of the outside of the gun-barrel measured behind the muzzle mouldings.

Dolphins. Ornamented handles styled as dolphins, placed at the point of balance to enable the cannon to be lifted.

Elevation. The angle between the horizontal and the highest point to which the muzzle can be raised.

Grommet. A rope ring placed in the bore after the cannon-ball to retain the ball when the cannon is moved.

Lay or *Train.* To aim a cannon.

Length. The overall distance between the front and back of the cannon, but not including the cascabel.

Muzzle. The front end of the cannon from which the ball emerges.

Point blank. The point where the ball would first strike when fired from a horizontal bore on level ground.

Quoin. A wedge placed under the breech of the cannon to alter its elevation.

Reinforcing Rings. Really decorations dating back to the days when cannon were bound in the manner of barrels—i.e., the early Lombards. Astragals and fillets are small mouldings going around the cannon in the same manner as the reinforcing rings. They served no purpose other than decoration. Reinforcing rings were cast with the cannon, and not applied after casting.

Touch-hole, or vent. A hole into the bore of the cannon from the outside, placed at the back or breech end of the gun to enable the powder to be ignited.

Trajectory. The path taken by a ball from the cannon's mouth to its target. The trajectory is curved.

Trunnions. Two integral parts of the cannon, one on either side, placed about midway along the cannon to facilitate the vertical movement of the barrel. They are cast with the gun, and are usually the same diameter as the bore of the gun.

Vent-field diameter is the diameter on the outside of the gun-barrel at the touch-hole.

Windage. The difference between the diameter of the shot and the diameter of the bore.

From the fifteen hundreds, cannon improved until each weapon could be used and moved by two horses and three men. Cartridges appeared, and these saved loading-time by allowing the charge to be rammed rather than ladled. Later, fixed ammunition with ball attached to the cartridge enabled guns to be fired even more rapidly. As cannon improved, so artillery units became more important to the campaigner, and the whole style of battle changed. As the cartridges changed, so did the shot. All sorts of variations came into use, from grape-shot, which was like a little bag with a wooden core around which were clustered musket-balls, rather like grapes on a bunch, to powder-filled and fused shells that exploded in the air or at the target. For sea warfare there was chain-shot, which was two round shot joined by a short length of chain, and bar-shot, which was a divided shot with a bar holding the two hemispheres apart, which were fired to break an enemy's rigging or masts. Canister-shot was similar to grape, but was contained in a can or case. Rifling of cannon-barrels, although understood long before, did not come into general use until the middle 1800's.

During the Armada campaign the cannon were of three main types. Luis Collado, a Spanish mathematician and Royal Engineer to His Most Catholic Majesty, agreed with this grading, and called culverins and sakers cannon of the first class; cannon, cannon of the second class; and periers or pedreros, cannon of the third class. First-class cannon were long pieces that could strike the enemy from long range, battering cannon of the second class were used to break down walls and smash other cannon batteries, while third-class cannon were defence cannon for installation in shore batteries against ships or advancing troops and machines. From now on the technique of cannon manufacture becomes very complicated. To illustrate this point, overleaf is a list of the principal English guns of the sixteenth century, together with their weights:

Name				Weight (in pounds)
Rabinet	..	..	..	300
Serpentine	..	..	..	400
Falconet	..	..	..	500
Falcon	..	..	..	680
Minion	..	..	..	1050
Saker ..	..	..	..	1400
Culverin bastard		..	..	3000
Demi-culverin		..	..	3400
Pedrero	..	..	..	3800
Basilisk	..	..	..	4000
Demi-cannon..		..	..	4000
Bastard cannon		..	..	4500
Culverin	..	..	..	4840
Cannon serpentine	..		..	5500
Cannon	..	..	..	6000
Cannon royal		..	..	8000

Each cannon had its pecularities in use, each a different size and weight of shot and powder, and as the history of cannon progressed, so even each type varied in length and weight. The list given above refers only to English cannon of a particular period. A Spanish list of first-class cannon for the same period contains names such as esmeril, pasavolante, sacre, moyana, culebrina, and doble culebrina, as well as many others. It can be seen that the classification of cannon now becomes the work of the specialist, and any wreck hunter who is fortunate enough to discover a cannon on the seabed should take measurements of bore, chase, chase diameter, position of trunnions, and markings embossed or carved on the gun, to enable the non-diving expert to work out what sort of a cannon has been discovered.

Concerning cannon markings, English cannon bore the crowned Tudor rose and the broad arrow of the Government mark, French cannon had cascabels in the shape of a tulip, Spanish cannon had markings like a pancake; but none of these identifying marks were uniform, and they can be used only as a general guide.

For ship recognition a cannon on the seabed can be a mixed blessing, as cannons were captured and often used on board an enemy ship to shoot back at their original manufacturers!

There is such a great amount of detail available about cannons that it is not at all surprising that a society for the study of cannon has been formed. During 1949 Donald H. Clark in Seattle decided that cannon study should be perpetuated through carefully checked records that would be available to all members of the association. The association he formed is known as the Cannon Hunters' Association of Seattle, which name gives the readily remembered and descriptive initials C.H.A.O.S.

Those interested in the association should write direct to Head Hunter Donald H. Clark, Cannon House, 4329 West Semple Street, Lawton Wood, Seattle 99, Washington, U.S.A. Don Clark is number one among some 1400 cannoneers. There is no restriction to membership, and to quote Don Clark's words: "There are no initiation fees, no dues, no obligations, no committees, and no meetings other than cannon hunts at odd times and in odd places. When an applicant is accepted by the Great Guns, a membership card is issued which entitles the bearer to hunt and recover old muzzle-loading cannon in any part of the world, with the stipulation that such activities be within the laws of the countries in which the hunting is conducted. Members are asked to report all cannon recoveries. Also any clues as to lost or misplaced cannon which might be the target for future search. Up to date, the record of recoveries by members is 473! Many have been immersed in salt water for long periods, and have been the subjects of rather long and careful chemical treatment to prevent destructive oxidization."

Various rewards to members for locating and salving cannon are presented by the association. Among these are cannonization, awarded for the recovery of a cannon by a member alone, and the Order of the Purple Lanyard, which is for outstanding work in research on cannon, or any notable assistance that furthers the aims of the association. Cannoneer Major Daniel Elvin was recently presented with this order for his valuable work in training gun crews in England with authentic British manuals on gun instruction that date back to the days of muzzle-loaders.

Although the association has its roots in Seattle, there is now a body of active British cannoneers who meet once annually for a celebration dinner in London. On these occasions information is exchanged concerning cannon, and a full report of the evening is sent to Cannon House.

Many divers are now finding cannon on the sea-floors about

the British Isles, and for information on how to preserve the guns once they are brought to the open air, and how to identify those which do not fall into a normal pattern, Cannon House provides a reference book that is second to none. This is becoming the world's clearing house for information, and although the information required may not actually be on file in Cannon House, the seeker will be recommended to a suitable source from the lists of active cannoneers.

The association also produces a magazine that appears with chaotic irregularity and gives information on the activities of C.H.A.O.S. members throughout the world, and also provides a valuable question-and-answer reference book.

For those whose interest goes beyond the recovery of the cannon, and this seems to happen more in the United States than it does in Great Britain at the present time, it is possible to obtain information on how to load, aim, and fire the recovered weapon! From time to time in Seattle cannon outings are arranged, and parties towing their pieces behind cars and lorries converge on a suitable practice area for a shoot-off. The afternoon's sport is punctuated by salvoes and volleys, while target practice and the occasional mock battle are staged to while away the day!

As far as Great Britain is concerned, the interested cannoneer must apply to the Chief Officer of Police, who can issue an authority, should the applicant be considered suitable, to keep for private use, and not for resale, thirty pounds of gunpowder. The licence issued will be for properly manufactured powder purchased from a reputable firm, and not for home-made stuff. If any reader is fool enough to make up quantities of powder without expert advice he will succeed only in blowing his head off, and maiming and disfiguring trees, animals, and other people into the bargain.

3 Underwater Archaeology

IF underwater archaeology was mentioned in recent years it was always taken to refer to the clear, almost tideless Mediterranean and the ancient wrecks with their cargoes of amphora or wine-jars still intact after centuries on the sea-bottom.

There in ideal conditions the archaeologist-diver slowly evolved a method of recording and excavating these old wrecks that could stand side by side with the high standards set today in land archaeological digs. Underwater archaeology in the Mediterranean so progressed from a haphazard lifting of the ship's cargo—which was promptly labelled looting by those not able to dive and see conditions for themselves—to a state in which the archaeologist-diver was on equal footing with his land-bound colleagues. Now recording and excavation can be as accurate and thorough as on land.

In this country it is only in the very recent past that underwater archaeology has begun to be taken seriously. The time-lag between acceptance of Mediterranean underwater archaeology and serious work around our coasts has been largely due to poor communications. By this we mean communication between the divers and the archaeologists. Many archaeological discoveries are made underwater, as on land, by pure chance. Unfortunately some of these discoveries have gone by default through lack of contact between the diver and the archaeologist.

Divers felt that archaeologists wanted to rob them of the opportunity to work on the sites they had discovered. They feared—as has happened on land in the past—that they would be pushed aside as of no importance by a team of archaeologists who would exploit the discovery. The archaeologists, in their turn, regarded the divers as just an ignorant bunch of muscle-men who would loot and destroy anything they found.

Fortunately this state of affairs did not continue for so long that the two sides could not be brought together. Much of the credit for doing so belongs to Miss Joan du Plat Taylor, of the Institute of Archaeology in London. Having worked on these ancient wrecks in the Mediterranean, she knew the views of both sides. She is an archaeologist, but has worked side by side with divers.

She encouraged British divers to bring their finds to her, and once these objects had been identified, recorded, and photographed, they were returned to the divers who had found them. And she sought a closer co-operation between all groups who had similar interests.

Her efforts coincided with the formation of the Scientific and Technical Groups of the British Sub-Aqua Club. Final result—the formation of the Committee for Nautical Archaeology.

Today the committee consists of archaeologists and divers, with representatives from the National Maritime Museum, British Museum, Science Museum, Institute of Archaeology, London University, Society for Nautical Research, the British Sub-Aqua Club, the Council for British Archaeology, and others.

The aims of the committee are:

(1) To promote research into all material aspects of nautical archaeology in the sea, lakes, rivers, and on land.

(2) To organize a wreck survey in and around the British Isles, noting such wrecks as are of historical and technical importance and which would repay detailed study.

(3) To promote the training of nautical archaeologists working on land and underwater, to promote good standards of recording and excavation, and to encourage the publication of results.

(4) To act as a channel of communication between field archaeologists, divers, local historians, and related scientists.

(5) To maintain files of wrecks, ports, harbours, and other nautical sites of archaeological interest both at home and abroad.

(6) To compile a bibliography of books and articles relating to nautical archaeology.

(7) To keep a list of specialists in all fields of related research, and of selected local representatives who will be informed of the committee's activities and who will advise the committee on local developments.

Mr George Naish, of the National Maritime Museum, is the chairman, and Miss du Plat Taylor the secretary. The address is c/o University of London, Institute of Archaeology, 31-34 Gordon Square, London, W.C.1.

The formation of the committee has been a most important step. Far from lagging behind, it now seems that Britain is speeding ahead. The first School of Nautical Archaeology in the world has been set up at Swanage, under the direction of Dr John Waechter, of the Institute of Archaeology. The school gives students practical underwater work to do as part of any course there. A barge has been sunk to act as a wreck near a pier in Swanage Bay, and the 'wreck' has been supplied with the sort of objects found underwater, so as to reproduce as nearly as possible the conditions under which marine archaeologists work. This artificial site is used for underwater surveying and recording, and also as an experimental station for trying out new techniques underwater.

London University is teaching suitable students of archaeology to dive, and evening classes are also held for divers and others on the "Archaeology of the Sea, Lakes, and Rivers".

The Nautical Archaeology Committee recently appealed to all divers to help pinpoint ancient and modern wrecks around the coasts of Britain.

Wreck hunters are asked to supply the following information:

(1) Date wreck was discovered. Ship's name if known.
(2) Name of finder and address.
(3) Exact position (chart references, bearings, a tracing of the chart showing its position in relation to the land).
(4) Depth of wreck, including state of tide and time when depth was recorded.

(5) Whether wreck was wood or iron.

(6) Estimated size of wreck or area covered by debris (*i.e.*, length, breadth, height).

(7) Estimated age of wreck.

(8) Sketches or photographs of any fittings of the ship

(9) What is visible.

(10) Conditions (*i.e.*, currents, seabed, weed, etc).

4 Learning to Dive

THE wreck hunters you have met in this book are no race of super-men, but they are all experienced divers. Most of them are amateur divers, and most of them can dive only in their spare time. In fact, you will find many of them seated behind a desk all the week, and only at weekends can they indulge in their sport.

So you can see that it is almost possible to say that anyone can dive. And anyone who is reasonably fit can. Age in itself is no bar. Doctors who are specialists in diving medicine—men like Surgeon Captain Stanley Miles, Director of Medical Research at the Royal Navy Medical School—will stress, however, that the fitter a man or woman is the happier he or she will be underwater.

It is important that the would-be diver should have no evidence of respiratory disease, that his ears should be sound (though a perforated eardrum need not disqualify), that there should be no evidence of heart trouble or fits or attacks of unconsciousness. Claustrophobia would certainly make safe diving impossible.

Anyone who would pass these standards of fitness can then move on to the next stage of actually beginning training.

There are some excellent training schools in the country, but by far the best of them all is the British Sub-Aqua Club. This is Britain's largest amateur diving organization.

At any one time its membership of active divers tops the 5000 mark, and its excellent training methods have resulted in about 30,000 divers passing through the organization. There are nearly 200 branches in this country and all over the world.

It is interesting to note that Prince Philip is a past president and honorary life member, and that the Prince was no mere figurehead. He did his early training in the use of the Aqualung, following closely the British Sub-Aqua Club's methods and tests.

The B.S.-A.C. is proud of the fact that its instruction manual is the accepted standard for many countries of the world, and that it is a leading organization among the world's divers. It was solely due to the efforts of club members that the 1962 World Congress of Underwater Activities was held in London, attracting the 'big names' of diving, such as Commandant Cousteau and Hans Hass, to give papers and lecture.

In countries where the waters are clear and warm there is little difficulty in forming diving clubs, but the British Club had no such advantages. It was a very frail organization indeed when first formed in 1953 by Oscar Gugen and the late Peter Small. Equipment was short, and only enthusiasm carried it forward to the strong state it is in today.

Diving accidents do, of course, occur, but the British Sub-Aqua Club's insistence on safety procedures has ensured that the number of accidents on club dives is exceptionally small. It is only when such safety procedures are ignored—as unfortunately they are by some amateur divers outside the club—that accidents frequently happen. The club stresses safe diving, and teaches the best-known techniques for even the very deep dives.

It was a great blow to the club's veteran divers when their friend and founder-member Peter Small died during the ascent from the Hannes Keller world-record dive of 1000 feet. Though the club sets great store by its technical and scientific work, this sort of scientific deep diving is, at the moment, outside its scope, and only the world's navies and large organizations have the facilities to pursue such great depths.

Quite recently the Executive Committee of the B.S.-A.C. have been able to award grants for scientific projects around the coasts of this country, there is a Duke of Edinburgh's Prize for similar projects, and a National Diving Centre on the coast is being set up. Each year the Brighton Branch, together with Club Headquarters, holds a conference at which the latest developments are

A rather fanciful drawing of the time showing divers at work on the wreck of the *Earl of Abergavenny*. The artist was obviously well ahead of his time with the 'bubble' of the diver shouting "Haul up." A copper and leather diving 'suit' was worn during salvage operations. (See p. 105.)

The *Lusitania*. She is now on the bottom in 300 feet of water. (See p. 130.)

(*Below*) The *Laurentic*. Torpedoed by a U-boat in 1917, she carried gold bullion worth nearly £5,000,000. Almost all was recovered by divers. (See p. 130.)

discussed, and a world competition of underwater photography is staged in collaboration with the club magazine *Triton* and its editor Bernard Eaton.

The strength of the club lies, however, in its branches and the voluntary workers in them. To explain how a branch works and the sort of training that is given let us suppose that you, having read this book, are keen to dive, and later, quite possibly, join the ranks of the wreck hunters.

First you can turn to the end of this appendix and find the nearest branch to your home. A letter to the branch secretary, whose name is shown, will discover where and when the branch holds its weekly meetings.

You will probably find that a local swimming-bath is the venue on one evening in the week, and the branch secretary will invite you to go along. This is your chance to look them over, and theirs to have a look at you. Take your swimming-costume and a towel, because they are going to want to see you swim.

Once again we come back to the same idea : they do not expect you to be a champion swimmer. If you are, so much the better, but there are a few simple swimming tests that the average swimmer can pass easily. Don't please expect them to teach you to swim. They won't do it.

In your next few visits to the bath—it will cost you about £3 a year to be a member, but this includes every issue of the club magazine and a diving manual—you will meet the branch officials.

There will be a branch chairman, a secretary, and a treasurer, just like any other club. But you will find and meet also the training officer, the diving officer, and the equipment officer. In a big branch—London Branch itself has over 300 members—these men will have a number of assistants. All will tend to treat you rather like a new boy at school—well, you are—but this will soon pass.

Basically the speed at which you progress in your training will depend to a large extent on yourself. Remember that these men are not paid to teach you to dive. They do it quite voluntarily because they like diving, and they like to pass on the pleasure in store to you—and someone else did exactly the same for them.

You will be taught the use of the basic equipment—the mask, fins, and snorkel or breathing-tube. Only when you are completely proficient in the use of these and able to dive happily down some feet below the surface just holding your breath will they start to teach you to use the compressed-air breathing apparatus or Aqualung.

You will be given a logbook in which to record your passing of set swimming tests, and you will be given talks about the technical and physical side of diving and be expected to answer questions on them.

Both the training officer and the diving officer will be watching your progress. Other people will be going through the same lessons and tests with you—both men and women. Yes, women make excellent divers.

When the training officer is quite satisfied that you are competent with the basic equipment, then you will be trained on the Aqualung. Now the floor of the local swimming-bath will become almost as familiar to you as the surface area, for a great deal of your baths' time will be spent sitting on the bottom underwater learning to cope with any kind of emergency. Soon the Aqualung will become as familiar to you as a bicycle. And you will start to think about buying your own diving equipment. Up to now, with the exception of mask, flippers or fins, and snorkel, which you will have bought for about £5, all the equipment you have used in your Aqualung training will have been branch equipment bought out of branch funds.

Some branches have only a few sets. Others have many, and a great deal of extra equipment such as an air-compressor and aquaplanes for underwater gliding. At any rate, for the absurdly low membership fee you have benefited greatly from all the branch-owned equipment. It is really up to you, if you can afford it, to buy your own equipment: the branch equipment will not always be available.

Soon it will be suggested—if you don't suggest it yourself—that it is time to leave the swimming-pool and venture into more open waters. The next step is usually carried out in a lake, a flooded quarry, or some other sheltered, not too deep water. Here you may be in for a shock or for a delightful surprise.

However competent you felt in the swimming-pool, it is not at all the same thing when faced with 'untamed' water. Still, here you are, and in you go. The shock may be that, unlike in the swimming-bath, you can't see a darned thing underwater, as the water is so cloudy, or the delight may be in finding yourself under-water among a cloud of quite unconcerned freshwater fish and able to see a reasonable distance.

In the lake more tests will be carried out and more instruction given. Suits of foam Neoprene will probably be worn to keep you warm in the cold water, and on the way home you will feel much more like a diver!

From a lake dive or two the road now leads to the sea. Here you will find visibility can vary enormously from one day to another. A miserable one-foot visibility can turn into an astonishing thirty feet the next day. And so you go on, never diving alone, always supervised, until the day comes when you are the dive leader and some new boy is making you all trail along much more slowly than you really want to!

The British Sub-Aqua Club grades its divers carefully. The three major categories are Third, Second, and First Class. The tests that you take as you go along count towards these categories. Certain of your branch outings will be specified "for Third Class Divers and above only", some "Second Class Only", dependent on the conditions and/or depth the diving officer expects to meet. First Class divers have each over 100 dives in their logbooks of varying conditions and depths.

You will meet in your branch an extraordinary mixture of trades and professions. All mix happily together. All have one thing in common: all want to dive. All have dived. Their en-thusiasm appears to be boundless, and you are almost certain to meet someone of similar interests to yourself. The scientifically minded group together, the underwater photographers will teach you as much as they can, the marine biologist will try and interest you in collecting his latest passion, and the wreck hunters will show you charts and talk airily of dives to come on a practically intact wreck. At the end of your training you will find yourself a diver and a member of the British Sub-Aqua Club branch that you think is the best of all!

If, however, none of the branches listed here is suitable for your purpose, then a letter to the Administrative Office of the Club at 25 Orchard Road, Kingston-on-Thames, Surrey, may provide the answer.

There are in addition to the normal branch instructors some Club recognized instructors who can give you a more concentrated course in diving, but you will, of course, have to pay much more for this sort of instruction. The Club has also been instrumental in getting a National Diving Coach appointed. In certain circumstances he could be obtained for instructional purposes.

B.S.-A.C. BRANCHES

Aberdeen (67): Alex Milne, 79 Cloverfield Gardens, Bucksburn, Aberdeen.

Banbury (74): G. J. Eastbury, 81 Manor Road, Banbury, Oxon.

Barnsley (95): S. W. Pickles, 44 Smithies Lane, Barnsley, Yorks.

Bath (33): A. D. Fleet, 5 Wayfield Gdns., Batheaston, Bath, Somerset.

Bedford (89): A. R. Bourlet, 33 Oldfield Road, Queens Park, Bedford.

Belfast (30): Miss H. P. McGuire, 104 Lansdowne Road, Belfast, N.I.

Bermondsey (42): Mrs C. Batey, 37 Belsize Avenue, London, N.W.3.

Birmingham (25): Mrs K. Mason, 39 Swindell Road, Pedmore, Stourbridge, Worcestershire.

Blackpool (4): Miss B. Crookes, 26 Toronto Avenue, Bispham, Cleveleys, Lancs.

Bognor (27): Mrs P. J. Claydon, 14 Shelley Road, Horsham, Sussex.

Bolton (84): Alan MacIvor, 20 Lovat Road, Bolton, Lancs.

Bournemouth (6): R. L. Willetts, c/o Hancocks Photo Supplies, Opposite Old Town House, High Street, Poole, Dorset.

Bradford (44): Miss W. G. Walton, Barnsley Cottage, Charlestown, Baildon, Yorks.

Bridgwater (128): Miss K. Lean, 61 Durleigh Road, Bridgwater, Somerset.

Brighton & Worthing (7): D. G. Allen, 8 Dower Walk, Gossops Green, Crawley, Sussex.

Bristol (3): W. J. Locke, 11 Mendip Road, Portishead, Nr. Bristol, Glos.

Bromley (26): B. J. Green, 6 Royal Road, Sidcup, Kent.

Burnley (143): Miss B. Perry, 39 Woodbine Road, Burnley, Lancs.

Chelsea (45): Mrs Lilian Stokes, 82 Urmstone Drive, London, S.W.19.

Coventry (58): Mrs J. McDonagh, Welcome, Birmingham Road, Warwick.

Crawley (148): B. Vickery, 118 Spring Flat, Pound Hill, Crawley, Sussex.

Croydon (23): W. J. Parish, 28 Lavender Avenue, Worcester Park, Surrey.

Darwen (47): Miss Hilary Latham, 36 Letchworth Drive, Chorley, Lancs.

Derby (72): Miss M. Hotson, 170 Western Road, Mickleover, Derby.

Doncaster (75): R. Robinson, 37 Ferrers Road, Wheatley, Doncaster, Yorks.

Durham City (104): W. J. Barnes, 11 Kiln Walk, Peterlee, Co. Durham.

East Anglia (11): John P. Anson, 9 Seafield Close, Great Yarmouth, Norfolk.

East Cheshire (100): P. M. Smith, 38 Bollin Grove, Prestbury, Lancs.

East Lancs (2): W. D. Stephenson, "Dale Edge", 2 Dalamere Avenue, Whitfield, Manchester, Lancs.

East London (15): A. W. Hayden, 21 Salcombe Road, London, E.17.

East Yorks (176): Miss K. Smith, c/o 26 Tindall Street, Scarborough, Yorks.

Edinburgh (21): Lieutenant-Colonel A. Gordon-Rogers (Retd.), O.B.E., T.D., 49 Falcon Gardens, Edinburgh, 10.

Folkestone (106): G. C. G. Prout, Ambry Court, St Nicholas-at-Wade, Birchington, Kent.

Furness (61): C. K. Scanlan, 12 McClintock Street, Barrow-in-Furness, Lancs.

Grays Thurrock (168): K. Jackson, Tirana, Ruskin Road, Stanford-le-Hope, Essex.

Grimsby (37): J. R. Elston, 5 Haile Road, Humberstone, Lancs.

Guildford (53): D. S. Allgar, 5 Hawthorn Way, Burpham, Guildford.

Gwynedd (71): J. B. Cale, Gweunydd, Llanbedr, Merioneth.

Halifax (48): Mrs A. Harris, 2 Stoney Road, Mytholmroyd, Halifax, Yorks.

Hampstead (179): M. Smith-Petersen, Flat 4, 8 East Heath Road, London, N.W.3.

Harlow (141): D. Johnson, 41 Vicarage Wood, Harlow, Essex.

Harrogate (39): S. Clarke, 21 Castle Close, Killinghall, Nr. Harrogate, Yorks.

Harwich (54): M. E. J. Mooney, 11 Market Street, Harwich, Essex.

Holborn (130): Miss D. Roberts, 10 Westbourne Grove Terrace, London, W.2.

Hounslow (55): A. R. Bance, 27 Pensford Avenue, Richmond, Surrey.

Huddersfield (18): K. Flinders, 15 Red Moles Road, Fartown, Huddersfield, Yorks.

Hull (14): G. A. Wright, 46 Seafield Avenue, B.O.C.M. Village, Hull, Yorks.

Ilford (49): R. F. Davison, 41 Selbourne Road, Cranbrook, Ilford, Essex.

Ilfracombe (86): R. D. Booker, 19 Slade Valley Road, Ilfracombe, Devon.

Ipswich (32): A. R. Todd, 66 Beachcroft Road, Ipswich, Suffolk.

Isle of Man (76): E. H. Maley, "Mount Vernon", Belmont Hill, Douglas, Isle of Man.

Keighley (117): R. Buffey, 5 Bradford Street, Keighley, Yorks.

Kingston (17): D. Pearce, 125a High Street, London, W.3.

Leeds (115): D. Porter, c/o 163 Manchester Road, Deepcar, Sheffield, Yorks.

Lincoln (109): A. C. Temperton, 7 St Nicholas Street, Lincoln.

London (1): Paul Howden, 9 Holland Park, London, W.11.

Lunesdale (138): R. Hargreaves, 36 Norton Road, Morecambe, Lancs.

Luton (105): Mrs O. Fidler, 125 Swifts Green Road, Luton, Beds.

Matlock (121): Mrs M. Hallam, Oker House, Oker Side, Matlock, Derby.

Medway (59): B. Lambert, 28 Sandown Road, West Malling, Maidstone, Kent.

Merseyside (5): M. R. Goodwin, 15 Mornington Avenue, Crosby, Liverpool 23.

Mexborough (41): Miss V. Whitehead, Kilnhurst, Nr Rotherham, Yorks.

Newport & Cardiff (35): C. Hyndman, 41 Herries Drive, Sheffield 5.

North Gloucestershire (80): A. Birchley, 56 Shearwater Grove, Innsworth, Glos.

Northampton (13): Mrs J. M. Warren, The Lodge, Brixworth Hall Estate, Brixworth, Northants.

North Staffs (12): Mrs Whitehead, 5 Eleanor Place, Westlands, Newcastle, Staffs.

Nottingham (16): A. H. Moore, 7 Pately Road, Woodthorpe, Nottingham.

Oxford (34): Miss A. Symons, Bramblefinch, Boults Lane, Old Marston, Oxford.

Penzance (116): Secretary Penzance Branch BS-AC, Pilots Lookout, The Wharf, Penzance, Cornwall.

Plymouth Sound (164): W. T. Jenkin, 23 Vanguard Terrace, Keyham, Plymouth, S. Devon.

Reading (28): G. O. Von Hoven, "Tamameh", Chiers Drive, Drayton, Abingdon, Berks.

Scarborough (83): The Secretary, Scarborough Branch British Sub-Aqua Club, 25 St Mary's Street, Scarborough, Yorks.

Sheffield (36): Mrs M. A. Allen, 5 Newhall Avenue, Wickersley, Rotherham, Yorks.

Southend (22): Miss H. Salmon, 16 Leigh View Drive, Leigh-on-Sea, Essex.

Southampton (139): R. Bryant, 20 Shakespeare Road, Eastleigh, Hants.

Southsea (9): Mrs J. S. Millgate, 23 Jubilee Avenue, Paulsgrove, Portsmouth, Hants.

Swansea (99): K. Hume, 7 Woodland Terrace, Swansea, Glamorgan.

Swindon (46): J. E. Hamilton, 11 Springfield Road, Swindon Old Town, Wilts.

Tamworth (137): T. Farmer, 121 Green Lane, Wilnecote, Tamworth, Staffs.

Taunton (10): I. G. C. Anderson, Henlade House, Henlade, Taunton, Somerset.

Tees-Side (43): D. Huppler, 653a Yarm Road, Eaglescliffe, Stockton-on-Tees, Co. Durham.

Torbay (8): Alan Webb, Lyndale, 17 Froude Avenue, Watcombe Park, Torquay, Devon.

Tunbridge Wells (149): C. C. Pratt, 20 Elim Court Gardens, Crowborough, Sussex.

Tyneside (114): B. C. Walker, 40 Grosvenor Place, Newcastle 2, Northumberland.

Wakefield (77): S. Webb, 53 Water Lane, Middlestown, Wakefield, Yorks.

West Bromwich (151): K. Cook, 17 Brockwell Road, Kingstanding, Birmingham 22c, Warwickshire.

West Lancs (153): Miss M. Slight, 27 Seafield Road, Blackpool, Lancs.

Westminster (159): L. Zanelli, 173 Newport Dwellings, Newport Place, London, W.C.2.

York (50): Mrs S. M. Storey, "St Fillans", Top Lane, Copmanthorpe, Yorks.

Overseas branches

Hillside-Rhodesia (163): J. R. Anderson, P.O. Box 8037, Sw.Dev. Sect. Causeway, Rhodesia.

Indianapolis-1st U.S.A. (154): W. R. Ross, 2607 E. Northview, Indianapolis 20, Indiana, U.S.A.

Jamaica (51): Miss L. Stockhausen, c/o Paul Methuen Ltd., 159 Orange Street, Kingston, Jamaica.

Salisbury-Rhodesia (63): The Secretary, Salisbury S.R. Branch BSAC, P.O. Box 3532, Salisbury, Rhodesia.

Sydney, N.S.W. (113): T. Grillo, 77 Banks Road, Earlswood, N.S.W.

Trinidad (129): Arthur Oliver, c/o Myerson Tooth Co. Ltd., P.O. Box 111, Port of Spain, Trinidad.

Special branches
Not open to General Public.

Adriatic (178): (U.S. Forces) R. E. Durkee, Box 525, C.P. 245, Brindisi, Italy.

A.E.E. Dounreay (119): H. Greenshiels, 27 Sweyn Road, Thurso, Caithness.

A.E.E. Sellafield (94): J. H. Howard, 11 Wodow Road, Thornhill, Egremont, Cumberland.

A.E.E. Winfrith (108): P. J. Riley, 14 Springfield Crescent, Broadway, Weymouth, Dorset.

Aquatic Group (180): Mrs J. E. Shiers, 11 Epping Way, London, E.4.

Battersea & Chelsea Colleges (123): Miss M. A. King, Lightfoot Hall, Manresa Road, Chelsea, London, S.W.3.

B.E.A. Silver Wings (146): J. W. Brinsden, 111 Long Lane, Stanwell, Staines, Middlesex.

Borough Polytechnic (186): D. J. Ball, 42 Elm Walk, Raynes Park, Surrey.

Bourneville (142): A. Rainsford, 54 Heathleigh Road, Kings Norton, Birmingham 30, Warwickshire.

B.P. Meadhurst (181): R. Tunesi, 12 Napier Road, Ashford Common, Middlesex.

1 (BR) Corps. (87): Major A. R. Dominy R. Sigs., H.Q. R. Sigs., 1 (BR) Corps, B.F.P.O. 39.

Bristol Aeroplane (88): K. Harse, 62 Wootton Cres., St Annes, Bristol, Glos.

British Timken (73): E. C. Wilkie, 29 The Greenways, Daventry, Northants.

Brunel College (144): B. D. Grimwood, 30 Birch Grove, Acton, London, W.3.

Cambridge University (52): J. Dent, St Catherine's, Cambridge.

Croydon Technical College (187): M. K. Todd, Dept. of Mech. Eng., Croydon Technical College, Fairfield, Croydon, Surrey.

Cyrenaica Area (131): Captain Greenwood, 67 A.E.C. Cyrenaica Area, Benghazi, B.F.P.O. 55.

De Haviland—Bolton (101): F. J. Lloyd, 26 Crescent Avenue, Ashton-in-Makerfield, Wigan, Lancs.

Dhekelia (120): British Sub-Aqua Club, Branch 120, c/o Lieutenant J. H. Upton WRAC, 27 Indep. Coy. W.R.A.C., Dhekelia, B.F.P.O. 53.

Episcopi T.S. (150): Sergeant L. Green, c/o Rx Troop, 259 Signal Squadron (Comcan) B.F.P.O. 53.

Farelf (152): Secretary, Farelf Sub-Aqua Club, H.Q. Singapore Base Area, c/o G.P.O. Singapore.

Flint College (167): A. G. D. Morris, Tyn-Y-Caeau, Llanasa, Nr Holywell, Flints.

H.M.S. Ariel (133): O. J. Alger, 66 Harold Road, Stubbington, Fareham, Hants.

H.M.S. Caledonia (184): Chief Petty Officer E. A. Bolton, Diving Instructor, H.M.S. Caledonia, Rosyth, Fife.

H.M.S. Condor (173): The Secretary, Sub-Aqua Club, H.M.S. Condor, R.N.A.S. Arbroath, Angus.

H.M.S. Fulmar (145): The Hon. Sec., H.M.S. Fulmar Sub-Aqua Club, R.N.A.S. Lossiemouth, Morayshire.

H.M.S. Goldcrest (103): Petty Officer Hodges, R.N.A.S. Brawdy, Haverfordwest, Pembs.

H.M.S. Heron (66): Sec. H.M.S. Heron, Sub-Aqua Club, R.N.A.S. Yeovilton, Somerset.

H.M.S. Seahawk (140): P. G. Hale, "Sunny Crest", Church Hill, Helston, Cornwall.

Ilford Films (177): T. W. Blake, 48 Westwood Road, Seven Kings, Ilford, Essex.

Imperial College (64): The Sec., I.C. Underwater Club, Imperial College Union, Prince Consort Road, London.

Leeds University Union (124): Mr. Philip Baker, 60 Harefield Avenue, Cheam, Surrey.

London University (69): J. B. King, 22 Greenlands Road, Staines, Middx.

Loughborough College (165): The Sec. (BS-AC) Loughborough College Branch, c/o Mr Millard, 47 Hold Drive, Loughborough, Leicestershire.

Massey-Ferguson (185): Miss C. Cooper, 146 Grayswood Avenue, Chapelfields, Coventry, Warwickshire.

New Cross Institute (102): Miss J. Knott, 21 Monmouth House, Avignon Road, Brockley, London, S.E.4.

Northampton College (70): Sub-Aqua Club, c/o Union Secretary, St John Street, London, E.C.1.

Oxford University (169): E. A. Drew, 2D Lathbury Road, Oxford.

R.A.F. Akrotiri (107): The Officer, I.C. Special Branch 107, British Sub-Aqua Club, R.A.F. Akrotiri, B.F.P.O. 53, Cyprus.

R.A.F. Benson (156): Corporal Dawe, C.E. 3526637, Police Section, R.A.F. Benson, Oxon.

R.A.F. Cosford (96): Flight-Lieutenant P. H. Crawshaw, Officers' Mess, R.A.F. Cosford, Wolverhampton, Staffs.

R.A.F. Falmouth (174): The Sec., Sub-Aqua Club, 1102 M.C.U., R.A.F. Falmouth, Cornwall.

R.A.F. Gan (126): Flight-Lieutenant R. Dyche, Officers' Mess, R.A.F. Gan, B.F.P.O. 180.

R.A.F. Geilenkirchen (110): Corp./T. R. Jones 682111, 3 Sqdrn., R.A.F. Geilenkirchen, B.F.P.O. 42.

R.A.F. Idris (155): 682287 J./T. Goward, Station Armoury, R.A.F. Idris, B.F.P.O. 57.

R.A.F. Laarbruch (132): Flight-Officer R. K. Jordan, Officers' Mess, R.A.F. Laarbruch, B.F.P.O. 43.

R.A.F. Marham (171): Flying-Officer I. H. Lewis, 147 Officers' Married Quarters, R.A.F. Marham, Kings Lynn, Norfolk.

R.A.F. Seletar (98): The Sec., R.A.F. Seletar Branch BS-AC, c/o P.F.O. Spts. Stre., R.A.F. Seletar, Singapore.

R.A.F. Tech. College (183): 685430 T/Cadet Lynch, M. Cadets' Mess, R.A.F. Tech. Col., R.A.F. Henlow.

R.A.F. Tengah (134): The Sec., Tengah Sub-Aqua Club, c/o Station Post Office, R.A.F. Tengah, Singapore.

R.A.F. Wyton (161): Squadron-Leader K. F. Ashley, Officers' Mess, R.A.F. Wyton, Huntingdon.

Regent Polytechnic (182): D. A. Jones, 13 Pine Walk, Woodmansterne, Surrey.

R.E.M.E. Terdendak (172): 23785327 Corporal Greenwell R., 2 Inf. Wksp., Terendak Camp, Malacca, Malaysia.

R.S.A.S.R.G. (91): D. A. Gay, 1 Claudina Close, Greendale, Salisbury, Rhodesia.

Scientific & Technical Group (158): D. R. Gray, The White House, Green Street, Sunbury-on-Thames, Middlesex.

Vickers Armstrong—Hurn (82): M. Davies, 12 Jubilee Road, Parkston, Poole, Dorset.

Woolwich R.I. (162): T. H. Simms, 347 Old Farm Ave., Sidcup, Kent.

Wycliffe College (68): J. Shirley, Wycliffe College, Stonehouse, Glos.

Affiliated bodies

(addresses may be obtained from Club Headquarters)

GREAT BRITAIN

Aylesford Paper Mills Swimming Club; Bournemouth County Borough Youth Committee; Guernsey Blue Dolphins Sub-Aqua Club; Leicester Underwater Exploration Club; Manchester Diving Group; Scottish Sub-Aqua Club; St Helens Underwater Club; Uxbridge Sub-Aqua Group.

OVERSEAS

Aquanauts Underwater Club, Umtali, Rhodesia; The Frogmen, Antwerp; Associated Divers, Durban, S. Africa; Atlantic Underwater Club, Capetown; Barbados Sub-Aqua Club; Hong Kong Underwater Club; Iscor Underwater Diving and Research Group, Pretoria; Malayan Sub-Aqua Club; Penguin Sub-Aqua Club, Tripoli; Transvaal Underwater Research Group; Underwater Research Group of Queensland; U.S.F.A. of Western Australia.

5 Sources for Wreck Location

THE anchor goes down. Minutes later so does our wreck hunter and his companion—only a fool dives alone—and they start their search. If they are fortunate the object of the exercise—the sunken ship—looms up ahead of them. It is a forbidding, forgotten thing, guarded by water, heavy growths on its sides, and silt, which whirls in misty clouds at a touch. . . . But this is the end of the hunt, not the beginning. The actual finding of the wreck is the climax. The first steps along the road to finding it are far behind. But those steps can be the most important. They can ensure success or failure.

Most important of the steps to wreck discovery is the discovery and checking of evidence that there is a wreck at all.

Vessels plying the trade routes these days are well insured, so that should a loss of ship or cargo occur, then the financial worry is removed from the shoulders of the shipping line to the insurance men. Hence an inquiry with the original owners into the loss of a certain vessel will often result in a reply such as this: "No great detail is available of the vessel in question as she sank some years ago and any loss to the Company was made good through insurance claims." To bother shipping companies for details of the ships they have unfortunately lost becomes, therefore, not only irksome to the inquirer, but dejecting to the shipping line.

It is probably easier to discover lost ships by asking people. Whom you ask depends on the area in which you want to search, but as wrecks have occurred on every headland and off practically every beach around the British Isles, it is only necessary to talk to the local fishermen to hear of their own wreck—which is sure to have something special or unusual about it—to realize that lost ships are in fact everywhere, and it is the local man who will have knowledge of them. Nearly every public-house that is in the remotest way connected with the sea fairly revels in displaying old prints of ships, charts, and the odd cannon or two, and once inquiry is made there, then half a dozen voices will offer information and argument, so that by the time an evening is over the wreck hunter will have details far beyond his wildest dreams. And in many cases just as wildly inaccurate.

Are there really all that number of wrecks around our coasts? The simple answer is 'yes'. For example, there is an old book that tells of more than a dozen wrecks along the short stretch of coast between Salcombe and Bigbury Bay, South Devon. The *Deventa,* the *Jane Rowe,* a trawler, H.M.S. *Ramillies,* the Armada ship *San Pedro el Mayor,* the *Herzogin Cecilie,* a ship laden with marble, the *Djebba,* the *Dragon,* the *Ruperra,* the Italian barque *Volere,* the *Halloween,* a clipper, all came to grief on the same cliffs. This short section of coast alone will give an idea of the fantastic amount of shipping scattered along our shores, and at the same time cover a fine section of maritime history from Elizabeth the First to Elizabeth the Second.

The *San Pedro el Mayor,* or *St Peter,* as she is locally known, was one of the two hospital ships attached to the Armada. She was lost during November 1588 at Hope Cove, Devon, and silver coins from her remains are still found on the beach. We have seen some, and the story of the ship is in this book. The *Ramillies* lies near by, lost in February 1760. She is on the bottom still, with her cannons by her: her story is here too. Farther around the coast at Anglesey the *Royal Charter,* laden with gold dust and nuggets from Australia, was wrecked near Moelfre Bay, and her story is in this book.

In Ireland the main part of the Spanish Armada lies on the bottom silted up, broken, and lost, but coins are discovered, and cannons too. In fact, many years ago a professional diver from Whitstable, John Gann, hearing of the reputed treasures that were carried in Armada ships, went to Galway and dragged the area with a net until he brought up a barrel-shaped lump composed of gold coins and pitch. He returned to Whitstable to build a row of houses, and was able to retire on the rents.

In Devon and Cornwall many wrecks await exploration; some have been looked at, others not, and the tales of the *Mohegan,* and *Maine,* and the *Anson* are all told in this book, each with details of how the wreck happened, why it happened, and finally how it looks today. These stories, however, are not just ramblings taken down from local fishermen, but are composed from actual experiences and from contemporary and historical accounts.

The story by the fireside is a good beginning, but the serious wreck hunter should regard such tales with some scepticism, as they are usually told to intrigue, and much of the fact will be buried in fiction. But such tales are never entirely without truth, and a small amount of careful searching based on the date of loss and the name of the wreck will bring the facts to light.

The greatest factor influencing the passage of a ship through the water is the sea itself. Vast areas of water can become spray-covered within moments, and after a few hours, under the effect of a strong wind, can turn into dark-green mountains of water that will toss even the largest vessels about like corks. Surface movement is apparent at once even to the most inexperienced sailor, and precautions can be taken directly, but under the surface, where currents run and water depths vary to suit the sunken contours, lie all the dangers of the deep. These effects of tide, wind, and underwater hazards account for about half the wrecks that have occurred around our coasts. The other half is due to human error or design—*i.e.*, negligence or war. Taking this reasoning a stage further, it is quite clear that half the wrecks will be in places most affected by bad weather, such as prominent headlands or tide-races, while the remainder will be scattered around harbours and in well-known shipping routes. There are always exceptions to this rule, and no hard-and-fast law can be laid down for deciding where a wreck should be, but the exceptions tend to make the hobby of wreck hunting all the more intriguing.

The manner in which a ship sinks need not be described in any detail here, it being sufficient to say that when a ship loses buoyancy past a certain critical figure it will sink; how this loss of buoyancy occurs need not concern us at the moment. However,

the place of sinking is of prime importance. A rough sight or
bearing is not good enough, and even first-hand accounts can
be misleading, as the survivor embellishes his own part of the
story and allows details of the ship to pass by.

Wreck hunting can be tackled in two ways. From the facts and
figures listed in records, documents, and newspaper accounts, or
by actual searchings of the seabed for remains of boilers, cannons,
and suspicious mounds.

The document approach is one that can well be carried out
during the dark days of winter, when diving, although possible
thanks to modern diving-suits, is to say the least uncomfortable.
Provided you have good reason to believe that the ship exists,
these are the places to try for more information:

Charted Wrecks

The Hydrographer to the Admiralty, Hydrographic Department, Oxgate Lane, Cricklewood, London, N.W.2, is a good
source.

Wartime Losses

The War Risks Insurance Office, Ministry of Transport, St
Christopher House, Southwark Street, London, S.E.1.

General

The Shipping Editor, Lloyd's, London, E.C.3.
The Secretary, Trinity House, Tower Hill, London.
The National Maritime Museum, Greenwich, London.
The Public Record Office, London.
Department of Sailing Ships, Science Museum, London.
The British Museum, London.

Local Sources

Do not forget your local newspaper office. It may surprise you
to find out just how long there has been a paper in existence.
Shipping losses are usually faithfully recorded.

Other local sources which are often forgotten are the local
archaeological society and local museums. They have access to
local records that are not always easily available to the general
public.

6 Wreck List

(Just a few of the losses around British coasts up to the First World War!)

20 July 1545.	*Marye Rose,* 60 guns (see Chapter Eleven).
1 September 1691.	*Coronation,* 90 guns, foundered off the Ramhead, but all crew saved.
	Harwich, 70 guns, wrecked on Mount Edgcumbe; crew lost.
29 January 1696.	*Royal Sovereign,* 100 guns; burnt in the Medway.
26 November 1703.	*Stirling Castle,* 70 guns.
	Mary, 70 guns.
	Northumberland, 70 guns, lost on the Goodwins.
	Vanguard, 70 guns, sunk at Chatham.
	York, 70 guns, lost near Harwich; all lost but four men.
	Resolution, 60 guns, coast of Sussex.
	Newcastle, 60 guns, at Spithead, 193 drowned.
	Reserve, 60 guns, at Yarmouth, 173 perished.
	Great storm caused loss of all above (see Chapter Four).
22 October 1707.	*Association,* 70 guns, and other vessels off the Scilly Isles (see Chapter Four).

15 October 1711.	*Edgar,* 70 guns, blew up at Spithead; all on board dead.
1711.	*De Liefde,* East Indiaman, sunk Shetlands with £500,000 on board (see Chapter Twelve).
21 September 1744.	*Colchester,* 50 guns, lost on Kentish Knock; 50 men lost.
5 October 1744.	*Victory,* 100 guns, near the Isle of Alderney; all drowned.
15 February 1760.	H.M.S. *Ramillies,* 90 guns, lost on the Bolt Head; only 26 sailors saved (see Chapter Four).
	Conqueror, lost on St Nicholas's Island, Plymouth.
1772.	*Chantiloupe.* Vessel returning from West Indies wrecked close to Bantham. All lost except one man. On board was a woman, who put on her richest gems and clothes, hoping that if she was washed on shore her appearance would help. Locals, however, waiting for loot, seized her, stripped her of clothes and gems. Even cut off fingers for rings, mangled her ears for earrings, and left her to die. Proved at inquiry that she was alive when she reached shore and was deliberately murdered.
4 August 1782.	*Swan,* sloop, off Waterford; 130 drowned.
29 August 1782.	*Royal George;* about 900 drowned (see Chapter Eleven).
24 August 1792.	*Impetueux,* 74 guns; burnt at Portsmouth.
4 May, 1795.	H.M.S. *Boyne,* by fire at Spithead. Man-of-war of 98 guns, destroyed by fire at Portsmouth by the explosion of the magazine; many killed. Portions were recovered June 1838 (see Chapter Five).
9-10 October 1799.	H.M.S. *Lutine,* 32 guns, was wrecked off Vlieland, coast of Holland; only one saved, who died before reaching England. *La Lutine* was a French ship captured by Admiral Duncan. She contained much bullion and money, belonging to merchants; a great loss to the underwriters at Lloyd's.

19 October 1799.	H.M.S. *Impregnable,* 98 guns, wrecked between Langstone and Chichester (see Chapter Five).
14 January 1800.	*Queen,* transport, on Trefusis Point; 369 dead.
19 January 1800.	*Mastiff,* gun-brig, on the Cockle Sands.
9 July 1800.	*Brazen,* sloop of war, off Newhaven; one man saved.
16 March 1801.	*Invincible,* 74 guns, near Yarmouth; Captain J. Rennie and crew drowned, 126 saved.
10 January 1803.	*Active,* West Indiaman, in Margate Roads (see Chapter Six).
11 January 1803.	*Hindostan,* East Indiaman, went to pieces on the Culvers (see Chapter Six).
16 November 1803.	*Circe,* frigate, 32 guns, off Yarmouth.
24 November 1804.	*Venerable,* 74 guns, at Torbay; lost 8 men.
6 February 1805.	*Earl of Abergavenny,* East Indiaman, on the Bill of Portland; more than 300 persons drowned (see Chapter Six).
21 December 1805.	*Aurora,* transport, on the Goodwin Sands; 300 dead.
28 November 1807.	*Boreas,* man-of-war, upon the Hannois Rock in the Channel.
29 December 1807.	H.M.S. *Anson,* 44 guns, wrecked in Mounts Bay; many lives lost (see Chapter Seven).
17 December 1814.	*British Queen,* packet, wrecked on the Goodwin Sands, and all on board lost.
23 October 1817.	*William and Mary,* packet, struck on the Willeys rocks, near the Holmes lighthouse, Bristol Channel; nearly 60 drowned.
8 August 1821.	*Earl of Moira,* on the Burbo Bank, near Liverpool; 40 drowned.
26 December 1821.	*Juliana,* East Indiaman, on the Kentish Knock; 40 drowned.
3 February 1822.	*Thames,* Indiaman, off Beachy Head.
13 July 1833.	*Earl of Wemyss,* near Wells, Norfolk; the cabin filled, and 11 women and children were drowned; all on deck escaped.
15 October 1833.	*United Kingdom,* W. Indiaman, with rich cargo; run down by the *Queen of Scotland* steamer off Northfleet, near Gravesend.

6 September 1838.   *Forfarshire,* steamer, on its passage from Hull to Dundee, was wrecked in a violent gale, and 38 persons out of 53 were drowned. The Outer-Fern Lighthouse-keeper, James Darling, and his heroic daughter, Grace, ventured out in a tremendous sea in a coble, and rescued several of the passengers.

4 January 1841.   *Thames,* steamer, Captain Gray, from Dublin to Liverpool, wrecked off St Ives; the Captain and 55 persons lost.

30 March 1850.   *Royal Adelaide,* steamer, wrecked on the Tongue Sands, off Margate; 400 lost.

24 December 1852.   *Lily,* stranded and blown up by gunpowder, on the Calf-of-Man; 30 lost.

29 September 1853.   *Annie Jane,* of Liverpool, an emigrant vessel, driven on shore on the Barra Islands, on the west coast of Scotland; about 348 lives lost.

19 October 1853.   *Dalhousie,* foundered off Beachy Head; the Captain (Butterworth), the passengers, and all the crew (excepting one), about 60 persons in all, drowned.

30 November 1854.   *Nile,* screw-steamer, struck on the Godevry Rock, St Ives Bay; and all drowned.

9 February 1855.   *Will o' the Wisp,* screw-steamer, on the Burn Rock, off Lambay; 18 lives lost.

25 February 1855.   *Morna,* steamer on rocks near the Isle of Man; 21 lives lost.

3 May 1855.   *John,* emigrant vessel, on the Manacle rocks off Falmouth; 196 lives lost (see Chapter Nine).

5 January 1857.   *Violet,* royal mail-steamer, lost on the Goodwins; many lost.

5-6 January 1857.   *Northern Belle,* a large American vessel, was wrecked near Broadstairs. The American Government sent 21 silver medals and £270 to be distributed among the heroic boatmen of the place, who saved the crew.

2 June 1859.   *Eastern Monarch,* burnt at Spithead; out of 500, 8 lives lost. The vessel contained invalid soldiers from India.

Can you tell from this picture that a wreck lies under the water here? Note the square-angled object sticking out of the sea beyond the near point and almost in line with the far headland. Rocks seldom make such clear angles.

(*Below*) You can see the wreck as she was when she struck. The cargo vessel *Louis Shied* ran aground at Thurlestone, South Devon, after being torpedoed in 1939. (See p. 194.)

(*Left*) Woman diver at work. Penny McDonald searching the seabed off the Sussex coast. Note the wrecking hook, or 'prodder', carried in her right hand. Jagged metal can cause serious cuts underwater, so some form of hook or rod is normally carried.
(See p. 197.)

(*Right*) Paying close attention to the seabed.

(*Left*) Reward for sharp eyes. An encrusted old anchor is lifted from its resting-place.

night of
25-26 October 1859.

Royal Charter, screw-steamer, Captain Taylor, totally wrecked off Moelfre, on the Anglesey coast; 446 lives lost. The vessel contained gold amounting in value to between £700,000 and £800,000; much of this has been recovered (see Chapter Eight).

31 January 1860.

Endymion, sailing-vessel, burnt in the Mersey; loss of above £20,000.

19 February 1860.

Ondine, steamer; lost through collision with the *Herione* of Bideford, abreast of Beachy Head; the Captain and about 50 lost.

28 February 1860.

Nimrod, steamer, wrecked on rocks near St David's Head; 40 lives lost.

April 1862.

Mars, Waterford steamer, struck on a rock near Milford Haven; about 50 lost.

20 December 1862.

Lifeguard, steamer, left Newcastle, with about 41 passengers, never since heard of; supposed to have foundered off Flamborough Head.

24 November 1864.

Stanley and Friendship, in gale off Tynemouth.

Dalhousie, screw-steamer, in the same gale, mouth of the Tay; 34 lives lost.

6-11 January 1866.

Many wrecks and much loss of life during gales, especially off Torbay.

23 March 1866.

Spirit of the Ocean, steamer; wrecked on Start Point, all lost except 4.

10 July 1866.

Amazon, H.M. screw-sloop, and screw-steamer *Osprey,* sunk by collision near Plymouth; several passengers and sailors drowned.

19 August 1866.

Bruiser, steamer, sunk by collision with the *Haswell,* off Aldborough; about 15 lives lost.

5 January 1867.

James Crosfield, iron ship; wrecked off Langness, Isle of Man; all on board lost.

7 March 1870.

Normandy, S.W. company's steamer, by collision with the steamer *Mary,* off the Isle of Wight; the Captain and 33 others lost.

22-23 November 1872.	Severe gales; many wrecks and many lives lost. *Kinsale,* steamer, off Waterford; *Albion,* schooner, off Looe.
25 November 1872.	*Royal Adelaide,* emigrant vessel, went ashore on Chesil beach, between Weymouth and Portland; 5 lost.
March 1873.	*Lalla Rookh.* From Shanghai, bound London. Wrecked March 1873 on Prawle Point. Cargo 1300 tons of tea and 60 tons tobacco. All crew, except Chief Mate, saved by rocket apparatus. Tea washed in and left in ten-foot-high wall at high-tide mark.
1 March 1873.	*Boyne,* barque; wrecked off Mohilo Bay, Cornwall; about 20 lost.
14 October 1874.	*Kingsbridge,* iron ship, sunk off the Lizard by collision with the *Candahar,* iron ship; the Master, his wife and daughter, and 8 others drowned.
6 December 1875.	*Deutschland,* Atlantic steamer, from Bremen to New York, went on sandbank, the Kentish Knock, at the mouth of the Thames during a gale; about 70 lost (many emigrants).
17 February 1876.	*Strathclyde,* Glasgow steamer, sunk by collision with Hamburg ship *Franconia,* in Dover Bay in daylight; about 17 lost. (Verdict of manslaughter against Kuhn, Captain of *Franconia,* quashed on appeal; 7 judges against 6 decided against British jurisdiction, 13 November 1876.)
3 September 1878.	*Princess Alice* by collision with the screwsteamer *Bywell Castle* in the Thames near Woolwich; between 600 and 700 lost.
25 November 1878.	*Pomerania,* Hamburg-American mail steamer, sunk off Folkestone by *Moel Elian,* iron barque, of Caernarvon a little after midnight; 162 saved by boats; about 48 missing.
13 August 1879.	*City of London* Aberdeen steamer; run down and sunk by the *Vesta(s)* in the Thames.
8 February 1880.	*Valentine* foundered in a gale near Falmouth; about 16 lost.

17 July 1880.	*Hydaspes,* sailing-ship, sank in collision with *Centurion,* screw-steamer, off Dungeness in a fog; both blamed; no lives lost.
29 April 1882.	*Alexandrovna,* Liverpool ship, wrecked off Swanage; crew all lost (see Chapter Eleven).
9 September 1882.	*Ponoma,* Glasgow iron ship, foundered off Yarmouth; about 20 lost.
16 October 1882.	*Constantia* and *City of Antwerp,* steamers, sunk by collision off the Eddystone; about 14 lost.
26 November 1882.	*Cambronne,* steamer, sunk by collision with *Marion,* near Lundy.
29 November 1882.	*St George,* steamer, lost off Portreath, Cornish coast; 11 dead.
7 January 1883.	*City of Brussels,* sunk by collision with the *Kirby Hall* in the Mersey; 10 drowned.
24 April 1883.	*British Commerce,* sunk by collision with *County of Aberdeen* off Selsey Bill; 25 lost.
2-3 August 1884.	*Dione,* steamer, sunk by collision with *Camden,* steamer, near Gravesend; about 17 persons drowned (Captain of the *Dione* punished for reckless navigation, August).
15 October 1886.	*Malleny,* Liverpool iron steamer, foundered on the Tuskar reef, Bristol Channel; all 20 hands lost in the gale.
15 October 1886.	*Teviotdale,* steamer, of Glasgow, lost on the Carmarthen coast; 18 lives lost.
8 March 1888.	*Lanoma,* iron barque, wrecked near Weymouth; 12 lives lost.
9 March 1888.	*City of Corinth* sunk by collision with *Tasmania* near Dungeness.
20 December 1889.	*Cleddy,* steamer, sank after collision with *Isle of Cyprus,* steamer, off St Catherine's; about 13 lives lost.
19 February 1890.	*Highgate,* steamer, and *Sovereign,* ship, both sunk by collision off Lundy Island; 12 lost.
21 March 1890.	*Ethel Gwendoline,* steamer, foundered off Rattray Head, Aberdeenshire; 7 drowned.
23 November 1890.	*Uppingham,* Cardiff steamer bound for China, struck on a rock below Hartland Quay, Cornwall; about 7 drowned.

24 November 1890.	*Calypso,* Bristol screw-steamer, by collision with *Pinzon,* Spanish steamer, off Folkestone.
1891.	*Marana* in snowstorm struck the Blackstone Rocks off Start Lighthouse. Went to pieces in minutes. Some thirty crew took to boats, but only four reached shore; they were Swedes (see Chapter Eight).
5 February 1891.	*Chiswick,* London steamer, struck on a reef off Scilly; 11 out of 19 drowned.
26 October 1891.	*Charlwood,* barque, sunk by collision with the *Boston,* near the Eddystone lighthouse; 15 lost.
11 November 1891.	*Benvenue,* full-rigged ship, bound for Sydney, wrecked off Sandgate; 27 persons suspended in the rigging for 16 hours were saved with great difficulty by the Sandgate lifeboat, and taken to Folkestone; Captain James Moddrel and 4 men drowned.
24 February 1892.	*Forest Queen,* steamer, sunk by collision with the *Loughborough,* steamer, near Flamborough Head; about 14 lives lost.
10 March 1892.	*County of Salop,* steamer, stranded in Widemouth Bay, Cornwall; the 30 persons on board saved by the Bude Rocket Brigade.
15 March 1892.	*Walmer Castle,* Deal lugger, foundered near the Isle of Wight; 7 drowned.
15 May 1892.	*Earl of Aberdeen,* barque, wrecked on the Pembrokeshire coast; 16 lives lost.
July 1892.	*City of Chicago,* Inman Atlantic liner, run ashore near Old Head of Kinsale, during a fog; passengers landed 1 July; totally wrecked, 7 July (see Chapter Eight).
14 August 1892.	*Thracia,* barque, capsized near Port Erin, Isle of Man, 17 lives lost.
9 December 1892.	*Dilsberg,* Glasgow steamer, wrecked on the Long Sands, Kent; about 7 deaths.
18 November 1893.	*Hampshire,* steamer, of London, owners Messrs MacBeth and Grey of Glasgow (Captain Weir and 22 men) sunk off St

Ives, Cornwall; all lost except Mr James Swanson, Chief Officer.

15 April 1896.

Elbe, North German Lloyd steamer, from Bremen to New York, sunk in collison with the *Crathie* of Aberdeen, off Lowestoft about 6 A.M.; 334 lives lost, including Captain von Gössel.

16 June 1897.

Susannah Kelly, steamer, sunk in a gale in Belfast Lough; Captain and 9 men lost.

1 February 1898.

Channel Queen, steamer, from Plymouth, wrecked on the Black Rock off Guernsey; 12 passengers and some of the crew drowned.

14 October 1898.

Mohegan, Atlantic Transport Company steamer, wrecked on the Manacles, off Cornwall by error of navigation; Captain R. Griffiths and 106 drowned (see Chapter Nine).

24 November 1898.

FitzJames, steamer, wrecked off Beachy Head, the Captain and 8 men drowned.

16 December 1898.

Ilios, steamer, sunk by collision with the *Pierremont*, steamer, off South Shields; 20 deaths.

11 February 1899.

Arno, steam collier, wrecked near Selsey Bill, 13 deaths.

30 March 1899.

Stella, excursion steamer from Southampton to Guernsey (S.W.R), wrecked at 4 P.M. while going at full speed in a fog on the Black Rock, near the Casquets, 8 miles off Alderney. Out of the 140 passengers and the 40 members of the crew 105 persons were drowned, including Captain Reeks. Great heroism was shown, and there was no panic; the ship sank in eight minutes.

16 September 1900.

Gordon Castle, Glasgow steamer, and the Hamburg steamer *Stormarn*, sunk by collision during a fog in Cardigan Bay; Captain Casey and 19 others from the *Gordon Castle* lost.

7 November 1900.

City of Vienna, Dublin steamer, sunk in collision with unknown steamer (believed to have also sunk) off Land's End; 20 deaths.

19 March 1901.	*Homer,* steamer, sunk in collision with the *Hopper,* Russian barque, off Spurn Head; 16 lost.
8 August 1901.	*Kincora,* steamer, sunk in collision with the *Oceanic,* Atlantic liner, in St George's Channel, 7 deaths.
4 November 1902.	*Defender,* fishing-boat, wrecked at Lowestoft; 6 deaths.
14, 15 January 1903.	*Manchester Merchant,* steamer, with 7000 bales of cotton on fire, scuttled in Dingle Bay, Kerry.
18 March 1904.	Submarine A.1 off Spithead; 11 lost.
18 August 1904.	H.M.S. Destroyer *Zephyr,* rammed in Portsmouth Harbour.
August 1904.	British barque *Inverkip,* sunk off Fastnet Rock; 25 lives lost.
4 April 1905	Destroyer *Spiteful* in collision off Yarmouth (I.O.W.); 2 drowned.
8 June 1905.	Submarine A.8 off Plymouth; 15 drowned.
16 October 1905.	Submarine A.4 sunk in Portsmouth Harbour after explosion.
2-3 December 1909.	The Manx steamer *Ellan Vannin* sunk at the mouth of the Mersey; 33 lives lost; the steamer *Thistlemoor* wrecked off the North Devon coast; 19 lives lost.
4 April 1910.	The *Kate Thomas,* from Antwerp, sunk in a collision with a steamer off Land's End; 19 lives lost.

Index

20 *Grâce Dieu.*　21 *Marye Rose.*　22 *Royal George.*　23 *Impregnable.*
29 *Preussen.*　30 *Stirling Castle.*　31 *Mary.*　32 *Northumberland.*　33 *Act*

A *City of Chicago.*　B *Gelph.*　C *City of Quebec.*　D *Conchee.*　E *Falls of*
J Spanish galleon.　K Spanish galleon.　L *Duquesa Santa Ana.*　M *La*